Designing and implementing virtual exchange – a collection of case studies

Edited by Francesca Helm and Ana Beaven

Published by Research-publishing.net, a not-for-profit association
Contact: info@research-publishing.net

© 2020 by Editors (collective work)
© 2020 by Authors (individual work)

Designing and implementing virtual exchange – a collection of case studies
Edited by Francesca Helm and Ana Beaven

Publication date: 2020/11/23

Rights: the whole volume is published under the Attribution-NonCommercial-NoDerivatives International (CC BY-NC-ND) licence; **individual articles may have a different licence**. Under the CC BY-NC-ND licence, the volume is freely available online (https://doi.org/10.14705/rpnet.2020.45.9782490057726) for anybody to read, download, copy, and redistribute provided that the author(s), editorial team, and publisher are properly cited. Commercial use and derivative works are, however, not permitted.

Disclaimer: Research-publishing.net does not take any responsibility for the content of the pages written by the authors of this book. The authors have recognised that the work described was not published before, or that it was not under consideration for publication elsewhere. While the information in this book is believed to be true and accurate on the date of its going to press, neither the editorial team nor the publisher can accept any legal responsibility for any errors or omissions. The publisher makes no warranty, expressed or implied, with respect to the material contained herein. While Research-publishing.net is committed to publishing works of integrity, the words are the authors' alone.

Trademark notice: product or corporate names may be trademarks or registered trademarks, and are used only for identification and explanation without intent to infringe.

Copyrighted material: every effort has been made by the editorial team to trace copyright holders and to obtain their permission for the use of copyrighted material in this book. In the event of errors or omissions, please notify the publisher of any corrections that will need to be incorporated in future editions of this book.

Typeset by Research-publishing.net
Credit illustration: iStockphoto.com/SB.
Cover layout by © 2020 Raphaël Savina (raphael@savina.net)

ISBN13: 978-2-490057-72-6 (Ebook, PDF, colour)
ISBN13: 978-2-490057-73-3 (Ebook, EPUB, colour)
ISBN13: 978-2-490057-71-9 (Paperback - Print on demand, black and white)
Print on demand technology is a high-quality, innovative and ecological printing method; with which the book is never 'out of stock' or 'out of print'.

British Library Cataloguing-in-Publication Data.
A cataloguing record for this book is available from the British Library.

Legal deposit, France: Bibliothèque Nationale de France - Dépôt légal: novembre 2020.

Table of contents

vii   Notes on contributors

xvii Acknowledgements

xix   Foreword
Sarah Guth

1   Introduction
Francesca Helm and Ana Beaven

Section 1. Teacher-designed

11   Combining expertise from linguistics and tourism: a tale of two cities
Judit Háhn and Katarzyna Radke

23   Immersive telepresence in theatre: performing arts education in digital spaces
Tom Gorman, Mikko Kanninen, and Tiina Syrjä

37   Virtual exchange: Romania and Hungary 100 years later
Andra Cioltan-Drăghiciu and Daniela Stanciu

47   The transnational job exchange project: a French-German TEP
Katja Auffret and Aloisia Sens

59   Multidisciplinary and international virtual collaboration on the "Shared Garden" between the Universities of Bordeaux and León
María Fernández-Raga and Thierry Villard

69   Mission (im)possible: developing students' international online business communication skills through virtual teamwork
Rita Koris and Jean-François Vuylsteke

81   Exploring foreign entrepreneurial ecosystems through virtual exchange
Nadia Cheikhrouhou and Małgorzata Marchewka

Table of contents

93   Virtual exchange for teaching EU economics: building enriching international learning experiences for European students
Rita Koris, Núria Hernández-Nanclares, and Francisco Javier Mato Díaz

105   E+VE-SFI: developing spoken interaction in a foreign language
Margarita Vinagre, Ciara R. Wigham, and Marta Giralt

117   Task-enhanced virtual exchange between University of Sfax, Tunisia, and Hacettepe University, Turkey
Asma Moalla, Nadia Abid, and Ufuk Balaman

127   How a multilingual project can foster and enhance international mobility
Lisa Griggio and Sara Pittarello

141   Recognising participation in virtual exchange: open badges and the CLAVIER contribution
Teresa MacKinnon, Simon Ensor, Marcin Kleban, and Claude Trégoat

Section 2. Ready-made

155   The Sharing Perspectives Foundation: a case study in blended mobility
Sophie C. Millner

167   Erasmus+ Virtual Exchange for internationalisation in besieged areas: a case study of the Islamic University of Gaza
Amani Al Mqadma and Ahmed Al Karriri

179   Implementing E+VE at the University of Bordeaux within English for specific purposes courses
Laüra Hoskins and Alexandra Reynolds

191   Communication across cultures: when the virtual meets the classroom
Marta Giralt

205 Integrating Soliya's Connect programmes into a language course and into a liberal arts and sciences degree
Tatiana Bruni

Section 3. Youth

219 Virtual exchange strengthens international youth work
Sandra van de Kraak and Jan Lai

231 Intercultural competence for youth workers
Daniel Dixon and Onur Tahmaz

241 Author index

Notes on contributors

Editors

Francesca Helm is Assistant Professor of English at the Department of Political Science, Law, and International Studies at the University of Padova, Italy. She is Chair of the Education Innovation working group of the Coimbra Group and research officer for UNICollaboration. Her research interests are in online intercultural communication and virtual exchange, critical education, ethical internationalisation, and academic freedom. She has been leading the monitoring and evaluation of the European Commission's Erasmus+ virtual exchange initiative.

Ana Beaven teaches English at the University of Bologna Language Centre. She is a trainer and dialogue facilitator for UNICollaboration. Her research interests are intercultural education, foreign language teaching and learning, and virtual exchange.

Invited author

Sarah Guth is the president of UNICollaboration and teaches English as a foreign language at the University of Padova, Italy. She was Program Coordinator at the SUNY COIL Center and designed their Professional Development Program. Her research focuses on intercultural communication and the normalisation of virtual exchange in higher education. She is the project manager for UNICollaboration's participation in the European Commission's pilot project Erasmus+ Virtual Exchange.

Authors

Dr Nadia Abid is Assistant Professor of applied linguistics at the Faculty of Arts and Humanities of Sfax, Tunisia. In her research, she is interested in intercultural language learning and teaching and related issues including: intercultural identity, intercultural citizenship, global issues, virtual cultural exchanges, English

Notes on contributors

as a foreign language textbook analyses, and their role in the development of intercultural communicative competence. Her research appeared in Language and Intercultural Communication.

Ahmed Al Karriri has a Master's degree in business administration. He joined the external relations office at IUG as Partnerships Officer in 2015 with responsibility, along with members of the external relations team, for building comprehensive strategic partnerships with the private sector, and for global partnerships with universities. Since last year, he has been managing the virtual exchange activities at IUG. Alkarriri is also involved in several projects of international, green, and social entrepreneurship in Gaza. He is the founder of the Green Knowledge Community in Gaza and a Caux Scholar alumnus 2018, Switzerland. Also, he is a Middle East Fellow at The Hunger Project; he has been part of the Community-Led-Development project since 2017. His main areas of interest include knowledge management, sustainable development, civic engagement, international development, and conflict resolution.

Amani Al Mqadma works as head of the International Relations office at the Islamic University of Gaza; she has a Master's degree in business administration. Amani has a wide range of expertise in international project management, she worked on projects funded by the European commission through Erasmus+ projects, TEMPUS, ERASMUS MUNDUS, in addition to other European funding by the Austrian Development Agency through the Appear programme, the Ministry of Foreign affairs in Finland through higher education's ICI programme, and others. Moreover, she has worked for the development of several manuals for international scholarships on gender and management of international projects. She has developed quality plans for several Erasmus+ CBHE projects. In these projects, she was responsible for managing quality and dissemination work packages. She is particularly interested in project management and sustainability, internationalisation of higher education, and how it affects students and universities. Her other research interest includes e-work and its effect on women's employability and gender equality and entrepreneurship.

Notes on contributors

Katja Auffret has studied environmental engineering in Germany and worked in engineering for 11 years in France. She is Lecturer for German since 2004 in several French engineering schools. She also coordinates an KA203 Erasmus+ project for IMT Mines Albi which develops language classes resources in engineering schools.

Dr Ufuk Balaman is Assistant Professor of English Language Teaching and Director of the HUMAN Research Centre at Hacettepe University. His research primarily deals with conversation analysis, CALL, and language teacher education. His work has appeared in Computer-assisted Language Learning, ReCALL, Language Learning & Technology, and Learning, Culture, and Social Interaction.

Tatiana Bruni graduated at Utrecht University in Italian language and culture, with a specialisation in translation. She teaches intercultural communication and Italian language and culture at University College Utrecht. She is also pursuing a PhD in intercultural education at Durham University, focusing on education for engaged citizenship and student voices.

Nadia Cheikhrouhou is Assistant Professor at the Higher Institute of technological studies of Béja, where she teaches business culture, development and management of innovative projects, and corporate communication. Her research interests include entrepreneurship and virtual telecollaboration. She has conducted four virtual exchange projects.

Andra Cioltan-Drăghiciu is a research assistant at the Graz University (Austria) and at the German speaking university in Budapest (Hungary) in the field of Central European history. She finished her PhD with a thesis on youth subcultures in Communist Romania and specialises in Cold War, youth cultures, oral history, and cultural memory.

Daniel Dixon is a project manager, professional trainer, language teacher, and coach with 25 years' experience and he has been involved in Erasmus+ projects for many years. He has been the president of ACSESO since its founding and is an expert in project management, non-formal education, cyberbullying, youth

Notes on contributors

empowerment, and critical thinking. Daniel has a wealth of experience working for the local government in the UK and Spain in the fields of education, training, and social services.

Simon Ensor, @sensor63, is an English as a foreign language teacher at the Université Clermont Auvergne in France, an associate member of the Laboratoire de Recherche sur Le Langage and works with friends in the CLAVIER network and further afield to grow transformative, connected environments for learning. His blog is Touches of Sense...

María Fernández-Raga is Associate Professor in applied physics, and Director of the International Affairs of the University of León, currently combining teaching, research, and management tasks. She has a broad experience in teaching since 2006, mainly in fluid mechanics and fundamentals of physics at the University of León, as well as similar subjects in five other international universities, obtaining several prizes. Her research career has recently focused on the characterisation of rain and in teaching in higher education, recently in virtual exchanges.

Marta Giralt is Lecturer in applied linguistics and Spanish at the School of Modern Languages and Applied Linguistics, University of Limerick, Ireland. She teaches Spanish, language studies, and technology and cross-cultural communication. Her research interests are in second language acquisition, computer-mediated communication, and intercultural communication. Recent publications list: https://ulsites.ul.ie/mlal/dr-marta-giralt-0

Tom Gorman is an academic and theatre director currently based at Coventry University. He studied English literature and language at Queen's University Belfast before completing a PhD in theatre at the University of Ulster. In 1990, after working for some time as a freelance actor, Tom co-founded Sightlines Theatre Company, Belfast, working with them as Artistic Director for six years. During this period, he also worked as a performer, writer and director with numerous theatre companies throughout Northern Ireland and as a writer/performer for BBC Radio Ulster. He was strand leader in drama at Birmingham

University from 1997-2005 and course director for Theatre Studies at Bath Spa University from 2005-2007. From 2007 onwards he has been working as Senior Lecturer on the BA theatre and professional practice degree at Coventry University. He is currently engaged in a research project in conjunction with the University of Tampere, Finland, using videoconferencing technology, bespoke network connections, rear-projection, and sound design to create immersive rehearsal spaces.

Lisa Griggio has been working at the language centre of the university of Padua for almost 20 years. She has worked as a language teachers trainer and an e-tutor. She is expert in peer-tutoring, gamification, intercultural dialogue, information and communication technology, as well as in multilingual and multicultural communities. She is involved in the fields of virtual exchanges, materials design, the use of new technologies for foreign language learning and teaching and is a trained E+VE facilitator.

Judit Háhn is Senior Lecturer of English linguistics at the Department of Language and Communication Studies of the University of Jyväskylä in Finland. She has arranged several online international projects for her students and conducted research on the participants' asynchronous interactions in the online learning environments.

Laüra Hoskins is an English for specific purposes teacher at the University of Bordeaux where she coordinates and teaches courses for students in health and human sciences. Her current interests are in blended learning and virtual exchange. She also coordinates and facilitates the University's professional development programme for internationalising learning and teaching through English, *Défi international*.

Núria Hernández-Nanclares is Associate Professor at the Applied Economics Department of University of Oviedo (Spain). She specialises in innovative teaching for higher education and economics, both fields on which she focuses her research currently. The main working areas are forms of assessment and alternative assessment methods, active methodologies in higher education, and

Notes on contributors

social and learning networks. She also focuses on pre-service teacher training in a Master's degree in teacher training in secondary education.

Mikko Kanninen is Senior Lecturer of Acting at The University of Tampere. He has been Artistic Director of Tampere Theatre Festival from 2011-2015 and is currently chairman of the board of TINFO Teatterin Tiedotuskeskus. He has worked as an actor and director across Europe and the USA and his research interests include the intersection between new technologies and actor training, recording possibilities of theatre performances, their digital life cycle, new forms of theatre in the environment of developing technology and the potential of such recordings to develop into new works of art, theatre videos, or theatre mediums.

Marcin Kleban, PhD, a senior researcher, teacher trainer, English as a foreign language teacher, and a coordinator of the teacher training programme at the Institute of English Studies, Jagiellonian University in Krakow, Poland. My research interests include applications of computer technologies in education, teaching English as a foreign language, teacher training, online intercultural exchanges, and developing digital literacies.

Rita Koris is Senior Lecturer at the Institute of International Studies at the Catholic University in Hungary where she teaches courses of English for specific purposes. She has been teaching English business communication courses for more than ten years now and has been involved in several VE projects with US and European partners. Before teaching, she worked as a business consultant for several multinational companies in Hungary, Italy, USA, Ireland. She is currently involved in the Erasmus+ Virtual Exchange Project as a co-trainer.

Jan Lai is a non-formal education trainer with 20 plus years of involvement in international youth work and intercultural learning. He has a strong interest in digital tools, critical thinking, and creativity. His education includes a Master's in international development and one in e-learning. He is a member of several organisations at regional, national, and international levels.

Notes on contributors

Katja Auffret has studied environmental engineering in Germany and worked in engineering for 11 years in France. She is Lecturer for German since 2004 in several French engineering schools. She also coordinates an KA203 Erasmus+ project for IMT Mines Albi which develops language classes resources in engineering schools.

Dr Ufuk Balaman is Assistant Professor of English Language Teaching and Director of the HUMAN Research Centre at Hacettepe University. His research primarily deals with conversation analysis, CALL, and language teacher education. His work has appeared in Computer-assisted Language Learning, ReCALL, Language Learning & Technology, and Learning, Culture, and Social Interaction.

Tatiana Bruni graduated at Utrecht University in Italian language and culture, with a specialisation in translation. She teaches intercultural communication and Italian language and culture at University College Utrecht. She is also pursuing a PhD in intercultural education at Durham University, focusing on education for engaged citizenship and student voices.

Nadia Cheikhrouhou is Assistant Professor at the Higher Institute of technological studies of Béja, where she teaches business culture, development and management of innovative projects, and corporate communication. Her research interests include entrepreneurship and virtual telecollaboration. She has conducted four virtual exchange projects.

Andra Cioltan-Drăghiciu is a research assistant at the Graz University (Austria) and at the German speaking university in Budapest (Hungary) in the field of Central European history. She finished her PhD with a thesis on youth subcultures in Communist Romania and specialises in Cold War, youth cultures, oral history, and cultural memory.

Daniel Dixon is a project manager, professional trainer, language teacher, and coach with 25 years' experience and he has been involved in Erasmus+ projects for many years. He has been the president of ACSESO since its founding and is an expert in project management, non-formal education, cyberbullying, youth

Notes on contributors

empowerment, and critical thinking. Daniel has a wealth of experience working for the local government in the UK and Spain in the fields of education, training, and social services.

Simon Ensor, @sensor63, is an English as a foreign language teacher at the Université Clermont Auvergne in France, an associate member of the Laboratoire de Recherche sur Le Langage and works with friends in the CLAVIER network and further afield to grow transformative, connected environments for learning. His blog is Touches of Sense…

María Fernández-Raga is Associate Professor in applied physics, and Director of the International Affairs of the University of León, currently combining teaching, research, and management tasks. She has a broad experience in teaching since 2006, mainly in fluid mechanics and fundamentals of physics at the University of León, as well as similar subjects in five other international universities, obtaining several prizes. Her research career has recently focused on the characterisation of rain and in teaching in higher education, recently in virtual exchanges.

Marta Giralt is Lecturer in applied linguistics and Spanish at the School of Modern Languages and Applied Linguistics, University of Limerick, Ireland. She teaches Spanish, language studies, and technology and cross-cultural communication. Her research interests are in second language acquisition, computer-mediated communication, and intercultural communication. Recent publications list: https://ulsites.ul.ie/mlal/dr-marta-giralt-0

Tom Gorman is an academic and theatre director currently based at Coventry University. He studied English literature and language at Queen's University Belfast before completing a PhD in theatre at the University of Ulster. In 1990, after working for some time as a freelance actor, Tom co-founded Sightlines Theatre Company, Belfast, working with them as Artistic Director for six years. During this period, he also worked as a performer, writer and director with numerous theatre companies throughout Northern Ireland and as a writer/performer for BBC Radio Ulster. He was strand leader in drama at Birmingham

Notes on contributors

Małgorzata Marchewka has a PhD in management and quality sciences (2019, Cracow University of Economics – CUE – Poland) and a Master's degree in applied psychology (2009, Jagiellonian University, Poland) and in controlling and corporate finances (2009, CUE, Poland). Her research interests include international management and modern work environments. She has conducted over ten telecollaboration projects.

Teresa MacKinnon, Associate Professor, University of Warwick, is a Certified Member of the Association for Learning Technology. She is experienced in technology enhanced learning design in secondary and higher education. She is resident on twitter as @warwicklanguage. An open educational practitioner, she is currently involved in the EVOLVE project supporting the mainstreaming of virtual exchange.

Francisco Javier Mato Díaz is Associate Professor at the Department of Applied Economics in the University of Oviedo. He holds a PhD in Economics from Oviedo, and an MSc in European Social Policy from the London School of Economics. His main research deals with the analysis of labour market and educational policies.

Dr Sophie C. Millner is Senior Partnerships Officer for the Sharing Perspectives Foundation where she designs the flagship Cultural Encounters course and supports higher education institutions across Europe and the Southern Mediterranean to implement virtual exchanges. Previously, Sophie worked as a parliamentary and non-government organisation researcher before completing a doctorate in national belonging and embodied citizenship.

Dr Asma Moalla is Assistant Professor of applied linguistics at the Faculty of Arts and Humanities of Sfax, Tunisia. Her research interests include: humour research, intercultural communication, conversation analysis, and interlanguage pragmatics. Her work appeared in the International Journal of Applied Linguistics, Journal of Pragmatics, and Journal of Intercultural Communication Research.

Notes on contributors

Sara Pittarello is Freelance Conference Interpreter and Expert in EU higher education and training projects; she is currently responsible for Erasmus+VE outreach with EU higher education institutions and national agencies for UNICollaboration. Expert Evaluator of EU higher education projects, co-tutor of the eTandem E+VE project. Trainer and speaker in national and international events.

Katarzyna Radke is Senior Lecturer of English at the Foreign Language Teaching Centre of Adam Mickiewicz University, Poznań, Poland. She teaches general English and English for specific purposes focusing on e-learning techniques. Her interests lie in the use of online tools for intercultural collaboration and virtual exchange in higher education.

Dr Alexandra Reynolds is Assistant Professor at the University of Bordeaux and a member of the LACES research department. Her research interests include language and identity, the use of English in professional contexts, and bilingual language practices.

Aloisia Sens has studied French, English, and Italian in Germany, Great Britain, and France. Since 1996, she has taught French as a foreign language at Trier University for Applied Sciences at the Environmental Campus at Birkenfeld. She was awarded the teaching price for innovative learning by her university in 2017.

Daniela Stanciu is Assistant Lecturer at the universities of Cluj-Napoca and Sibiu, in Romania. She focuses her research on the field of urban and social history, being interested in the history of the German community in Romania, urban development, and leisure activities in the Hapsburg Monarchy.

Tiina Syrjä is Doctor of Arts in theatre and drama, a speech therapist, vocologist, yoga teacher, and teacher of the Alexander technique, working as a university lecturer in voice and speech in the School of Communication, Media, and Theatre of Tampere University, Finland. She is also an actress and conductor in Tampere Playback Theatre. Tiina has worked with stage voice for almost 30 years and has given presentations and workshops in various universities and theatre schools in Finland and also in Denmark, Germany, Iceland, Italy, Norway, Russia, Spain, Sweden, and Switzerland (to name a few). Her current research interests include vocal extremes, (online) acting in a foreign language, representations of female sexuality in the voice, and telepresence aided rehearsals.

Onur Tahmaz has worked with several international non-government organisations as a trainer, fundraiser, and coordinator in European Union projects for ten years. He graduated from Universidad de Cordoba in the M.A. Culture of Peace, Conflicts, Education and Human Rights. He has publications on migration studies, youth work, and intercultural dialogue. He speaks English, Turkish, Spanish and German.

Claude Trégoat is Associate Professor at the University of Warwick and a French subject leader at the Language Centre. She is a pedagogical lead engaged in action research specifically in innovative assessment and virtual exchange. She has been part of the CLAVIER network since its inception in 2011 and has been initiating and collaborating on multiple virtual exchanges.

Sandra van de Kraak is a creative perseverer, who is very keen to offer young people the opportunities they themselves want to achieve. As an international youth worker and trainer she likes to think outside the box in order to tackle innovative projects together with young people. She was named Youth Worker of the Year for her successful participation projects.

Thierry Villard is a language teacher in charge of incoming and outgoing mobility at Institut de Technologie, the applied sciences institute at the University of Bordeaux. He is involved in virtual exchange programmes with European and Japanese universities. He is also an elected EAIE Steering Group member of the Language and Culture Expert Community.

Margarita Vinagre is Associate Professor at Autónoma University of Madrid where she teaches Educational Technologies and English Language and

Notes on contributors

Linguistics. Her main research interests are the integration of technologies in the foreign language classroom, computer-mediated communication, and the implementation of intercultural exchanges for the development of transversal competences. She has published widely on these topics and is a member of the Editorial Boards of the EUROCALL Review and CALICO (Computer-Assisted Language Instruction Consortium) journals. She is currently the coordinator of the VELCOME project on the integration of virtual exchange for key competence development in higher education, with 20 participating researchers from five countries.

Jean-François Vuylsteke is a passionate, senior language lecturer with more than 30 years of teaching experience at Bachelor level at the Ecole Pratique des Études Commerciales (Belgium) where he teaches business English and cross-cultural business management. He has developed numerous offline bilingual collaborative projects for the last 25 years, first with Belgian universities, then, shifting to online experiences with international partners in the UK, US, Hungary, and Palestine. For the last two years, he has been an Erasmus+VE project trainee and co-organiser of transnational virtual exchange projects.

Ciara R. Wigham is Senior Lecturer in English and applied linguistics at Université Clermont Auvergne and a member of the research laboratory Laboratoire de Recherche sur le Langage. Her research is in the field of computer-assisted language learning and looks at the contribution of multimodality to pedagogical interactions. Ciara has studied this specifically within the context of virtual exchange, content and language integrated learning, and online teacher training. She has been running virtual exchanges in spoken English classes for her applied foreign languages students since 2010.

Acknowledgements

We would like to thank all of the authors of the case studies for their contributions and also the peer reviewers listed below for their invaluable support in providing feedback on the case studies. Thank you also to the Department of Political Science, Law, and International Studies (SPGI) of the University of Padova for the financial contribution which made the publication of this volume possible.

- Alvarez, Inma; *The Open University, Milton Keynes, United Kingdom*
- Arnó-Macià, Elisabet; *Universitat Politècnica de Catalunya, Vilanova i la Geltrú (Barcelona), Spain*
- Bacino, Lorenza; *Unicollaboration, León, Spain*
- Beaven, Tita; *Sounds-Write, Buckingham, United Kingdom*
- Dalziel, Fiona Clare; *University of Padova, Padova, Italy*
- Davies, Gillian; *Università degli Studi di Padova, Padova, Italy*
- Ensor, Simon; *Université Clermont Auvergne, Clermont Ferrand, France*
- Finardi, Kyria; *Federal University of Espirito Santo (UFES), Vitória, Brazil*
- Gimeno-Sanz, Ana; *Universitat Politècnica de València, València, Spain*
- Guth, Sarah; *University of Padova, Padova, Italy*
- Gutiérrez, Begoña F.; *University of León, León, Spain*
- Hauck, Mirjam; *The Open University, Milton Keynes, United Kingdom*
- Johnston Drew, Liz; *Birkbeck College, University of London, London, United Kingdom*
- Koris, Rita; *Pázmány Péter Catholic University, Budapest, Hungary*
- McKinnon, Sabine; *Consultant in internationalisation of the curriculum, Edinburgh, United Kingdom*
- Mertens, Katrien; *KU Leuven, Leuven, Belgium*
- O'Dowd, Robert; *University of León, León, Spain*
- Pittarello, Sara; *Freelance interpreter and expert in EU HE projects, Padova, Italy*
- Plowright-Pepper, Linda. C.; *The Open University, Milton Keynes, United Kingdom*

Acknowledgements

- Sawhill, Barbara; *Bowdoin College, Brunswick, Maine, United States*
- Simon, Nicole; *SUNY-Nassau Community College, Garden City, United States*
- Soulé, Maria Victoria; *Cyprus University of Technology, Limassol, Cyprus*
- Van de Ven, Stephan; *Université de Bourgogne, Dijon, France*
- Van Maele, Jan; *KU Leuven, Leuven, Belgium*

Francesca Helm and Ana Beaven

Foreword

Sarah Guth[1]

This collection of case studies could not come at a more auspicious time, and not only because of the global pandemic that is affecting all of our lives. Virtual exchange is often presented as an innovative approach to teaching and learning across cultures, but inherent in the word 'innovative' is the concept of something being 'new'. As a practice, as well as a focus of research, different forms of virtual exchange have been around for over three decades. What is perhaps 'new' is the exponential growth of the field in the past five years, and the coming together of a community of practitioners, researchers, and funders who now place their different models under the umbrella term of 'virtual exchange'.

As early as the 1990's, when the Internet began to make it possible for people who were geographically distant to communicate more easily, teachers across the globe and across disciplines saw the value in using this new tool to connect students. Of course it took hold more easily in some areas than others. For example, foreign language teachers saw the value in giving their students access to authentic conversation and dialogue with peers who lived in countries where the target language was spoken. This practice was called 'telecollaboration'. At the turn of the century, other forms of this type of activity began appearing in different contexts, with different names. Educators at McGill University in Canada began engaging their learners in 'globally networked learning', others at the State University of New York (SUNY) in Collaborative Online International Learning (COIL) and others yet at East Carolina University in 'global classrooms', to name just a few. At the same time, not-for-profit organisations such as Soliya (USA) and Sharing Perspectives Foundation (Europe) were developing programmes to bring together young people to engage in facilitated dialogue on sensitive topics such as tensions between the Middle East and the 'West' and hate speech. The practice had different names, but the aims were similar: to offer

1. University of Padova, Padova, Italy; sarah.guth@unipd.it

How to cite: Guth, S. (2020). Foreword. In F. Helm & A. Beaven (Eds), *Designing and implementing virtual exchange – a collection of case studies* (pp. xix-xx). Research-publishing.net. https://doi.org/10.14705/rpnet.2020.45.1109

© 2020 Sarah Guth (CC BY)

Foreword

intercultural, international experiences to students and young people in general, as a complement to mobility for those who are fortunate enough to travel, and as an opportunity for a meaningful international experience for those who are not.

What was *not* happening was communication amongst these different practitioners, educators, and researchers. This inevitably led to people reinventing the wheel without the benefit of learning from the experience of others who had already been engaging in this type of activity for some time. Although experience and research were often disseminated through publications, these were almost exclusively in discipline-specific journals thus inhibiting learning across disciplines. The founding of the SUNY COIL Center in 2006 in the United States and UNICollaboration in 2016 in Europe, and their respective conferences and professional development opportunities, began to break down these barriers. But perhaps what truly led to the boom the field has seen in the past five years were the government-funded Stevens Initiative in the United States (2015) and Erasmus+ Virtual Exchange (2018) in Europe. It is in many ways thanks to the latter that we are fortunate to have this collection of case studies. A volume such as this one *is* innovative because it will allow practitioners, researchers, administrators, and decision makers to be inspired, and to not have to continue reinventing the wheel. Although each case study is situated in a different context, two of the fundamental characteristics of virtual exchange are creativity and flexibility. So I invite you, reader of this collection of case studies, to read through them and while doing so imagine how what others have done before you may be applied in your specific context to enrich teaching, learning, and internationalisation. Only by listening to one another and learning from one another may we hope to create future generations equipped with the skills needed to face the many challenges that we are experiencing now and those that the future holds.

Introduction

Francesca Helm[1] and Ana Beaven[2]

Virtual Exchange (VE) is a pedagogic practice based on values such as reciprocity and mutual learning, offering young people opportunities to engage with multiple perspectives on particular issues or disciplinary areas, and to interact and collaborate with distant peers within structured educational programmes in formal or non-formal contexts. VE is not a novel practice, as it has been implemented in a variety of contexts and academic disciplines for nearly 30 years (O'Dowd, 2018), since the Internet made it possible to connect classrooms. In recent years, VE has become recognised as a way to internationalise the curriculum (Leask, 2015), as a form of 'internationalisation at home'.

The recent Covid-19 pandemic has led to a heightened interest in VE, due no doubt to the halt and predicted reduction in student and staff mobility for the near future. Yet this growing interest may also be a response to the need for more environmentally sustainable, and also more accessible and equitable ways to offer meaningful international and intercultural experiences to both students and staff (De Wit & Altbach, 2020). The need for international collaboration is stronger than ever – but experiences of international collaboration based on principles of mutuality and reciprocity are somewhat lacking.

This volume brings together a series of case studies which illustrate how VE projects have been developed and implemented in a range of different settings. Most of the case studies presented were developed in the context of the Erasmus+VE project (2018-2020), a pilot project funded by the European

---

1. University of Padova, Padova, Italy; francesca.helm@unipd.it; https://orcid.org/0000-0003-2197-7884

2. University of Bologna, Bologna, Italy; ana.beaven@unibo.it; https://orcid.org/0000-0003-3289-3010

How to cite this case study: Helm, F., & Beaven, A. (2020). Introduction. In F. Helm & A. Beaven (Eds), *Designing and implementing virtual exchange – a collection of case studies* (pp. 1-8). Research-publishing.net. https://doi.org/10.14705/rpnet.2020.45.1110

Introduction

Commission[3]. The aims of the project are to offer young people in Europe and in Southern Mediterranean countries opportunities to engage in a meaningful cross-cultural experience, as part of their formal or non-formal education. The project's specific objectives include:

- encouraging intercultural dialogue through online people-to-people interactions;

- promoting various types of VE as a complement to Erasmus+ physical mobility, allowing more young people to benefit from an intercultural and international experience;

- enhancing critical thinking and media literacy, and the use of the Internet and social media;

- fostering the development of soft skills, notably to enhance employability;

- supporting the objectives of the 2015 Paris Declaration; and

- strengthening the youth dimension of the EU Neighbourhood Policy.

The E+VE project was accompanied by monitoring and evaluation of activities by a research team, and impact reports have been published every year (see Helm & van der Velden, 2020). The case studies in this volume, however, bring to the fore the voices of some of the beneficiaries of the project, that is educators and youth workers who implemented VE. Their case studies present two main models of VE, as outlined in Table 1 below.

---

3. E+VE is a pilot project established under a contract with the Education, Audiovisual, and Culture Executive Agency (EACEA), financed by the European Union's budget. It is implemented by a consortium composed by Search for Common Ground (Search), Sharing Perspectives Foundation (SPF), Anna Lindh Foundation (ALF), UNIMED, Soliya, UNICollaboration, Kiron Open Higher Education (Kiron), and Migration Matters.

Table 1. Models of VE

'Ready made', facilitator-led dialogue exchanges	Co-designed exchanges
These exchanges are developed and implemented by organisations that have specialised in this activity. Universities have students participate in these projects, which are integrated into curricula, and students may be awarded recognition for their participation. Examples of these are the Connect Programme, a facilitator-led dialogue exchange developed and implemented by Soliya[4] and thematic, dialogue-based exchanges such as those developed by the Sharing Perspectives Foundation[5].	These 'grassroots' exchanges are collaboratively designed by educators who develop a shared curriculum for (part of) their course. Activities or projects are designed so that students in partner classes interact and collaborate with one another in order to meet the learning objectives. In non-formal education contexts these activities are collaboratively designed by youth workers.

In the context of E+VE, training courses were offered to university staff (both educators and administrative staff, mostly but not only international relations officers) and youth workers interested in developing and/or implementing VEs to meet their specific needs and target groups. Based on an experiential and collaborative approach, these courses allowed the participants to have an experience of VE, engaging in both synchronous and asynchronous activities as well as in facilitated dialogue sessions, and exchanging knowledge, experiences, and perspectives. In the advanced training and the course for youth workers, participants collaborated in the design of a Transnational Exchange Project (TEP). However, not all educators and youth workers that took part in the training events actually went on to develop exchanges for a range of reasons, including the difficulty in finding a partner, changes in their working situations, lack of time to invest, not feeling prepared for it, and perhaps not fully understanding how it would fold out.

The idea for this collection of case studies came above all from the strongly perceived need for concrete examples of VE which would help educators and

---

4. Developed by the non government organisation Soliya.

5. https://sharingperspectivesfoundation.com/

Introduction

youth workers to get a sense of what VE actually 'looks like'. The case studies are therefore examples of how VEs have been designed and/or implemented in different settings, to meet the needs of specific target groups. They are not intended as models of 'best practice' or ideal scenarios for VE, but rather 'real life' contextualised examples of how VE has been designed and implemented.

The authors of the case studies were asked to provide some information about the settings in which their exchanges were developed and/or implemented, the aims of their VE, information on the different steps taken in the design and implementation of their project, and how the participants' learning was assessed. They were also asked to write about the lessons learnt, and reflect on how they would change the exchange if they were to repeat it. VE is an often 'messy' endeavour: whilst interactions and activities may be structured and planned, the outcomes are unpredictable and depend on a multiplicity of factors. Yet it is often the unexpected and the challenges that lead us to reflect and learn.

The case studies in this volume illustrate various different 'models' of VE. The majority fall into the category of co-designed or 'grassroots' VE projects. These are generally developed in collaboration by partnering educators or youth workers around a specific theme, disciplinary area, or set of competences. However there are also several case studies (**Al Mqadma & Al Karriri**; **Hoskins & Reynolds**; **Giralt**; **Bruni**) which report on how some of the 'ready made', dialogue-based VEs developed by Soliya and Sharing Perspectives have been integrated in courses in different disciplinary and geographic contexts. In addition, **MacKinnon, Ensor, Kleban, and Trégoat** describe how they used digital badges as a way to acknowledge the skills developed by their students.

Most of the case studies presented come from the Higher Education (HE) sector, first of all because the majority of VEs in the context of E+VE have been developed in HE contexts, and also because writing about and publishing their work is a more common working practice for lecturers. However we have included two case studies which look at VE in the context of youth work (**Dixon & Tahmaz; van de Kraak & Lai**) and are sure that in the near future there will be more VEs in this sector, as well as trans-sectoral exchanges which bring together universities and youth organisations.

VE has been practiced in some disciplinary areas for decades and there is a considerable amount of research literature in particular on foreign language and intercultural learning, where it is known as 'telecollaboration' (Guth & Helm, 2010) or 'online intercultural exchange'(O'Dowd & Lewis, 2016), and management or business studies (Jimenez, Boehne, Taras, & Caprar, 2017). In this collection we have actively sought case studies from other less represented disciplinary areas, such as tourism (**Háhn & Radke**), performing arts (**Gorman, Kanninen, & Syrjä**), history (**Cioltan-Drăghiciu & Stanciu**), and STEM (**Fernández-Raga & Villard**; **Auffret & Sens**, two examples of trans-disciplinary projects), in addition to language and culture (**Vinagre, Wigham, & Giralt**; **Moalla, Abid, & Balaman**) and business (**Koris & Vuylsteke**; **Koris, Hernández-Nanclares, & Mato Díaz**; **Cheikhrouhou & Marchewka**).

Several of the VEs reported in the case studies can also be considered examples of what is now referred to as 'blended mobility', that is the combination of VE with short-term mobility projects, a format which will become more common in the upcoming Erasmus programme[6]. **Gorman et al**'s telepresence in theatre project was intended to culminate with a short-term mobility of students from Coventry (UK) to Tampere (Finland) but this was thwarted, like all student mobility, by Covid-19. **Cioltan-Drăghiciu and Stanciu**'s history project succeeded in its second iteration to secure funds for students to cross the border and actually meet one another in both universities and participate in events in which students collaboratively presented their research projects to the host universities, expanding the understanding of VE to their institutions. **Griggio and Pittarello**'s VE was specifically designed for incoming international students, to support their social, linguistic, and academic integration on arriving at the host university through contact with local students before their arrival, and to prepare outgoing students for their upcoming mobility. **Millner**'s case study describes how a large scale VE project integrated a 'mobility for some'

---

6. http://www.erasmusplus.it/wp-content/uploads/2019/12/Bruno-Castro_DG-EAC.pdf

component whereby one or two participants from each partner university took part in a one-week trip to Brussels. Whilst this brought tangible benefits for the direct beneficiaries, the majority of participants were excluded, and the viability of the model of 'mobility for some' is discussed.

VE provides an opportunity for reflection and research on educational practice, but for some of the authors it has also opened up avenues for collaborative research in their subject disciplines: **Cioltan-Drăghiciu and Stanciu**, for example, report how their three-year project is embedded in a research study on cultural remembrance and the construction of history in their respective contexts. Similarly, **Cheikhrouhou and Marchewka** found that an additional benefit of their VE project was the possibility of scientific cooperation. By working together on the contents of their TEP, they discovered shared topics of interest and have since expanded their academic cooperation.

Co-designed VEs can also be seen as a form of continuous professional development – as the process of developing an exchange entails reflecting on and discussing one's pedagogic practice and context, and learning about one's partners'. Through the E+VE project, a community of practice has emerged, many of these case studies have been presented and discussed virtually, and an ethos of collaboration and sharing has developed.

The case studies in this volume cover a wide range of countries: from Finland, Poland, the UK, Hungary, Romania, France, Spain, Germany, Belgium, Ireland, Italy, The Netherlands, to Turkey, Palestine, and Tunisia. The geographical scope of this collection is limited to Europe and Southern Mediterranean countries as this is the area that the E+VE project targeted. This is no doubt a limitation, as the collection is somewhat Eurocentric. In addition, the majority of the authors are from the field of HE. What we would like to see in the future are more case studies from non-European countries including, for example, sub-Saharan Africa, Southeast Asia, and Central and South America, and covering a wider range of languages, since the majority of exchanges reported were carried out in English. We also hope that future collections will gather examples from a wider range of disciplinary areas, in particular the hard sciences and STEM as this is where there is a considerable gap. Finally, we would like to see more case studies involving youth work, as well as studies of VE across educational sectors.

The case studies can be read in any order. We have divided them into three groups: teacher-designed VE projects, ready-made options, and projects in youth work. The structure of the case studies is similar, facilitating comparison between them. For this reason, we believe the book would be particularly useful to educators in HE institutions looking for inspiration, international relations officers looking for ideas to implement in their own institutions, youth workers wishing to understand how they can integrate VE into their work, and finally teacher trainers looking for examples of innovative teaching practices.

We would like to express our gratitude to the authors who were willing to share their experiences with us and you, our readers. We believe their studies show the many ways in which VE can enrich university curricula and non-formal education alike, offering young people around the world opportunities to connect and develop meaningful relationships online.

References

De Wit, H., & Altbach, P. (2020, January 11). *Time to cut international education's carbon footprint*. University World News. https://www.universityworldnews.com/post.php?story=20200108084344396

Guth, S., & Helm, F. (2010). (Eds). *Telecollaboration 2.0: languages, literacies and intercultural learning in the 21st century*. Peter Lang.

Helm, F., & van der Velden, B. (2020). *Erasmus+ virtual exchange: intercultural learning experiences. 2019 impact report*. Publications office of the European Union. https://op.europa.eu/en/publication-detail/-/publication/0ee233d5-cbc6-11ea-adf7-01aa75ed71a1/language-en

Jimenez, A., Boehne, D., Taras, V., & Caprar, D. (2017). Working across boundaries: current and future perspectives on global virtual teams article reference. *Journal of International Management, 23*(4), 341-349. https://doi.org/10.1016/j.intman.2017.05.001

Leask, B. (2015). *Internationalization of the curriculum in context*. Routledge.

Introduction

O'Dowd, R., & Lewis, T. (2016). (Eds). Online intercultural exchange. Routledge.

O'Dowd, R. (2018). From telecollaboration to virtual exchange: state-of-the-art and the role of UNICollaboration in moving forward. *Journal of Virtual Exchange, 1*, 1-23. https://doi.org/10.14705/rpnet.2018.jve.1

Acronyms and abbreviations

CEF or CEFR Common European Framework of Reference (for Languages)
E+VE Erasmus+ Virtual Exchange
EC European Commission
ELF English as a Lingua Franca (not sure we have it, but just in case)
HE Higher Education
HEI Higher Education Institution
TEP Transnational (Virtual) Exchange Project
VE Virtual Exchange

Section 1.
Teacher-designed

1. Combining expertise from linguistics and tourism: a tale of two cities

Judit Háhn[1] and Katarzyna Radke[2]

Abstract

This case study presents the results of an interdisciplinary Virtual Exchange (VE) that was arranged between Finnish and Polish students in 2019. During their six-week collaboration, the students of language studies at the University of Jyväskylä, Finland, worked in teams together with their Polish peers specialising in information and communications technology and management in tourism at Adam Mickiewicz University in Poznań, Poland. The international teams combined their linguistic and tourism-promotion expertise, and, using collaborative digital tools, grappled with the tasks of analysing the official municipal city websites and promoting the lesser-known aspects of their sister cities (Jyväskylä and Poznań) in jointly created videos.

Keywords: virtual exchange, interdisciplinarity, employability skills, digital literacy, promotional discourse.

1. Context

Most of today's workplaces require competent, tech-savvy, and culturally aware graduates who are able to collaborate online, going beyond geographic, political, and cultural borders (Turula, Kurek, & Lewis, 2019). VE is defined as "online

---

1. University of Jyväskylä, Jyväskylä, Finland; judit.hahn@jyu.fi; https://orcid.org/0000-0003-1784-3541

2. Adam Mickiewicz University, Poznań, Poland; karad@amu.edu.pl

How to cite this case study: Háhn, J., & Radke, K. (2020). Combining expertise from linguistics and tourism: a tale of two cities. In F. Helm & A. Beaven (Eds), *Designing and implementing virtual exchange – a collection of case studies* (pp. 11-22). Research-publishing.net. https://doi.org/10.14705/rpnet.2020.45.1111

© 2020 Judit Háhn and Katarzyna Radke (CC BY)

Case study 1

intercultural interaction and collaboration with students from other cultural contexts or geographical locations as an integrated part of their education programmes" (O'Dowd, 2018, p. 1). Paradoxically, despite its virtual nature, VE prepares the students for the real world by enhancing their working life skills, such as digital literacies, intercultural collaboration competencies, and foreign language skills.

VE projects allow for interdisciplinarity because students from different degree programmes can work together. This way the students broaden their multiliteracy repertoires (Luke, 2002) by building on their peers' expertise and viewing problems from new perspectives. As pointed out by Neumeyer and McKenna (2016) and Bosque-Pérez et al. (2016), members of interdisciplinary student teams engage in authentic dialogues, improve their communication skills, solve problems in a holistic way, and gain unique insights.

This case study discusses an interdisciplinary VE which involved students of language studies (n=12) from the University of Jyväskylä, Finland, and students specialising in information and communications technology and management in tourism (n=13) from Adam Mickiewicz University in Poznań, Poland. The Finnish students were majoring in foreign languages and had expertise in the study and analysis of language use and discourse. The Polish students were in the second semester of their four-semester graduate studies (MA), doing a language course, *English for Tourism*.

The project was called 'Combining expertise from linguistics and tourism: a tale of two cities told in videos' and lasted for six weeks during the spring term of 2019. The international teams of four to five students had to explore, discuss, and promote the lesser-known aspects of their cities, Jyväskylä and Poznań. As the main outcome of the collaboration, each group created a joint promotional video of the two sister cities. The project had relevance for both the tourism and the language students. The Polish students had an opportunity to work in English on a real-life scenario in the field of tourism. The language majors from Finland could apply their knowledge of foreign languages and discourse theories in practice.

The teachers had met in 2018 during an online course on VE, which was offered by EVOLVE (Evidence-Validated Online Learning through Virtual Exchange). EVOLVE is an initiative that aims to mainstream VE as an innovative form of collaborative international learning across disciplines in higher education. Both teachers saw interdisciplinary collaboration as a great opportunity for their students to internationalise at home and to practise 21st century skills (Beelen, 2019; Rubin, 2019). Their idea was supported and later mentored by two experts, Mirjam Hauck and Juan Alba Duran from the EVOLVE team, who provided guidance and regular feedback prior to, during, and after the project.

2. Aims and description of the project

Building on the sister city connection between Jyväskylä and Poznań, the VE aimed to enhance the students' online intercultural collaboration skills by bringing their educational experience as close to real life as possible. By working in autonomous international teams, they could develop the skills essential in any career: critical thinking, creativity, collaboration, communication, digital literacy, as well as interpersonal skills, such as initiative, flexibility, and productivity.

Another important aim was to raise the students' awareness of promotional discourse in tourism by exploring the potentials of multimodal meaning-making through a critical analysis of the official websites of their respective cities. In this way the students were meant to gain new insights in multimodal content creation and use them in practice. By the end of the project, students from both countries were expected to be able to formulate critical views of municipal website discourse, produce their own creative promotional materials with a new digital tool, and reflect critically on the experience of intercultural online collaboration. The project description was published by EVOLVE on their website (https://evolve-erasmus.eu/collaboration/jyu-amu-1000/).

With regard to the learning outcomes, the emphasis was placed on foreign language skill improvement, especially in the case of the Polish students, who had been taught English in monolingual classes and had not had many opportunities to use English in authentic and meaningful communicative situations. An intercultural project such as this proved ideal for them since it ran parallel to the core subject module involving the current tourism trends and promotion of Poznań among international tourists. For the Finnish students, who did the VE as a separate module, the project was a form of internationalisation at home (Garam, 2012; Weimer, Hoffman, & Silvonen, 2019) and an opportunity to work with students outside their discipline. For them, the main learning outcomes were to learn how to use their linguistic expertise in a supportive way and to get experienced in collaborative video-creation.

To ensure that the students were on the right track to achieving the intended goals, the Finnish and Polish teachers regularly met their students during on-campus classes to offer pedagogical mentoring and to discuss various aspects of teamwork, and technology-mediated and intercultural communication (O'Dowd, Sauro, & Spector-Cohen, 2019).

3. Pedagogical design and tools

The teachers chose to use Gilly Salmon's (n.d.) *five stage model* as a scaffold for a structured sequence of the online activities. The model emphasises the need for easy access of students to the VE platform, a range of well chosen team-building activities, collaborative tasks that strongly focus on the learning outcomes, team-orientated knowledge construction, and – last but not least – review and reflection (Salmon, n.d.). The values that the teachers of the present project selected to serve as the pillars of VE were trust, communication, clarity, and predictability.

When it came to the choice of social networking tools to be used during the project, the teachers opted for Google Suite, as most participants had already had access to and experience with some of its applications. Google Classroom was chosen as the main hub for information exchange between teachers and students, and Google Hangouts for group (teacher-students) video-meetings. As the recourse to Google tools required disclosure of personal gmail addresses, the teachers asked the students for their consent and informed them about the General Data Protection Regulation (GDPR) policy adopted in the project. The students also signed privacy waivers for research purposes.

It was decided that the student output (introductions, weekly reports, final products) would be presented on a Padlet, since this application was free and very intuitive for novice users. It also allowed to display information in various modalities and kept all student work neatly organised in one place. In addition to the three tools that were mandatory (Padlet, Google Classroom, and Google Hangouts – later replaced by Zoom), the students were free to choose the applications for their team communication and collaboration (Messenger, WhatsApp, Facebook, Skype, Google Docs, Vimeo, YouTube, etc.). The students were also allowed discretion in deciding how to share the workload in their groups, determining their weekly work schedules, and choosing the themes to be pursued. The need to negotiate various project-related aspects of their group collaboration mirrored the challenges which real-life office teams deal with on a regular basis.

As successful group work depends heavily on group dynamics (Becker, 2003), great emphasis was placed on the team-building activities. Student introduction took place in three stages: introductions in the form of text and image on a Padlet, oral presentations during the opening video-conference with all participants and the teachers present, and finally, more personal exchanges in their groups' virtual meetings. It was in their small groups that the students got to know each other and created a group identity. Among the first tasks was choosing a group name, having a small talk on hobbies, and sharing the results of a survey they had conducted in their own country prior to the start of the project. The survey's aim was to find out how much the students in Poznań or in Jyväskylä knew about the other country and the sister city, and what potential motivation they might have for making visits there.

As the next step, the students analysed and compared the two cities' official websites, focusing on the language, graphic design, professed values, and the marketing strategies. The students were asked in particular to evaluate how much the municipal website of their partners appealed to potential young visitors from their own country. They also had to make suggestions on remedying the deficiencies of the official city website. Each group presented their conclusions in a comparative report, which was shared on the project's Padlet.

As the work progressed, the group activities became more complex and required more creativity. When designing their own promotional materials, the students were encouraged to present their respective cities in a new light. Of particular importance was showcasing those aspects of their cities that were not well known but had a potential to attract young visitors. After some brainstorming, each group had to agree on a common theme and then do some fieldwork to collect the necessary materials by taking photos and recording short videos with authentic scenes of city life. They also had to find suitable background music published on free licences, devise text graphics for the video, and combine all these elements into one convincing, multimodal piece of promotional material revolving around a chosen theme. The latter part was a particularly challenging and stressful element of the project due to the tight deadlines. The workload was intense, but all the groups succeeded in creating the promotional videos, which were shared on a Padlet.

The final stage of the project focused on evaluation and reflection. During the closing video-conference, the students discussed their VE experience and compared their strategies of coping with the challenges. They evaluated their own promotional materials as well as those of their partners. They also expressed their emotions about what they deemed useful and difficult by drawing their own mind-maps and commenting on the maps made by their fellow participants. When asked to focus on a critical moment of the collaboration process, they closely examined an event of their choice and discussed it with the teachers and their peers. Both activities were adopted from Małgorzata Kurek's (2015) rich repertoire of collaborative tasks. The individual e-portfolios completed weekly by the students showcased their activities, attitudes, expectations, and lessons learnt at each stage of the six-week VE, creating a vivid record of the progress made during the project.

4. Evaluation, assessment, and recognition

Despite numerous obstacles (inclement weather, illnesses, misunderstandings, local holidays, unreliable Internet connections, and other technical issues), all the teams managed to produce their promotional videos on time. Only one out of the six videos was patched up from two separate parts about Jyväskylä and Poznań, as the students involved ran out of time in snowy weather, did not get the right footage, and were unable to discuss a better combination of images. All the groups focused on diverse aspects of their sister cities. They were proud of the final products and drew enormous satisfaction from successful overcoming of linguistic, intercultural, interpersonal, and technical issues which cropped up along the way.

In order to get credit for the VE project, the students were required to complete all individual and group assignments, such as posting their personal introductions on a Padlet, presenting the results of the introductory survey on the two cultures, and completing the six weekly reports on international collaboration with records of synchronous and asynchronous group communication and online meetings (e.g. group photos, screenshots of messages, and students' quotes). The students were also required to actively participate in the opening and closing video-conferences and individually submit a full reflective e-portfolio. The pass/fail grading system was used.

Both the Finnish and Polish participants were volunteers and, as such, were highly motivated to engage in interactions with international students using English as a lingua franca. As a form of international recognition, all participants received digital badges issued by EVOLVE to be displayed on social media platforms such as LinkedIn. They also received official certificates, issued by their respective universities, acknowledging their participation in VE. Both the certificates and the digital badges were highly appreciated by the students and some participants used them later in the job recruitment process, in scholarship and Erasmus+ grant applications, and in other situations. For the Polish students the VE project was worth 50% of the total credit for their English course (spring semester), which is two ECTS points. The Finnish students got three ECTS points.

Case study 1

Student feedback on the collaboration process was extremely positive. The anonymised individual e-portfolios provide vivid testimony that teamwork was going well in most cases. There were difficult times at the production stage, but all the groups were able to overcome their problems using various group-developed strategies. The class discussions, the students' reports, and e-portfolios reveal that the overwhelming majority of participants felt that VE was an extremely valuable experience. They believed it was relevant for their future working lives and saw it as a great opportunity to develop their transversal and intercultural skills. Let us share some excerpts from the individual e-portfolios.

One Finnish student wrote:

> "From the entire virtual exchange project, I learned that working in a multicultural team using only technology can be challenging at times but it is also rewarding as you can save time, money, and meet new people and learn more about other countries and cultures by sitting at your computer at home. It was nice to see how we were able to help each other see things we might not have thought about otherwise. The Polish students are tourism majors, whereas the Finnish students are language students, and because we represented different study fields, we were able to utilize our personal skills and combine our knowledge to produce a promotional video for the two cities. This demonstrates well how a team does not have to meet physically in person in order to work well together, and this experience also shows how intercultural communication does not always have to mean miscommunication".

Another one observed:

> "I learned from this experience that it is important to view familiar things through the eyes of a tourist/stranger to get a new perspective and notice things I hadn't noticed before. I also learned that in different cultures the same assignment can be understood very differently or the effort may differ. I stayed calm and thanked for the effort even if in my mind I felt slight irritation. It resembled working life, I guess, but also

> taught me group work skills: you have to get results with what you have and you cannot control everything, despite that, the result may be good because the other party has done their part nevertheless".

And still another noted:

> "I felt a bit sad that the project is over. It felt like it would take a long time and suddenly it was over. However, I am happy I participated in this project. It is a useful skill to learn to communicate and plan things together with people you are not able to see".

One Polish student observed:

> "To sum up the project was very interesting, I'm glad that I took part in it. I can meet new people and new culture [sic], I'm so happy. Thank you! We made [a] really nice movie and thanks to this I am more confident using English".

5. Lessons learnt and conclusion

What the participants of the Polish-Finnish VE seemed to cherish the most was the chance to use English in an authentic setting and the opportunity to work in autonomous teams. The students' sense of agency and the ability to communicate across cultural divides significantly boosted their self-esteem and helped them to see the value of their own linguistic skills. The promotional videos, which were the final outcomes of the project, showed that the students enjoyed the collaboration. They could overcome disciplinary, cultural, and language barriers when engaging in creative teamwork. Most of them gave very positive feedback on the project, pointing out its relevance for working life.

As the teachers of the project, we learnt about the importance of having a similar level of commitment and work ethics. The project required a jointly developed pedagogical design, which meant a lot of planning and negotiation. The chosen tasks had to be challenging but attainable and, whenever possible, simulate real-life scenarios. It was also worthwhile to have the support of the EVOLVE mentors and more experienced colleagues. It was essential that both of us had a clear overview of the schedule, the assignments, and the assessment. We also learnt that the students need constant support and encouragement from their teachers. On-campus guidance combined with emailing and reminders posted in the project's online platform proved to work well.

VE requires a great deal of commitment, discipline, and patience from both the teachers and students. VE projects are meant for individuals who are willing to put their heart and soul in the process. Trust and close collaboration are the keys to successful completion of the tasks (Rico, Alcover, Sánchez-Manzanares, & Gil, 2009). Notwithstanding the effort, VE is extremely rewarding and provides opportunities for personal and professional growth for everyone (Hauck, 2007).

VE offers something that traditional classes organised for monolingual and mono-disciplinary groups at the same fluency level are unable to provide: authentic language use, curiosity about the outside world, an opportunity to see your own culture from a new perspective, and a genuinely international experience. VE is a cost-effective way of bringing schools closer to real life and it prepares graduates for the demands of future culturally diverse societies and the globalised labour market. Although VE is unlikely to replace physical mobility, it can still offer real-life intercultural experiences at home to a vast majority of students and motivate them to venture outside of their comfort zone.

References

Becker, K. L. (2003). Just tell me what to do: group dynamics in a virtual environment. In *Proceedings Women in Research Conference, Rockhampton, Australia.* https://eprints.qut.edu.au/12187/1/12187.pdf

Beelen, J. (2019). Employability skills as guiding principles for internationalising home curricula. In R. Coelen & C. Gribble (Eds), *Internationalization and employability in higher education* (pp. 200-212). Routledge. https://doi.org/10.4324/9781351254885-16

Bosque-Pérez, N. A., Klos, P. Z., Force, J. E., Waits, L. P., Cleary, K., Rhoades, P., Galbraith, S. M., Bentley Brymer, A. L., O'Rourke, M., Eigenbrode, S. D., Finegan, B., Wulfhorst, J. D., Sibelet, N., D., & Holbrook, J. (2016). A pedagogical model for team-based, problem-focused interdisciplinary doctoral education. *BioScience, 66*(6), 477-488. https://doi.org/10.1093/biosci/biw042

Garam, I. (2012). Internationality as part of higher education studies. *FAKTAA. Facts and Figures 1B/2012*. CIMO. https://lemonoc.eu/sites/default/files/26139_Faktaa_1B.pdf

Hauck, M. (2007). Critical success factors in a TRIDEM exchange. *RECALL, 19*(2), 202-223. https://doi.org/10.1017/s0958344007000729

Kurek, M. (2015). Designing tasks for complex virtual learning environments. *Bellaterra Journal of Teaching & Learning Language & Literature, 8*(2), 13-32. https://doi.org/10.5565/rev/jtl3.633

Luke, C. (2002) Cyber-schooling and technological change: multiliteracies for new times. In B. Cope & M. Kalantzis (Eds), *Multiliteracies: literacy learning and the design of social futures* (pp. 67-88). Routledge.

Neumeyer, X., & McKenna, A. (2016). Entrepreneurial thinking in interdisciplinary student teams. *Advances in Engineering Education, 5*(1), 1-20. https://advances.asee.org/?publication=entrepreneurial-hinking-in-interdisciplinary-student-teams

O'Dowd, R. (2018). From telecollaboration to virtual exchange: state-of-the-art and the role of UNICollaboration in moving forward. *Journal of Virtual Exchange, 1*, 1-23. https://doi.org/10.14705/rpnet.2018.jve.1

O'Dowd, R., Sauro, S., & Spector-Cohen, E. (2019). The role of pedagogical mentoring in virtual exchange. *TESOL, 54*(1), 146-172. https://doi.org/10.1002/tesq.543

Rico, R., Alcover, C. M., Sánchez-Manzanares, M., & Gil, F. (2009). The joint relationships of communication behaviors and task interdependence on trust building and change in virtual project teams. *Social Science Information, 48*(2), 229-255. https://doi.org/10.1177/0539018409102410

Rubin, J. (2019). Collaborative online international learning (COIL): now preparing students for international virtual work. In R. Coelen & C. Gribble (Eds), *Internationalization and employability in higher education* (pp. 189-199). Routledge. https://doi.org/10.4324/9781351254885-15

Turula, A., Kurek, M., & Lewis, T. (2019). (Eds). *Telecollaboration and virtual exchange across disciplines: in service of social inclusion and global citizenship*. Research-publishing.net. https://doi.org/10.14705/rpnet.2019.35.9782490057429

Case study 1

Salmon, G. (n.d.). The five stage model. https://www.gillysalmon.com/five-stage-model.html

Weimer, L., Hoffman, D., & Silvonen, A. (2019). *Internationalisation at home in Finnish higher education institutions and research institutes*. Ministry of Education and Culture, Helsinki. http://julkaisut.valtioneuvosto.fi/bitstream/handle/10024/161606/OKM_2019_21_Internationalisation_at_Home.pdf

2. Immersive telepresence in theatre: performing arts education in digital spaces

Tom Gorman[1], Mikko Kanninen[2], and Tiina Syrjä[3]

Abstract

This case study examines a joint project in performer training and rehearsal conducted between Coventry University (UK) and Tampere University (Finland) using a variety of telepresence and app-based technologies. In this project, two identical spaces, equipped with rear projection screens and linked by videoconferencing technology, were created in both institutions. This study reports on the adaptation of the pedagogical practices to a digital setting.

Keywords: theatre, telepresence, COIL, rehearsal, Shakespeare, Beckett.

1. Context

Theatre traditionally has had a somewhat problematic relationship with online learning. Students of theatre "often select performing arts programmes at university because of the promise of the viscerality and the co-present experience with fellow actors and an audience" (Crossley, 2012, pp. 171-172). Most online practical work in the performing arts tends to be of an experimental nature, work that embraces the limitations of the laptop/mobile screen and the variable nature of home and academic networks.

---

1. Coventry University, Coventry, United Kingdom; aa4084@coventry.ac.uk; https://orcid.org/0000-0003-0175-2602

2. Tampere Theatre, Tampere, Finland; mikko.kanninen@tampereenteatteri.fi; https://orcid.org/0000-0002-8947-0804

3. Tampere University, Tampere, Finland; tiina.syrja@tuni.fi; https://orcid.org/0000-0002-9545-371X

How to cite this case study: Gorman, T., Kanninen, M., & Syrjä, T. (2020). Immersive telepresence in theatre: performing arts education in digital spaces. In F. Helm & A. Beaven (Eds), *Designing and implementing virtual exchange – a collection of case studies* (pp. 23-35). Research-publishing.net. https://doi.org/10.14705/rpnet.2020.45.1112

Case study 2

At the moment (March 2020), I am writing this under lockdown in the UK due to the current Coronavirus crisis. As my university closed three weeks ago, there was a last-minute scrabble to refocus teaching and assessment for online consumption with many of my colleagues having to come to terms with moving their teaching online for the very first time and many students genuinely distressed that their performances and productions, some of them planned for over a year, have now been replaced by online written assessments and presentations using videoconferencing. Facebook groups of theatre practitioners struggling to cope with this new online paradigm have sprung up and Twitter feeds showing photographs of Zoom theatre tutorials have now become ubiquitous.

The COVID-19 crisis interrupted (and continues to disrupt) any concept of performances for live audiences occupying the same physical space. As a result, practitioners and educators have turned to techniques that were previously the domain of more experimental practitioners, largely unknown outside of specialist circles. The largely physical experience of a theatre degree found itself forcefully moved into the digital space with all performance and rehearsal venues closing their doors to both performers and public alike.

The biggest problem that theatre teaching faces when moving online is that the subject mostly involves group activity, relying on work created in physical spaces. Online work requires a holistic understanding of how a digital space operates and theatrical work using these strictures needs to be planned and crafted with the dynamics of the networked world in mind from the outset. The virus outbreak and necessary social distancing has meant that many courses (including my own) have struggled to get work refocused to cope with the very different dynamics of digital learning. Theatre as a communal activity faces the challenge of moving traditional theatre work and teaching online whilst attempting to replicate the sense of belonging that comes from the rehearsal room.

This was a problem that we struggled with back in 2016 when we started the Immersive Telepresence in Theatre project. The course developed initially as a joint initiative between Coventry University (UK) and Tampere University (Finland) to explore acting in a foreign language but eventually mutated into a course that explored performances of Shakespeare in both English and Finnish. The concept of this stemmed from the idea that acting in Shakespearean blank verse would be equally challenging for both English speaking and Finnish students. Tampere had experience in conducting research into teaching actors techniques to cope with acting in an unfamiliar tongue, so the combination of expertise in Shakespearean acting from the Coventry side, coupled with the Finnish research into acting in a foreign language seemed like an ideal combination of our specialisms.

Since the initial trial version in 2016, collaborations under the umbrella term 'Immersive Telepresence in Theatre' have occurred with The University of the Arts, Helsinki, Gothenburg Theatre Academy, Adam Mickiewicz University, Poznan, and Purdue University in the United States. Just as the pandemic prompted a shutdown in campuses worldwide, Tampere and Coventry were completing the most recent iteration of the project, a two-week exploration of the text of Samuel Beckett's 'Waiting for Godot'.

For the initial project, we adopted the term 'virtual stage' to describe our system until a colleague pointed out that there was, in fact, nothing 'virtual' about the space. Both sets of participants were physically present in their own campuses – they were not occupying a 'third space' even in a theoretical sense. A decision was made to adopt the term 'immersive telepresence' to refer to future versions of the project as it was felt that this was a more accurate description of the space. Telepresence (or telematics) as a term was first coined by Marvin Minsky (1980) in reference to the remote operation of robots, but has since taken on the wider definition of using internet related technologies to give the participants the sense of 'being there' in remote spaces, whether actual or virtual (Parker-Starbuck, 2011). Many researchers in the field have stressed that *liveness* is key to telematic communication and, as a result, live-streams do *not* constitute telepresence collaborations, nor do recorded performances – synchronous interaction is key to the experience.

2. Aims and description of the Erasmus+ Virtual Exchange

In June 2015, the initial meeting between theatre staff from Coventry and Tampere universities rather naïvely suggested a series of online rehearsals to explore, rehearse, and perform selections from the text of Shakespeare's 'Coriolanus'. The course was to be delivered synchronously, but we faced a problem in that we had not considered which digital platform could best replicate the sensations of a physical rehearsal process in a virtual setting.

> "Performance and performer training requires both intimacy and openness – the ability to simulate/recreate emotions and to be comfortable with both physical and emotional intimacy in order to re-create this in a public performance situation" (Gorman, Syrjä, & Kanninen, 2019, p. 238).

We often hear talk of 'chemistry' between performers, a phenomenon that occurs when actors have developed a strong working relationship, and are used to each other's speech patterns and physicality. However, it is very challenging to attain this online, with participants who had never actually met face to face before the start of the project.

The initial idea was to have students collaborate together in small groups working via Skype or Google Hangouts, but this solution turned out to be immediately problematic. Laptop screens and the technological limitations of webcams made it difficult to discern facial expressions, and the added latency of these platforms made real time communication frustrating when trying to follow the rhythms and patterns of Shakespearean dialogue.

There was an additional problem in that the rooms that students traditionally engage with these software packages (labs, bedrooms, student flats) lack space for performers to move around. Even if the performers are able to move, their images become so tiny that any real rehearsal work becomes almost unwatchable. The more users occupy these spaces (as you will be aware from Zoom meetings), the smaller the image becomes as the screen fills with windows. Using any of these formats meant that full group work would be impossible.

Eventually, a rather ambitious (and naive) decision was made to create a space in both countries that would allow us to have a synchronous experience for both groups. We decided to support this work with Adobe Connect[4] for contextual lectures and small specific scene rehearsals[5]. Inspiration for this spatial design came from an installation by a Coventry colleague, Joff Chafer, who, in collaboration with the Australian performance artist, Stelarc, had created a physical space in the Herbert Art gallery, Coventry, that linked to the online virtual world, Second Life. Called 'Extract/Insert', participants entered the physical space in Coventry and interacted with a virtual recreation of that same space on a large rear projection screen. They were able to interact with avatars on this screen by stepping onto a plinth that "would insert their image, captured by an infra-red camera, onto a separate screen in the Second Life space visible on the screen" (Chafer, 2015, p. 249).

The basic physical architecture of this installation would be adapted to create two identical spaces in Tampere and Coventry both with carefully balanced lighting, sound, and camera positions to give the occupants the illusion that they were occupying the same space in real time. The set up occurred over one week in February 2016 using H.323 videoconferencing technology[6] and large rear projection screens with the bulk of the technology (bar the camera) hidden behind both screens. This camera, situated at waist height in the centre of the screen, was the focal point for interaction and play between the students and is still the piece of technology that encourages the bulk of experimentation (Figure 1).

---

4. For more recent versions of the project we have switched to Zoom for this aspect of the course. Adobe Connect, although effective for our initial projects, proved to be too expensive and complex when compared to other software solutions.

5. Students were split into six scene groups of two Tampere students and three Coventry students. Adobe Connect was also seen as a 'fall back option' in case the larger space proved to be unworkable.

6. Polycom in Coventry, Cisco in Tampere. Both systems use the same H.323 protocols which enables higher speed transfer of data back and forward between sites. This technology was chosen as it is the simplest and most affordable solution for first time users engaging in this type of task. For low latency it does need some fairly advanced networking skills and the bulk of the set up (to this day) involves testing the latency between both sites and tweaking the network connections on both sides. For the most recent iteration of the project (Godot Online) we have switched to the NIMBRA media server from NetInsight which allows us to experiment with low latency cameras.

Case study 2

Figure 1. Set up of screen with camera slightly above waist height[7]

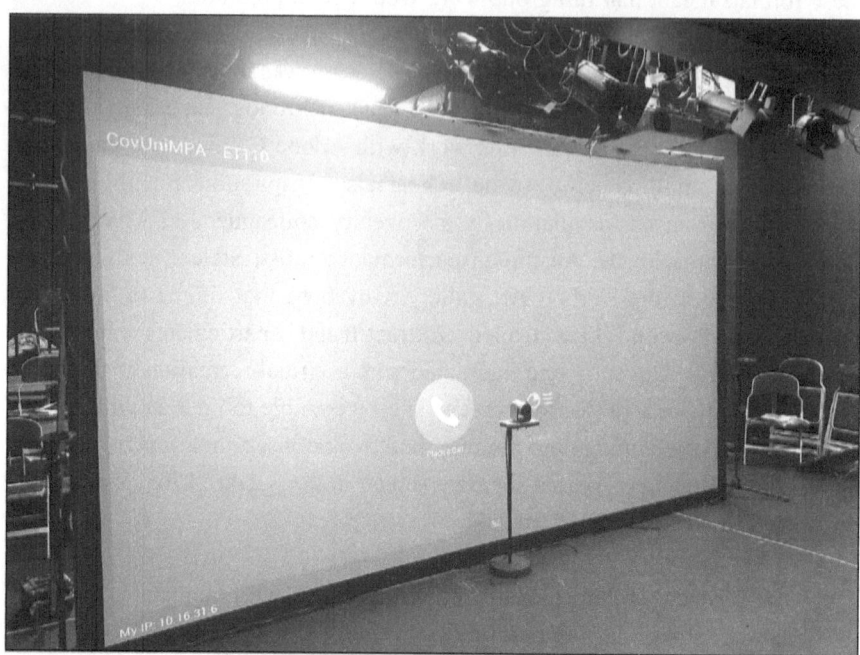

Adobe Connect was also used to give each scene group (consisting of two Tampere and three Coventry students) their own individual 'rooms' to work independently on their scenes. Facebook was also utilised for scheduling details, sharing research materials, and to provide a quick way for students in each location to share photographic and video material of the ongoing work.

3.   Nuts and bolts

Coriolanus Online, the first iteration of the project, threw up some interesting and unexpected problems for both students and staff new to working in this fashion. I am sure that now, since we have all been working remotely, readers

---

7. Published under CC BY in Gorman, Syrjä, and Kanninen (2019, p. 243).

of this article are painfully familiar with the twin concepts of bandwidth and latency. These problems were amplified in the first incarnation of the telepresence experiment due to the sheer scale and ambition of what we were attempting. Research conducted into latency in online collaboration in the performing arts suggests that a latency of 20 milliseconds gives the impression of participants being 20 feet apart (Miske, 2016)[8]. Once latency goes above 40 milliseconds, playing instruments, singing, and synchronous performance becomes problematic – imagine having to communicate with another person across a large room. During Coriolanus Online, we faced latency times of over 600 milliseconds meaning that synchronous activities had to be adapted to cope with this delay between sites[9].

This issue of latency initially had an effect on pedagogy, especially in terms of what could be achievable in the space during the first iteration of the project. A synchronous session on Finnish folk dancing led by Tampere choreography tutor, Samuli Nordberg, managed to cope with the delay between both sites as Tampere students were demonstrating unfamiliar steps to the Coventry students who were attempting to replicate these moves (Figure 2).

It was when we moved to other activities which would be standard practice during theatre teaching that the issue of latency proved rather more problematic. A session in which both groups attempted to sing an Elizabethan 'round song' proved to be impossible as both were completely out of synch with each other and the activity had to be adapted to take this into account. A simple game of 'grandmother's footsteps' in which participants attempt to sneak up on 'the grandmother' and must freeze when he/she turns had to be altered in

---

[8]. Miske's research mainly deals with instrumental collaboration which requires much lower latencies than acting as performers need to be perfectly in synchronisation. Dialogue can cope with higher latencies as thought and response need to come into play. However, when looking at the rhythmical patterns of blank verse (which is not naturalistic dialogue) there is a certain point where high latencies can cause problems for the performers.

[9]. In later incarnations, we have shaved valuable milliseconds from the latency between both sites. Some of this was due to better communication with the teams that administrate the campus networks, getting dedicated ports for the project and not sharing bandwidth with the general traffic on the campus. In 2020, the switch to the NIMBRA media server (primarily designed for live streaming of broadcast television) improved the stability and latency of both connections. Because of the manner in which this system encodes sound and video we found that, during Godot Online, latency had been reduced to around 40 milliseconds.

Case study 2

consideration that the students on both sides could see each other move due to the delay[10].

Figure 2. Finnish folk dancing lesson conducted by Samuli Nordberg: Coriolanus Online 2016[11]

During this initial version of the project, students were given free rein to play with the technology, exploring the limitations and advantages of this technologically enabled space for rehearsal and teaching. We started each day with a one hour warm up using the whole group in both campuses. These workshops/warmups were the most 'experimental' aspects of the course and remain so in each subsequent incarnation. Over the five years of the project, we have invited guest artists and academics to participate in these sessions, teaching a wide variety of

---

10. https://www.youtube.com/watch?v=67nxQTkCZsM&t=1s – first half shows a demonstration of latency between Hong Kong and Tampere and the second half shows the attempt to play 'grandmother's footsteps'.

11. Reproduced with permission from © Immersive Telepresence in Theatre: http://telepresenceintheatre.coventry.domains/iterations/coriolanus-online/

skills including dance, voice, yoga, asahi[12], a skiing lesson and, with Purdue, a burlesque masterclass[13].

Each group would then have an hour in the main telepresence space to develop their scenes before moving on to continue this work in their individual Adobe Connect spaces. Whole group communication, schedule changes, and research materials were uploaded to a private Facebook group (which, rather surprisingly, continues to operate). Facebook also gave us the ability to share images and video clips from both locations in real time, giving each group an immediate sense of what the other side could see and hear. It also became an important 'back channel' for communication between groups if any of the technology failed at any point[14].

4. Evaluation

As mentioned in Lindén, Kanninen, Kupiainen, and Annala (2019),

> "[t]he students moved rather easily from one technological environment to another and even introduced new ways of using personal social media to solve study-related problems. Second, the usually very daunting experience of throwing oneself into acting in a foreign language with a 'native speaker' did not seem to be a long-term issue. [...] The international co-operation did not happen in a strange cultural space but in a neutral place created by everyone's bodily presence" (p. 91), see Figure 3.

---

12. A form of martial arts and relaxation techniques developed in Finland.

13. https://www.youtube.com/watch?v=8zA52730D-g From 3.50 - 5.44 King Lear Online (2017) singing sessions led by vocal tutor Soila Sariola (Tampere) and Sam Fox of Kiln Theatre (UK).

14. On the 2nd of February 2016, the UK academic network was hacked and the internet went down for the afternoon. Two days later Adobe Connect decided to update their software meaning that the platform went down for the day. Students switched (without prompting) to other platforms such as Skype or Facebook messenger to continue the work and made new arrangements through the Facebook group.

Case study 2

Figure 3. Coventry and Tampere students greet each other in Godot Online 2020

Over the five years of the project we have continued to refine both the technology and pedagogy that involves teaching in mediated spaces such as these. The traditional teaching methods that we would use in a live space had to be slightly adjusted to cope with this semi-digital method. At the beginning of the process it is tempting for the tutor to focus on the participants onscreen as this object is such a dominant presence in the space. One also gets the initial sense that these onscreen students are international visitors to your 'home space' and not just one half of the whole group. We found it necessary to try and psychologically overcome the temptation to deliver everything to the screen at the expense of ignoring the home students. The optimal position for the tutor in this space became either at the side of the group standing diagonally so that both groups could view his/her face or standing at the back of the space (Figure 4).

An unforeseen aspect of the initial course is that, as work continued in the Adobe Connect spaces, the team noticed a shift in the dynamics between the students in the main space. As they got to know each other through their own individual rehearsals using the app, they became much less self-conscious about interacting together in the main area. The Facebook group began to fill with pictures of students spending time and talking to one another in Adobe Connect. In terms of engagement, this level of informal interaction (either digitally or in person) outside the classroom is almost as important as the formal interactions within the campus space (cf. Krause, 2007). We were delighted when we discovered that the students had even shared a 'virtual beer' together over Adobe Connect. What was unusual back in 2016 has now become commonplace for us all during the pandemic (Figure 5).

Figure 4. Galileo online 2019, tutor positioned in the centre of the semi-circle and further back than the participants[15]

Figure 5. Virtual Beer Coriolanus Online 2016

---

15. Reproduced with permission from © Immersive Telepresence in Theatre: http://telepresenceintheatre.coventry.domains/uncategorized/galileo-online/.

5. Lessons learned and conclusion

Recreating the physical rehearsal space through telepresence technologies may be time consuming and technically rather complex, but the benefits to international collaboration between academic institutions, especially during the current pandemic, are vast. Not only have we saved money on expensive hotels/hostels during field trips, but we have effectively doubled our staff teams during these projects, enabling true international collaboration at a fraction of the cost. Of course, this digital experience does not replace the experience of travelling to another country and, in the past, we have adopted a blended experience with students working online for two weeks before travelling to the partner institution to continue the work and, on some occasions, to stage a performance with both casts.

With our most recent project the plan was, after the two weeks online work, to gather in Tampere to continue rehearsals and develop the piece for performance in 2021 as part of UK City of Culture. Of course, the global pandemic derailed those plans. As we continued rehearsals whilst watching case numbers rise, there was a sense that we might not be able to conclude the project in the way we intended. At the start of each session the students discussed the pandemic with increasing concern. Eventually Finland closed all schools and universities on the 16th of March with the UK following suit on the 20th of March. There was a sense of gloom as both groups of students realised that the trip would not occur.

Both casts had never met in person – and still have not[16], although there are plans to regroup in March 2021 to finish the work for performance in both cities either live or live-streamed.

Telepresence technologies encourage students to "broaden their horizons, [permit] discipline based academic theories to be contrasted with practice and, in addition, [allow them] to have greater confidence in assessing how theatre is created in other countries [and cultures]" (Kanninen, Syrjä, & Gorman, 2016,

---
16. https://youtu.be/e6_81P43-qg - Godot Online documentary consisting of interviews conducted via Zoom, rehearsal footage filmed on iPhones and the final sharing of work between both casts on the last day before both institutions closed due to COVID-19. It shows the work in progress which was still at an embryonic stage as well as discussions with students about working during a global pandemic

p. 226). The desire to co-create across borders is a strong enough justification for the existence of telepresence enabled theatre and performance and can be a rich field for theatre pedagogy advancing both rehearsal and pedagogical methodologies. As our connections with each other redefine what we think of as 'presence', perhaps digital solutions on this scale for performing arts education can offer new ways to preserve our live work for the future.

References

Chafer, J. (2015). Blended reality performance. In D. Doyle (Ed.), *New opportunities for artistic practice in virtual worlds*. IGI Global.

Crossley, M. (2012). From LeCompte to Lepage: student performer engagement with intermedial practice. *International Journal of Performing Arts & Digital Media, 8*(2), 171-188. https://doi.org/10.1386/padm.8.2.171_1

Doyle, D. (2015). (Ed.). *New opportunities for artistic practice in virtual worlds*. IGI Global.

Gorman, T., Syrjä, T., & Kanninen, M. (2019). Immersive telepresence: a framework for training and rehearsal in a post-digital age. In G. Ubachs & F. Joosten-Adriaanse (Eds), *Blended and online education within European university networks*. EADTU. https://core.ac.uk/download/pdf/304335206.pdf

Kanninen, M., Syrjä, T., & Gorman, T. (2016). The coriolanus online project. In *Proceedings of the 20th International Academic Mindtrek Conference*. AcademicMindtrek. https://doi.org/10.1145/2994310.2994352

Krause, K.-L. (2007). Social involvement and commuter students: the first-year student voice. *Journal of the First Year Experience and Students in Transition, 19*(1), 27-45.

Lindén, J., Kanninen, M., Kupiainen, R., & Annala, J. (2019). Sensing the same space – spatial understanding and engagement in higher education. D*ansk Universitetspædagogisk Tidsskrift, 15*(27).

Minsky, M. (1980). Telepresence. *Omni Magazine*. https://web.media.mit.edu/~minsky/papers/Telepresence.html

Miske, G. (2016). *Feasibility study for using music to introduce technology: the Kentucky initiative*.

Parker-Starbuck, J. (2011). *Cyborg theatre: corporeal/technological intersections in multimedia performance*. Palgrave Macmillan.

3 Virtual exchange: Romania and Hungary 100 years later

Andra Cioltan-Drăghiciu[1] and Daniela Stanciu[2]

Abstract

The aim of this Virtual Exchange (VE) project was to bring together students from the Andrássy Gyula German speaking university (AUB) in Budapest, Hungary, and Lucian Blaga University in Sibiu (LBUS), Romania, in order for them to get to know their neighbors and reflect on the way the end of WWI is remembered 100 years later. In this case study, we discuss the way we conceived the three iterations of the VE (2018-2020), the challenges we faced on different levels, as well as the value of this teaching method for the academic field of history.

Keywords: cultural memory, culture of remembrance, central European history, Romanian history, Hungarian history, cultural studies.

1. Context

The last three years, including 2020, have been years both of celebration and of mourning in Central Europe. While some nation states commemorated their coming into existence in the aftermath of the First World War, others lamented the consequent loss of territory and population. The governments organized celebrations on a national scale, people gathered in public demonstrations, politicians spoke about the events, while historians wrote about them; works of

---

1. Graz University, Graz, Austria / Andrássy University Budapest, Budapest, Hungary; andra.draghiciu@uni-graz.at

2. Sibiu University, Sibiu, Romania / University of Cluj-Napoca, Cluj-Napoca, Romania; danamstanciu@yahoo.ro

How to cite this case study: Cioltan-Drăghiciu, A., & Stanciu, D. (2020). Virtual exchange: Romania and Hungary 100 years later. In F. Helm & A. Beaven (Eds), *Designing and implementing virtual exchange – a collection of case studies* (pp. 37-46). Research-publishing.net. https://doi.org/10.14705/rpnet.2020.45.1113

© 2020 Andra Cioltan-Drăghiciu and Daniela Stanciu (CC BY)

art were created and private companies used the symbolic value of these events to sell products. The series of three VE between AUB and LBUS was aimed at students in the neighboring countries Romania and Hungary with the purpose of addressing three historical events and their remembrance from an analytical and scientifically critical point of view.

In this context, we analyzed, together with the student-participants, the events that happened 100 years ago (Boia, 2017) from the point of view of cultural remembrance (Assmann, 2008). The purpose of the three iterations of the VE was to combine historical facts, the concept of cultural remembrance and discourse analysis as a research method to question the way history is constructed in Central Europe.

The idea for the exchange arose when Robert O'Dowd spoke about the possibilities offered by VE in a course Andra Cioltan-Drăghiciu attended at the University of Graz in spring 2018. Finding the concept fascinating and very fitting for a history class, she proceeded in looking for a partner, which she found in Daniela Stanciu, a historian she had known since high-school. Thus, a 'robust partnership' (O'Dowd, 2013) was created by means of personal networks, which enabled the two teacher-partners to repeat the exchange successfully.

Under the guidance of the UniCollaboration team, the first exchange of the series began in autumn that same year. The concept of the course and the idea of the VE was very appealing to both historians, as it represented a good opportunity for lecturers and students to cooperate in a virtual classroom, and reflect on topics of great importance to their field.

As neither of the universities had ever been involved in such a project before, we had the opportunity to offer our students something new and exciting, while also raising their awareness about stereotypes and the ways the two nations had created 'mutually incompatible fairy tales' (Hobsbawm, 1996) to legitimize their existence. The biggest challenge in the beginning of the course was for the students to acknowledge that the cultural and historical stereotypes they had grown up with merely represent social constructs and that communication is the best way to overcome them.

Participating in the course from the AUB were Master students enrolled in the cultural diplomacy and/or Central European history programs. The exchange was integrated in the curriculum as part of the class 'Transculturality and Cultural Conflict', for which the students received credits.

Students from LBUS were Bachelor students from the Department of History, Heritage Studies, and Protestant Theology. Unfortunately, the LBUS' fixed curriculum did not permit the integration of the course, so the students and the lecturer did not receive any credit or remuneration for participating – they did it voluntarily in their own time. As remarked by O'Dowd (2013), university management has yet to recognize the value of these activities and incorporate them into the syllabi.

A very interesting, but also difficult part was the fact that the participants from the AUB were of different nationalities, from Hungarians and Germans to a student from Tajikistan. This meant that they had different levels of knowledge about Central European history and culture, but also, as it turned out during the exchange, a very different set of language and analytical skills. The students from the LBUS, on the other hand, came from a homogenous milieu, with limited multicultural experience or contact with students from other universities. Since most of them were young undergraduate students, the VE allowed them to appreciate the contact to other cultural milieus and broaden their horizon. In this respect, the exchange was of great help for the Romanian students in developing not only their language skills, but also their understanding of multicultural societies and universities. Moreover, as undergraduate students, the participants from LBUS had to catch up with the historical information; this is the reason why we insisted on including a theoretical part in the very first VE.

One challenge was the significant differences in knowledge and English language skills among the students.

Case study 3

In the first iteration of the exchange, a total of nine students attended the courses and worked together in mixed teams on some specific themes, such as *analysis of the political discourse* regarding the events happening 100 years ago (1918), advertisements inspired by these events, and remembering 1918 in art and artistic festivals, happening in Sibiu and Budapest in 2018. This was also a 'blended exchange' in that we managed to organize a mobility so the groups of students could visit each other's universities and present the results of their projects in the frame of two workshops we organized in Sibiu (17th of December 2018) and Budapest (23th of March 2019).

The second iteration of the VE took place in the first semester of the academic year 2019/2020 and brought together eight students from the two aforementioned universities. In the last iteration of our three-semester series, nine students from the two universities came together, to discuss the ways in which the Treaty of Trianon is currently remembered.

2. Aims and description of the project

The main goal of the exchange was to bring students from these neighboring countries together and thus create a dialogue on some of the most controversial events of their history, to discuss the ways in which history is constructed and exploited for political or financial purposes, how narratives are created in order to serve a particular agenda, and that historical facts are not objective realities, irrefutable truths, but subjective constructions, which can be bent to accommodate specific needs. As well as acquiring communication and online skills, the main aim was for students to understand that history is shaped by different perspectives, not only by the academic point of view.

3. Pedagogical design and tools

The exchanges combined a theoretical and a practical, collaborative component. In each iteration, students were first equipped with the necessary background historical knowledge and analytical frameworks. Subsequently they worked in transnational groups, exploring and analyzing specific historic events and how these events are remembered and reconstructed in different contexts.

The first iteration of the exchange took place in 2018, the year which symbolically marked 100 years since the Unification of the Romanian Provinces. The students were divided into three groups (one student from the AUB and two from the LBUS in each group). For this first exchange, which lasted throughout the winter semester, we applied the blended learning method (O'Dowd, 2013), which meant that the online classes were integrated in the usual classroom activities. Each lecturer discussed the theoretical part with her own students in the physical classroom and all the participants together with the teachers subsequently met four times in a Zoom virtual classroom for a total of 90 minutes per session in order for the students to get to know each other and pick the topics for their common presentations. The three major themes addressed were culture of remembrance (Assmann, 2008) on Trianon and Greater Romania in advertisement, arts, and politics.

Allowing them the freedom to choose their topic unfortunately led to very unbalanced groups in terms of language and analytical skills. Even though each group contained one master and two undergraduate students, the participants with better English and analytical skills were interested in the same topic and thus ended up in the same group.

To prepare their presentations, the participants communicated with their group via Google Drive, Messenger, and WhatsApp. Whenever they needed help or had any questions about the task, they turned to the lecturers for guidance, but other than that, they were encouraged to work independently, without direct supervision. At the end of the semester, each group presented the result of their project in Zoom meetings.

To avoid the aforementioned imbalance, for the second iteration of the exchange in 2019 on the topic of the occupation of Budapest by the Romanian Army (1919), we decided to do the theoretical work together asynchronously.

Case study 3

This was done via a Facebook group, which we preferred to Moodle because we did not want to overwhelm the students with new technologies. Each lecturer posted a task such as reading specialized texts and then answering the teacher's questions regarding those texts. The students responded by commenting on each post, then received feedback from the lecturer who created the task. Having their work assessed by someone other than their own teacher stimulated the students and confronted them with a new teaching approach and a different set of expectations.

Reading their written answers allowed us to better assess their English and analytical skills, but also their knowledge on the subject. It was important for us to examine each participant's skills both in terms of language and of methodological knowledge in order to pair them up in balanced groups and to make sure they could keep up with the tasks.

This time there were four groups of two, one student from the AUB and one from the LBUS. What we observed, however, was that this approach was not ideal either, as pairing up a student with a solid knowledge base and good English skills with a student without these characteristics prevented the former from reaching their full potential. This is certainly something we had to work out for the third VE on the Treaty of Trianon (1920), which started in March 2020 with nine students, three of which had participated in the second iteration of the exchange. We solved the problem by carefully assessing their English and analytical skills, then pairing them up in one group of three and three groups of two by adjusting the subjects and difficulty of the respective projects to their skills.

While diligent collaboration among the students seemed like a given during the first iteration of the exchange, there was a group in the second iteration which faced some communication issues with one of the students trying to contact the other repeatedly and not receiving any answer until the lecturers stepped in. This made us realize how important the interest of each individual is in sustaining a VE, especially when they are not motivated extrinsically by the perspective of grades or credits. To avoid this issue in our last exchange, we created group chats with each group and the lecturers, so whenever communication issues arose, the participants could write in those groups, making sure both their teammates and the lecturers saw their attempt at communicating.

For this third and last exchange of our series, we invited a guest lecturer, Dr Florian Kührer-Wielach, a specialist from the Institute for South-Eastern Culture and History in Munich, to observe the course by taking part in the Zoom sessions and creating tasks for the participants. He took over the practical part of our introduction and gave the students materials on discourse analysis, then had them answer some questions and analyse texts using this method. The concept of VE was new to him, as it is among our research community. By offering him, the director of a prestigious historical institute, a glimpse into our class, we hope to introduce VE among historians and promote it as an innovative means of teaching history especially in neighboring countries with competing historiographies, as is often the case in Central Europe.

4. Evaluation and assessment

In the first VE, the joint presentations were assessed after their completion by taking into consideration criteria such as form, content, and critical analysis. During the semester, the students worked on the following topics: cultural remembrance in advertisement, commemorative performances in Budapest and Sibiu, and political discourse of Hungarian and Romanian politicians. The students sent their PowerPoint presentations to the coordinators, who made suggestions, comments, and spelling checks. Thus, they were able to update their slides before presenting them to the other participants in the Zoom virtual classroom. After each final presentation, the groups received written feedback from the coordinators, which consisted in remarks regarding the methodology used, the flaws in their analysis, and suggestions regarding historical sources.

After the first VE, we asked for funding from Erasmus+ teacher mobility and our respective departments and were able to organize two workshops, one in Sibiu, in December 2018, and the second one in Budapest, in March 2019.

This way, the students had the opportunity to meet in person and discuss the project but also to form a deeper, personal relationship. Each group presented their project again in front of students and professors from the LBUS and AUB, who were very excited and curious about the VE. The coordinators presented short introductions and conclusions, whereas the highlight of the workshops consisted in the Zoom presentations made by UniCollaboration experts. The aim of these presentations was to introduce VE to students and professors at both universities, as they had never been confronted with this type of teaching before. Having VE experts contribute to the workshops gave the events authority in the face of our program directors, who could thus convince themselves that our virtual classes were part of a larger endeavor on a European scale, supported by European institutions.

At the end of the second iteration in the 2019 semester, each of the four groups presented the results of their research. The first group focused on the topic of international press and cultural memory of 1919 in Hungary and Romania, the second one analyzed Hungarian and Romanian history textbooks, whereas Groups 3 and 4 researched historical journals. In the end, the comparative approaches and analyses presented by the students were thoroughly documented, most of them with strong, well-structured arguments. After presenting their projects, the students received written feedback from the coordinators, which contained some suggestions and recommendations for the future.

As mentioned above, the students from the AUB received grades and credits for taking part in the VE, as opposed to the students from LBUS. The ideal circumstances for VEs described by O'Dowd (2013), training and support of teachers, and integration of VE in the department's curriculum, were not given, but the institutions contributed financially by enabling the physical mobility of the participants, a method they were more comfortable with. Thus, the workshops financed by the two universities were meant as a reward for the participation in the first VE. All the participants in the exchanges received Erasmus+ badges, which they were happy to include in their resumes. Aside from the content, historical, and methodological skills they acquired during the course, the students benefited from learning to work online via tools like Zoom and Google Drive.

Student feedback:

"Erasmus+ VE was an amazing experience, one that truly impacted the manner in which I see European history in general and interethnic relations in particular. Being part of this project gave me the huge opportunity of seeing things objectively, of knowing students from other countries and of using tech means I did not use before. Moreover, I got to understand different points of view and manners in which one approaches history today through the eyes of past events that scarred the collective memory. With all my heart, I would recommend VE to all the students that want to expand their knowledge and to know amazing people".

"As far as I am concerned, the exchange was an enjoyable and fulfilling experience. Through this project, I was able to meet new people with whom I could exchange ideas and opinions. This project also introduced me to an interesting video conference app called 'Zoom' which proved to be very reliable during the realization of our project. The subject chosen for this project allowed me, as a Romanian history student, to see another side of the discourse regarding these events and made me realize that such controversial events cannot be analyzed just from one perspective. This project also allowed me to assess and improve my communication skills in the English language. VE also helped me to refine my teamwork skills, but also my time and task management capabilities. This project also made me realize that in this day and age, thanks in part to advancements in telecommunications technology, anything can be done with a stable internet connection and a lot of communication".

This experience is proving of great value now, in times of world-wide quarantine, when all classes are held online. The students who have participated in our exchange have shown greater flexibility in solving tasks online, they are familiar with tools such as Google Drive and Zoom, which others (professors and students alike) were just beginning to master. The same is true for us as lecturers. We did not have any difficulties making the transition from physical to virtual classes, we did not need to invest time in learning how to use the proper tools and our colleagues turned to us for advice in managing classes online.

5. Conclusion

Our conclusion as lecturers in the field of history is that VE is a viable, refreshing, and fruitful alternative teaching method which enriched both the didactical experience of the coordinators and the communicative, technical, and linguistic skills of the students. Addressing sensitive historical topics through the eyes of students with different cultural and intellectual backgrounds allows for a holistic approach of the subject and for the broadening of the individual perspective, a fact which undoubtedly enriches the academic experience for both lecturer and student. Moreover, we were privileged enough to be able to implement the three iterations in the three most important consecutive years for Central European history, thus going full circle in analyzing cultural remembrance in Romania and Hungary one hundred years after these symbolically charged events occurred.

References

Assmann, J. (2008). Communicative and cultural memory. In A. Erll & A. Nünning (Eds), *Cultural memory studies: an international and interdisciplinary handbook*. Walter de Gruyter.

Boia, L. (2017). Istorie și mit în conștiința românească. *Editura Humanitas, Bucarest*. https://humanitas.ro/assets/media/istorie-si-mit-2017.pdf

Hobsbawm, E. (1996). The stories my country told me. *Arena, BBC*. https://www.youtube.com/watch?v=OyO2hbvxx8s&t=5s

O'Dowd, R. (2013). Telecollaborative networks in university higher education: overcoming barriers to integration. *The Internet and Higher Education, 18*, 47-53. https://doi.org/10.1016/j.iheduc.2013.02.001

4. The transnational job exchange project: a French-German TEP

Katja Auffret[1] and Aloisia Sens[2]

Abstract

The technical institutions Institut Mines Télécom in Albi, France (IMT) and Trier University for Applied Sciences at the Environmental Campus of Birkenfeld, Germany (UCB) have been running Virtual Exchange (VE) projects since 2013. These projects allow the French and German students to use the vocabulary learned in class in a real context and to develop their interaction competencies. This case study reports on the latest project about job searches, in which teams with a German and a French partner were formed and different activities were created to gain insights into the job application procedure.

Keywords: tandem project, job research, language for specific purposes, German, French.

1. Context

IMT and UCB have in common one of the major aims of higher education institutions: to prepare students for the world of work in an increasingly globalized world. For this reason, the two institutions involved offer their students the possibility to do an internship in the partner country.

---

1. Institut Mines Télécom, Albi, France; katja.auffret@mines-albi.fr; https://orcid.org/0000-0001-9641-0925

2. Trier University for Applied Sciences, Birkenfeld, Germany; a.sens@umwelt-campus.de

How to cite this case study: Auffret, K., & Sens, A. (2020). The transnational job exchange project: a French-German TEP. In F. Helm & A. Beaven (Eds), *Designing and implementing virtual exchange – a collection of case studies* (pp. 47-58). Research-publishing.net. https://doi.org/10.14705/rpnet.2020.45.1114

Case study 4

Nevertheless, these students are often faced with intercultural differences they had not been aware of and for which they were not prepared, thus resulting in misunderstandings.

VE has shown to help students develop employability skills (Guadamillas Gómez, 2017; O'Dowd & Lewis, 2016), which is one of the reasons why it has been implemented in this context.

IMT and UCB are partner universities and signed Erasmus+ mobility agreements more than ten years ago. The lecturers contacted each other within this Erasmus+ cooperation and since 2013, tandem projects between the two partner universities in which the students collaborate on technical as well as business topics have been integrated in the language classes, mainly at the B1 and B2 levels – Common European Framework of Reference for languages (CEFR).

The two authors, one a lecturer in German at the French institution, and the other a lecturer in French at the German university, decided to integrate a bilingual VE project into their teaching to raise their students' awareness of intercultural differences and thus prepare them better for their period abroad.

The two lecturers decided to follow specific training programs offered within the Erasmus+ VE (E+VE) initiative to design their Transnational Exchange Project (TEP) collaboratively. The E+VE program also offered their students the opportunity to obtain their first virtual badges for their participation.

2. Aims and description of the project

As the students have to do an internship abroad, and will potentially do it in the partner's country, the two lecturers decided to use their TEP to prepare their students to enter the graduate job market. The intended learning outcome of the project was to learn more specific vocabulary for the job search in the partner country and to gain self-confidence for real job interviews, as well as to improve students' global competence (Asia Society/OCDE, 2018).

Focusing on this goal, the lecturers set up the course on the learning management system OpenOLAT of the UCB, with the following structure for a seven-week VE project (see Figure 1).

- In the first week, each student presented another student of their country in the foreign language. In the weekly forum, they discussed their fears and expectations.

- In the following six weeks, teams of two to three students from both countries worked both synchronously and asynchronously on the topics of the project (employment opportunities in their country; mock job interviews; and preparing for the first day of work in the partner's country). They had to deliver three recordings of synchronous video-meetings as evidence of their collaborative work.

- Finally, the students provided feedback in class and in a common survey to express their opinion concerning the project and to reflect on the learning experience.

The objectives of the weekly activities were described briefly before each activity was explained in detail – step by step what was asked for and which Information and Communication Technology (ICT) tool to choose. In the platform there was also a special tab containing important information, such as the dates and logins for the common synchronous sessions on Zoom, and a link to the weekly forum for the discussion of intercultural topics and awareness. Instructions were given in French and German.

The VE was accompanied by classroom lessons once a week for 90 minutes. Here the linguistic preparation for the different activities took place, and new vocabulary was established and shared between all students of the two countries

Case study 4

through Google Sheets and revised and trained by playing quizzes like Kahoot prepared by the lecturers and the students.

The lecture time was also used to share experiences, to ask questions, to give support, and especially to discuss upcoming problems, such as when agreed virtual meetings have repeatedly not taken place without being cancelled by the partner/s or when the required task could not be solved within the allowed time. The questions were also discussed under the focus of intercultural misunderstandings.

Three facilitated sessions were offered by UNICollaboration in which the students met in groups of 8-10 and were encouraged to get to know each other on a personal level in order to engage in meaningful intercultural dialogue with their partners during their collaboration.

Figure 1. The structure of the TEP project on OpenOlat

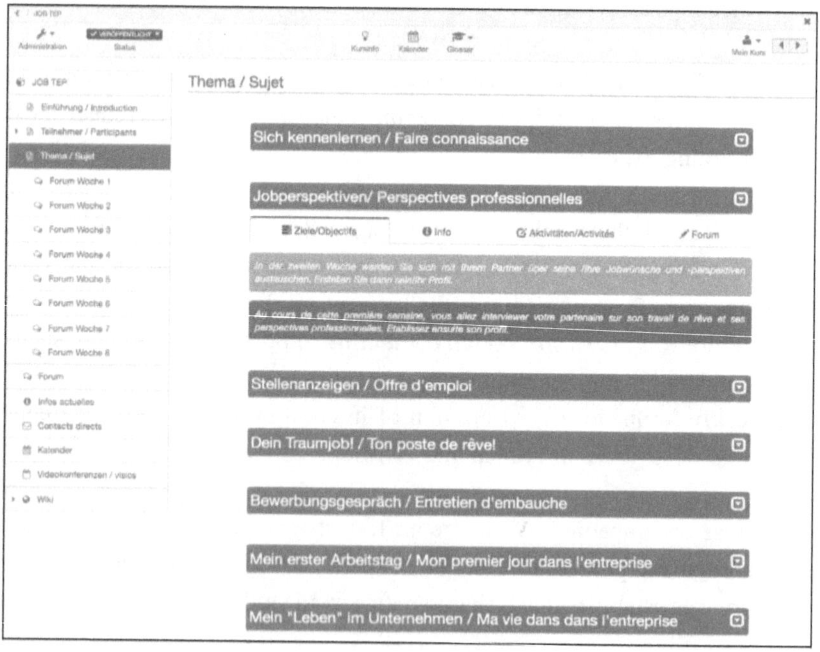

3. Pedagogical design and tools

As to the organization of the project, it was set up on one learning management system, in the case of this project OpenOlat, which served as a supply for the activities and all organizational aspects. The ICT tools which had to be applied were explained to the students before they had to use them.

The following tools were used for this project:

- Zoom as a tool for video conferences (https://zoom.us/meeting);

- OpenOLAT as a learning management system: organization, information and telecollaboration in the forum as a tool for asynchronous communication and in the wiki (https://olat.vcrp.de/);

- Padlet as a collaborative working space and for sharing documents and information (https://padlet.com/);

- genial.ly as a telecollaboration and presentation tool (https://app.genial.ly/); and

- Mentimeter as a survey tool (https://www.mentimeter.com/).

The VE project started with a self-portrait: on a Padlet, a virtual pinboard which had been integrated in the course, the students and lecturers presented themselves. The layout of this pinboard allows all students' profiles to be visible on one page and to easily integrate images and photos.

In a second step, the students were asked to talk about their expectations and fears regarding the TEP in the course's forum – an ideal tool for asynchronous communication and discussion.

As the lecturers knew the language level of their students and considering their studies and interests, they formed the tandems (or sometimes groups of three) between a German and a French partner. The groups were asked to find a name and a picture representing their team.

During the synchronous session of that week, the pictures of the teams were analyzed using the *DIE method* (Paige et al., 2002), which stands for Describing, Interpreting, and Evaluating. Here, the lecturers asked the students to describe only what they saw on the image representing the team. The students had to interpret the image by answering the questions: who, what, when, where, and why. The lecturers also asked the students to put the interpretation in an intercultural context. Finally, the students had to deconstruct the interpretation by evaluating it. They had to answer the following questions: Why did you interpret the image like this? Could there be other interpretations? Is your interpretation positive or negative? The pedagogical goal of this exercise was to create awareness of intercultural differences but also common values.

In the following week, the real VE started when the students had to exchange information about their studies and their job wishes and perspectives. On a poster, they presented their partner regarding their job perspectives. The students used genial.ly (https://www.genial.ly) to create this poster, an Internet site for interactive presentations and infographics.

During the next weeks, the students gained insights into the job application procedure. Each student had to find three real job offers in their own country suitable to the profile of their partner(s). In a word cloud on Mentimeter, the most requested skills were collected and discussed during the lecture time. Mentimeter allows users to create interactive live polls, quizzes, word clouds, Q&As, and more (see Figure 2 below).

The groups moved on to the presentation of their offers. In a Zoom meeting which had to be recorded, the French students presented the selected French job advertisements to their German partners speaking German and vice versa. The links to the recorded meetings were shared in a wiki that was integrated in the online platform. One page was provided for each group in order to facilitate collaboration and the sharing of documents.

Figure 2. The most important soft skills wordcloud on Mentimeter

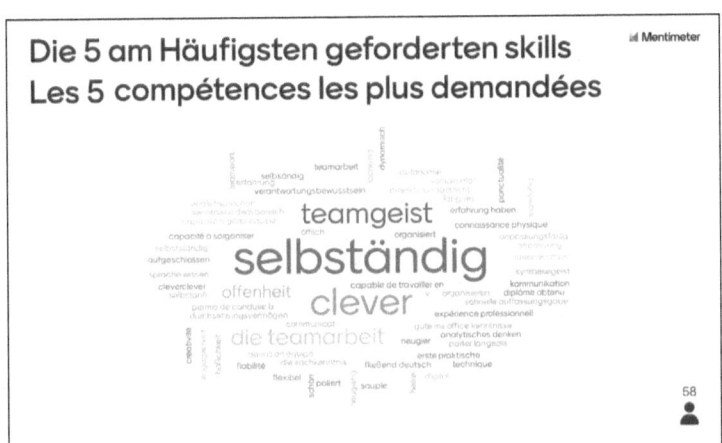

After the presentation of the three offers, each partner selected the most suitable one and, as an activity for the following week, mock interviews had to be planned, one in French and one in German. Thus, the German students were interviewed in French by their French partners in the role of interviewers, and the French students then acted as interviewees in German. The students were again asked to record the meetings on Zoom. The vocabulary and important questions were learned in class by brainstorming and watching example videos of job interviews. The students prepared the mock interviews by means of their choice (email, Messenger, or videoconferencing), but they had to produce a 15-minute recording of both interviews on Zoom.

The next topic was 'How to prepare one's first day in a new company'. This question was asked in the forum and three tips in the foreign language were expected from everyone. Hints regarding clothes, form of address, time aspects, social behavior, and conduct toward colleagues and a superior were given in this asynchronous communication.

This was transformed into a task on work etiquette. Intercultural differences became evident and were discussed in the lecture time. Whereas the German

Case study 4

students focused mainly on aspects like the dress code, time aspects, and relation toward colleagues, nearly all the French students pointed out the significant role of the supervisors and the importance of hierarchy in French companies – which was unknown and strange to their German partners.

Finally, being virtually employed by the company, the students had to talk about their tasks in the new job, the atmosphere, and the netiquette in the company. The conversations also took place on Zoom and had to be recorded. Here the intercultural differences that were pointed out in the previous activity were again addressed. The German students for example complained about the rigid atmosphere in the French company, while the French students felt very comfortable in the relaxed environment of a German company – not only concerning the social relationships but also regarding the dress code.

4. Evaluation, assessment, and recognition

The TEP ended officially at the end of January 2020. In their last shared lesson, the students were asked to complete the evaluation sheet co-developed by the two lecturers. This evaluation sheet, a Google Form, included questions about the management of the project (how much time did it need per week? Did you prefer synchronous or asynchronous sessions?...), the learning outcomes (did you learn relevant professional vocabulary? Which intercultural differences did you come across?...), and also asked for suggestions to improve the project.

Analyzing the evaluation, the feedback is mainly positive – besides the progress in especially oral production, the students welcomed the collaboration in an international team and the critical reflecting or thinking on stereotypes or prejudices. They also appreciated being creative at the beginning of the TEP. Besides the improvement of their language skills, they highlighted the soft skills they acquired during the TEP as good preparation for their future jobs, such as learning to collaborate with an international partner respecting their working time and manners, and applying digital tools to discuss and come to a conclusion. The students did particularly mention the difference of working and hierarchic styles in Germany and France. One student's quote: "We don't have the same way of working, that's evident. I think that the Germans are more punctual and disciplined".

The students spent between one hour and one and a half hours on the project per week and estimated this time was suitable to the project needs.

The participants liked the synchronous sessions and appreciated the combination of both synchronous and asynchronous work (see Figure 3).

Figure 3. Final evaluation: did you prefer synchronous or asynchronous sessions or the combination of both?

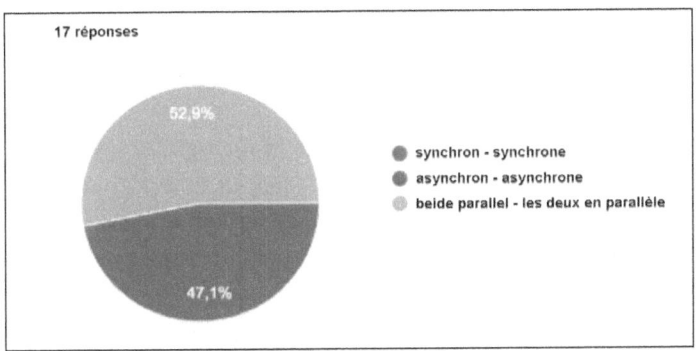

One of the quotes of the students[3]:

> "Mir hat die Eigenständigkeit der Teams gut gefallen, denn es ist nicht immer einfach, v.a. zu dritt, Termine zu finden und Abgaben abzuliefern, wenn einer aus dem Team gerade nicht kann/sich nicht meldet, etc. Also alles toll! :)".

It confirms the two lecturers' opinions that the students need not only online tasks but also training in class with face-to-face activities and synchronous video

---

3. Translation: I liked the independence of the teams, because it is not always easy, especially with three of them, to find dates and deliver documents when one of the team members cannot/does not report, etc. So everything is great! :)

conferences with their partners. As a matter of fact, online activities are very useful because students can manage their time individually (how often they watch a video and how much time they invest to learn vocabulary or to prepare synchronous sessions). They can also more easily compensate for the different systems in the two partner institutions. But to improve their oral competencies and ability to interact with a partner, it is necessary to combine the asynchronous online work with synchronous sessions where the students can apply what they have learned.

Almost three quarters of the participants highlighted not only their linguistic progression during the TEP, but also the international collaboration with all its advantages and misunderstandings as the best preparation of 21st century workforce skills. They especially welcomed the fact that vocabulary was acquired and practiced through exercises during the lecture time which they could apply immediately.

In the discussions of intercultural differences in their groups, with their French and German partners, the students needed this vocabulary and they had the chance to turn the passive vocabulary into actively used vocabulary. Although they complained on the one side about the amount of work, they were all in all happy about having participated in the TEP and proud of their badges distributed by Erasmus which they can link for example to their LinkedIn profile. The fact of being rewarded with such a badge by an official organization with the European Commission logo on it was all in all a determining point in their decision to choose the project. Furthermore, the badge can be added to an application which especially regarding the geographical location of the German university can be of advantage: on the one side, the attractive labor market in Luxemburg and on the other side, the French strategy of the Saar Government and its effort to become bilingual German/French by 2043[4].

Working in Germany and gaining initial professional experience in a German company as an engineer is very motivating for the French students. The TEP

---

4. https://www.saarland.de/stk/DE/service/publikationen/_documents/Frankreichstrategie.pdf?__blob=publicationFile&v=1

was thus designed to reflect their future professional life – collaborating in international teams on a project – and to gain their first experience in a transnational working environment. They benefited from being supported by their lecturers and by the E+VE facilitators on linguistic, intercultural, and organizational aspects.

5. Lessons learned

As to the opinion of the lecturers, the two great challenges of digitalization and internationalization which determine the European higher education program are combined in VE projects. Beyond the fact that they offer the possibility of integrating the challenges of innovative didactical methods – namely the four Cs (communication, collaboration, creativity, and critical thinking) – in their teaching, an international context is provided. Participating in TEPs, the students gain soft skills such as working in international teams, which due to globalization is increasingly demanded in their future professional life.

A lot of students stated that one of the big challenges was the involvement of students in the project. This was due to intercultural issues, like different understandings of time management and discipline and to the fact that, in Germany, students choose this module and get more credits.

For their next project, the two lecturers plan to establish rules every student has to respect during the project, a 'netiquette' and to carry out a pre-survey in addition to the post-survey, to measure the development of intercultural awareness. They still need to explore tools to measure this awareness, which is currently done only by comparing comments and analyzing the post-survey.

6. Future plans

The two lecturers will continue to implement VE projects, but try to further improve them.

In addition to the netiquette to be written by the students at the beginning of the project and a pre-survey, the activities in the forum need to be further developed. As a matter of fact, the students are not really interactive in the forum, they need to be motivated.

The lecturers are also thinking of integrating more scientific subjects in the VE projects and seeking to cooperate with science lecturers as they both work with engineering students.

References

Asia Society/OCDE. (2018). *Teaching for global competence in a rapidly changing world.* https://doi.org/10.1787/9789264289024-en

Guadamillas Gómez, M. V. (2017). Building global graduates and developing transnational professional skills through a telecollaboration project in foreign language education. In C. Álvarez-Mayo, A. Gallagher- Brett, & F. Michel (Eds), *Innovative language teaching and learning at university: enhancing employability* (pp. 49-58). Research-publishing.net. https://doi.org/10.14705/rpnet.2017.innoconf2016.654

O'Dowd, R., & Lewis, T. (2016). (Eds). *Online intercultural exchange: policy, pedagogy, practice.* Routledge.

Paige, R. M., Cohen, A. D., Kappler, B., Chi, J. C., & Lassegard, J. P. (2002). *Maximizing study abroad: a student's guide to strategies for language and culture learning and use.* Center for Advanced Research on Language Acquisition, University of Minnesota.

5. Multidisciplinary and international virtual collaboration on the "Shared Garden" between the Universities of Bordeaux and León

María Fernández-Raga[1] and Thierry Villard[2]

Abstract

This case study describes two iterations of a cross-disciplinary Virtual Exchange (VE) project developed between the Universities of Bordeaux (France) and León (Spain), involving students of Applied Physics and Measurement Engineering (APME), and Electrical Engineering. The students worked together on designing a real garden in Bordeaux within ecological and sustainable parameters. This Project-Based Learning (PBL) activity helped them develop both their content knowledge and their competences in English, teamwork, time management, and self-evaluation.

Keywords: virtual exchange, science competences, intercultural competences, transnational exchange projects, project based learning (PBL), engineering.

1. Context

This VE project, entitled the Shared Garden, is the result of a fruitful collaboration between the University of León in Spain and the Institute of Technology of Bordeaux, part of the University of Bordeaux in France. This collaboration

---

1. University of León, León, Spain; maria.raga@unileon.es; https://orcid.org/0000-0002-8228-6705

2. University of Bordeaux, Bordeaux, France; thierry.villard@u-bordeaux.fr

How to cite this case study: Fernández-Raga, M., & Villard, T. (2020). Multidisciplinary and international virtual collaboration on the "Shared Garden" between the Universities of Bordeaux and León. In F. Helm & A. Beaven (Eds), *Designing and implementing virtual exchange – a collection of case studies* (pp. 59-68). Research-publishing.net. https://doi.org/10.14705/rpnet.2020.45.1115

© 2020 María Fernández-Raga and Thierry Villard (CC BY)

began in 2018 after the two authors followed a training program to develop transnational exchange projects, and has seen two iterations of the VE project, one in the academic year 2018-2019 and one in 2019-2020.

The French students taking part in the project are undergraduate students and more precisely second year students enrolled in the APME department. The students in Spain are also undergraduate students but from the fourth year of the Degree in Electrical Engineering of the University of León. They are studying Fluid Mechanics Engineering in English, which involves six ECTS. As part of their studies, they participate in one PBL activity which develops their theoretical and practical knowledge as well as their competences in English, teamwork, deadline tracking, and self-evaluation methods.

In the French department, some students follow the international track, which provides 30% of science classes taught in English. These students also get extra classes to help them upgrade their scientific vocabulary, improve their communication skills, and prepare them for their mobility since all the students have to do their compulsory internship abroad. As part of the project, the students had to carry out a tutored project, which gave them a first impression of their future placement. Indeed, they had to organize themselves to complete various tasks.

Developing VEs is not a new activity for language teachers (Guth, Helm, & O'Dowd, 2014); many people may still remember their penfriends from all over the world. But this project goes one step further since it combines science and intercultural competences (Lewis & O'Dowd, 2016). The teachers involved in this project are interested in working with other countries, so it has enabled teachers from different scientific areas to take part in an international experience. It is supervised by three academics: on the French side a language teacher (Mr Villard, researcher) and a science teacher (Mrs Taris); and on the Spanish side, an associated professor specialized in fluid mechanics (Dr Fernández-Raga, researcher) who also manages the project. The three teachers share a passion for environmental issues.

2. Aims and description of the project

The international VE is part of a compulsory tutored project proposed to the second year students of the APME department.

The project, called Shared Garden, is centered on a physical area situated on the campus in Bordeaux, given to the students in order to allow them to design a garden under the philosophy of ecological and sustainable parameters. They can plant, design their watering system, measure humidity and production, and use all these ideas to discuss and explore the possibilities and consequences of their decisions. Because the French participants are second year students, they have less experience in technical solutions, so the Spanish students help them to design elements to allow them to save water in their garden. It is called Shared Garden because of the collaboration of students of different years and countries working together.

There have been two iterations of the project, one in the academic year 2018-2019 and the second one in 2019-2020. In both cases the aim was twofold. First, the goal was to help our students (nine in total the first year with three French and six Spanish, 15 in total the second year, with six French and nine Spanish) get a better insight into water shortage issues by imagining a cheap eco-friendly watering system, which could be used for our Shared Garden. Secondly, the project was also designed for our students to improve their communication skills by working in English and to work with an international team; thus, working on their soft skills, such as communication, team work, and problem solving, would be helpful to navigate their future professional life. Because of different academic calendars at the University of León and the Institute of Technology in Bordeaux, the project ran from October to May. It was organized into three different steps: first, the French students worked on their own from October to late January. They familiarized themselves with the subject by doing some research on water consumption in general, and by trying to find innovative eco-friendly watering systems. Then, from February to early April, the French and Spanish students worked together on their ideas through the VE. Finally, the

Case study 5

Spanish cohort worked on their own from April to May, creating scale models of the irrigation systems and testing them. The reason for starting at different moments was because the teachers involved needed to adjust the project to the timetable or their subjects, so the French students started during the autumn semester while the Spanish students started their fluid mechanics module in February.

Because of the size of the group, the French students worked in three pairs, each group working on a part of the project. Some students focused on the soil and its quality by interviewing farmers to assess the water shortage issue and come to conclusions on the type of plants that needed to be planted in the garden. Two other students worked on the irrigation system and another pair worked on the valve system. During all this period, not only were the students supervised by their French teachers, but also by the Spanish colleague several times using Zoom, which helped her get to know the students, discuss with them the various issues, and help them in deciding about the irrigation system.

As the Spanish teacher is specialized in fluid mechanics, she was able to help the students decide on which system to adopt; the French science teacher helped the students with the sensor technology, while the English language teacher made sure that the communication went smoothly. The French students communicated mostly in French but wrote in English so the international experience with VE forced them to use more specialized English. Luckily for the project, Mrs Fernández-Raga was able to visit Bordeaux in the middle of January to meet the French team, see the garden, and check on the students' ideas. This visit was very much appreciated both by the students and the French team, and it helped to explain to the French students the details of the next collaboration with the Spanish students.

In February, the French students presented their ideas and progress to their Spanish peers, and together they decided on some ideas to improve their projects, taking into account that the Spanish participants were fourth year students of Electric Engineering, so they had greater knowledge of fluid mechanics. The role of the Spanish students was to listen to the oral presentations of the French students and to give them ideas for possible improvements of the projects (improvements in the watering systems, ideas to recover water from the rain, or similar). The presentations, which were organized in plenary groups, lacked a structure. As the Spanish students also had more experience in presenting projects, these presentations offered a good opportunity to show the French students that structure is essential for presentations to be clear.

3. Pedagogical design and tools

As was said previously, the French students' activities done from October until January were presented to the Spanish students in February, to allow them to think about ideas to improve the work done. Just after that, the students were divided into small groups of four students depending on the number of students in each year (three Spanish and one French, or two Spanish and two French), in order to make well-balanced international groups.

After the presentations, a PBL activity was proposed to the students, who had to decide on a challenge or improvement of the project that they would like to develop together. The ensuing discussion allowed the students to exchange opinions with peers, organize how to deal with the challenge as a team, think about each-other's abilities, skills, and weaknesses, and manage the time working in a group. The teams communicated in English, which is highly relevant in terms of developing their ability to work in an international environment where English could be used as an international language. Other abilities were also developed, because time management, resources, efforts, and schedules had to be adjusted to an international context. Therefore, the members of these teams organized meetings through the Zoom platform, which allows to hold and record video conferences, to chat, to share documents, and to make presentations to share their results with other teams in a plenary meeting with all the Spanish and French students.

Following the teachers' instructions about how tasks should be accomplished, each international team of four students needed to elaborate a PowerPoint presentation about an improvement in the Shared Garden, testing their ideas and showing their results to the rest of the class involved in the PBL in May. The idea was that all the students had to evaluate the work of the other students. Each student had to give a mark to the peers of their own group, and to the other teams' presentations.

To develop the PowerPoint, each group of students was allowed to use any available tools such as WhatsApp videos, Google Docs, Zoom, Skype, Trello, or any other means they found relevant. They needed to provide answers to a challenge that could be either scientific (answering a question about fluid mechanics) or linked to engineering (construction and testing of a prototype). In both cases, they needed to communicate in another language (English), so the students involved in this activity had to develop skills such as communicating in a foreign language to a non-expert audience (since French students had less training in fluid mechanics than their Spanish peers). Furthermore, during the two months of this activity, students had to resolve small conflicts, organize meetings, and plan assignments. Teachers acted as guides, and were able to participate and contribute to the students' knowledge despite the distance, integrating knowledge from their different fields (language and engineering). In addition, the project was integrated with an activity of co-teaching, where the French science teacher traveled to teach the Spanish students in March, and the Spanish engineering teacher went to Bordeaux to teach the local students for a week. One of the main advantages was the interdisciplinary approach to this activity, which combined English and Science, allowing a more comprehensive, ecological, and valid solution to a complex problem like the global awareness of drought issues.

4. Evaluation and assessment

One of the most difficult parts that we had to design in this activity was the evaluation process, because of several aspects such as the distance, the different grades of the students, and the different criteria of the teachers involved. Participation in this activity was voluntary for all the students. They were informed of the activity, and the possibility to improve their ability to work in European teams, adapting to different schedules, ways of working, and ways of expressing themselves. During the first iteration, the French students did not take this activity seriously since there was no formal assessment. If students are not highly motivated, their skills will not improve much. So, in the second iteration, we proposed to have some academic assessment, maintaining the activity voluntary for the Spanish students but compulsory for the French students. The final PBL presentation that the students had to produce at the end of the project on the application of fluid mechanics concepts accounted for 15% of the global grade, but this mark was the result of the combination of the evaluation given by all students and teachers involved. The mark obtained by each student was made up of the average grade given by the teachers, as well as marks given by the other groups and by the participants of the same group (accounting for 50%, 30%, and 20% of the final mark respectively) following the instructions and rubrics showed in Fernández-Raga et al. (2019). Peer evaluation makes students more aware of their ability and performance on their tasks.

One problem with this activity was that a part of the students were not involved from the first moment. In general, the collaboration between the Spanish and French students of both countries was active during the two months when they worked together.

Most of the students started with a lot of enthusiasm, thinking they would get to know other people. But when they started group work they were confronted by some difficulties they had not taken into account, like reaching an agreement on the topic or on the methodology to use as a team with people that they did not know, and in another language. Their first reaction to these problems was to ask their teachers for help; however, the teachers needed to guide them but without taking decisions so that students could decide by themselves. Our experience shows that after teachers listened and analyzed the situation with them, students managed their teamwork without any trouble.

Another difficulty in our activity was the different background knowledge. Our students belonged to different courses (second and fourth year) and this meant that fourth year students were thought of as leaders of the project, a role they did not always want to accept. The solution was again negotiation within each group. This issue was addressed by highlighting that the VE part would be done only during the months of February and March, when the international teams had to design a common project, which could be added to the ones developed previously in the Shared Garden. Sometimes, however, the French students felt demotivated and were losing momentum because they considered they had finished their practical work in February, while the Spanish students were getting ready to start the project. During the first year, this issue was solved by talking with their respective teachers, and in the second year by informing the students of the complete calendar of the project. After the final presentation, the perspective of all the students was more positive about the activity because the results were evident. After asking them through a questionnaire to provide their personal opinion about the activity, and the evaluation by their peers, they provided positive answers, and their self-evaluation made them conscious of their improvement. An increase in student motivation and involvement was noticed, as well as an improvement in their communicative ability in English. In addition, this VE project reinforced their teamwork abilities, and their use of new technologies, which are the basis to allow communication between team members who are in two different countries. As mentioned in Fernández-Raga et al. (2019), it also allowed the development of other skills such as better time management, individual responsibility in the assigned tasks, and improved communication with non-experts, since the teachers who collaborated in the project belong to different complementary areas and these aspects were valued in the evaluation rubrics.

Also, another advantage was the introduction of instructions on how students should be evaluated and evaluate their peers, because this allows the students to feel empowered in their learning (see Fernández-Raga et al., 2019, for the rubric). And the last advantage was that the objective of each iteration of the VE project was to contribute to a more sustainable garden, which will be developed with the ideas of the students year after year, developing and implementing the strategic objectives of Agenda 2030.

5. Lessons learned and conclusion

This project was highly valued by the students from both institutions since it prepared them for their future professional life in many ways. Indeed, the students have to be autonomous and come up with new ideas, which they have to share and communicate using a foreign language. They also have to work in teams, which might be difficult for some of our students, especially for the French cohort, who are younger. All these activities helped the students become aware of the others' working culture and gave them some keys to a successful professional career. Companies are now looking for students and professionals who are flexible, versatile, and open to others, and this project helps them face these challenges. So even if these activities did not exactly fit in a language course or in a fluid mechanics course, the project showed the students how enriching interdisciplinary projects can be both personally and professionally.

The specificity of this PBL is that it includes collaborative work in teams using English, incorporating VE activities. This means that it enriches the number of skills developed thanks to the combination of PBL with intercultural interaction, like improvement in language skills or work in international environments.

This activity allows the project to adapt to different time frames, different specialties, and different numbers of students. The objectives have been fully achieved since the students indicated that they felt that they had learned to express themselves better when communicating with non-experts, had lost their fear of expressing themselves in a foreign language, and were better able to evaluate themselves and their peers. During the second iteration, carried out in the academic year 2019-2020, the realization of PBL with the French students was easier because the students themselves transmitted the objectives pursued to the younger students and they were more involved from the beginning. In any case, a longer period doing PBL (from two to four months working all together for example) will help in the development of competences such as teamwork, better organization, and cooperation.

Our opinion is that this activity should be enriched with a blended mobility of a week for the students in each country. This would be very attractive for the students, and would help develop strong bonds with their project peers. It would also develop the internationalization of both institutions.

In any case, this initiative can be easily adapted and launched in any other degree course and subject, by searching for challenges that may be attractive to students, and looking for students and teachers willing to collaborate internationally. There is no requirement for teachers to belong to the same area, since a multidisciplinary focus represents the general environment of a company where there are many more multicultural and multidisciplinary teams that allow carrying out projects with greater complexity.

References

Fernández-Raga, M., Villard, V., Palencia, C., Castañón, A. M., Viejo, J., & Gómez Fernández, F. (2019). Virtual exchange in engineering to realize a learning experience based on projects using ICTs. *TEEM'19: Proceedings of the Seventh International Conference on Technological Ecosystems for Enhancing Multiculturality* (pp. 689-695). https://doi.org/10.1145/3362789.3362790

Guth, S., Helm, F., & O'Dowd, R. (2014). Telecollaborative foreign language networks in European universities: a report on current attitudes and practices. *Bellaterra Journal of Teaching and Learning Language & Literature, 7*(4), 1-14. https://doi.org/10.5565/rev/jtl3.609

Lewis, T., & O'Dowd, R. (2016). Introduction to online intercultural exchange. In R. O'Dowd & T. Lewis (Eds), *Online intercultural exchange: policy, pedagogy, practice* (pp. 3-20). Routledge. https://doi.org/10.4324/9781315678931

6. Mission (im)possible: developing students' international online business communication skills through virtual teamwork

Rita Koris[1] and Jean-François Vuylsteke[2]

Abstract

This case study outlines an example of cooperative online learning for teaching business communication skills at a Hungarian and a Belgian university. During this eight week long Erasmus+ Virtual Exchange (E+VE) project, students collaborated online in virtual teams on a weekly basis to complete the following main missions: (1) giving constructive feedback; (2) creating an elevator pitch; (3) promoting themselves by creating a digital CV; (4) preparing for a job interview; and (5) participating in a real online job interview with a professional recruiter. Not only does this case study describe the planning, design, and implementation of the project from a pedagogical perspective, but it also details its challenges and outcomes.

Keywords: international collaboration, Erasmus+ virtual exchange project, online intercultural exchange, business communication, virtual teamwork.

1. Context

Graduate students lacking relevant work experience are often at a disadvantage when they step out into the European job market (EPSC, 2019). European higher

---

1. Pázmány Péter Catholic University, Budapest, Hungary; koris.rita@btk.ppke.hu; https://orcid.org/0000-0003-1912-8744

2. École Pratique des Hautes Études Commerciales (EPHEC) University College, Brussels, Belgium; jf.vuylsteke@ephec.be

How to cite this case study: Koris, R., & Vuylsteke, J.-F. (2020). Mission (im)possible: developing students' international online business communication skills through virtual teamwork. In F. Helm & A. Beaven (Eds), *Designing and implementing virtual exchange – a collection of case studies* (pp. 69-79). Research-publishing.net. https://doi.org/10.14705/rpnet.2020.45.1116

education institutions have a key role in equipping graduate students not only with marketable knowledge, but also with skills to facilitate their school-to-work transition. Efforts have been made by European educational institutions and instructors to react to this need and incorporate skills development courses into their graduate programs (Carretero et al., 2018). At Pázmány Péter Catholic University (PPCU) in Hungary and École Pratique des Hautes Études Commerciales (EPHEC) University College in Belgium, we have also taken up on this challenge and redesigned our business communication curriculum to cover and teach new sets of skills to boost students' English business communication competences with digital and transversal skills, hence making them highly competent job applicants (Burke, 2019; EPSC, 2019). Job-seekers in Europe also need to acquire intercultural or rather intra-European cultural competence as they need to respond to culturally-different requirements depending on the country where they are applying for vacant positions. All these should be taken into account when preparing for job interviews, very often done online and in English. Also, job applications and CVs are scrutinized by the recruiters for proof of digital skills, English language proficiency, and business soft skills to identify the best candidates for job interviews matching their strict selection criteria. Therefore, new graduates need to acquire a new skills set and be able to demonstrate them effectively during the recruitment process.

Our unique online virtual exchange project was born out of an informal partnership between two professors at PPCU and EPHEC. The project was designed and implemented during the fall semester of 2019/2020 as an E+VE project and was embedded into two BA-level English business communication courses run in tandem at the Belgian and the Hungarian universities. Thirty-four students participated in the first cycle of the project: ten Hungarian students were from PPCU, one Russian student was studying at PPCU on Erasmus exchange, and 23 students were international students studying at EPHEC on Erasmus or Campus Mundi programs. The latter group represented ten different nationalities. The students at EPHEC were business administration majors, while the students at PPCU were majoring in international studies.

2. Aims and description of the project

Our VE project brings together graduate students across Europe to work in virtual teams, acquire and develop skills they need for a successful job interview, and provide the opportunity to try themselves out in the real European job market. The participants brought 12 different nationalities and multiple perspectives into the project, which created a culturally-diverse learning environment reflecting multicultural diversities in Europe. During this eight week long project, students worked online in mixed virtual teams on pre-set assignments, while also attending in-class sessions with their teacher. Five to six students were assigned to a multicultural team, representing at least four to five nationalities each and a variety of cultural backgrounds.

The project aimed to develop, practice, and demonstrate students' English business communication skills in an intra-European virtual setting. During the individual and team assignments, students had the opportunity to (1) develop intercultural competences, (2) practice international online collaboration and teamwork, (3) apply digital technologies and master digital skills, (4) organize and manage online meetings, (5) promote professional skills, (6) prepare for an online job interview, and (7) prepare a team charter, team performance reviews, team reports, and a final digital personal portfolio.

At the beginning of the project, students were assigned to teams, and were then encouraged to get to know their team members. In the first week of the project, students participated in an online facilitated dialogue session with a professional external facilitator and engaged in ice-breaking and team-building activities online. During the project, student teams had to accomplish the following five main missions: (1) give constructive feedback, (2) promote themselves by creating an elevator pitch, (3) promote themselves by creating a digital CV, (4) prepare for a job interview, and (5) participate in a real online job interview with a recruiter. Each mission comprised both individual tasks and team assignments. Student teams had to organize and manage weekly online team meetings to discuss individual tasks and complete their team assignments. Their findings, task completion, and lessons learned, together with the meeting minutes, were then documented and shared with the tutors in the weekly team reports. The project concluded with an online facilitated session, where students could share their individual experiences of the job interviews with their peers and reflect on their learning outcomes. At the end of the project, students had to write and present a digital portfolio on the successful completion of their assignments, document the professional and soft skills they had developed, the challenges they had faced, and provide examples for their intercultural learning.

3. Pedagogical design and tools

It was important to involve all our students not only in meaningful oral and written activities, but also to develop their online communication skills. They were all studying English business communication and their English language proficiency levels ranged from intermediate to advanced[3]. We encouraged them to apply a professional business communication discourse in the way they collaborated with their peers. Students had a series of tasks and research activities to perform, designed to develop their reading, writing, and speaking skills. As a pre-project task, students were invited to contribute to a web magazine and write a small biographical sketch. The magazine was published before the first online meeting and this gave them the opportunity to read about the other students they would be working with. It turned out to be a very useful task in raising students' awareness of the cultural diversity of the group and at the same time it proved to be an excellent ice-breaking activity. Before the teams started to work on their missions, they had to schedule weekly virtual team meetings and organize themselves and their teamwork so that they could accomplish their team assignments together. After their first meeting, the virtual team had to define their team charter in which they laid down the ground rules and organization principles for a successful online collaboration.

---

3. Equivalent to the Common European Framework of Reference for languages (CEFR) B2 level and above.

As giving feedback underpinned each activity of the project, participants learned how to give constructive feedback professionally in English and explored cultural differences when giving feedback, making a complaint or providing criticism. During Mission 1, students had to read and explore pre-set background materials on how to give positive feedback and how to provide constructive criticism. At the online team meeting, they could discuss their findings and ideas, and learn from one another. During Mission 2, students focused their attention on optimizing not only their personal virtual image, but also their professional one. They produced and shared a one minute personal elevator pitch promoting their professional qualities and skills. Team assessment enabled them to give performance reviews and professional feedback to each other. Mission 3 concerned preparing and finalizing their creative online CVs, which they discussed online within their teams. The purpose of the team discussion was to give each other advice on how to improve their digital CVs and also to practice giving constructive feedback. Mission 4 allowed the students to explore how to succeed at a job interview before facing the challenge of having a realistic one with an external recruiter. In order to prepare for this, the students had to watch a selection of small videos on interviewing techniques, prepare a shortlist of functional tips, and have an online discussion to exchange views and opinions to learn from one another. Also, they discussed possible cultural differences and the challenges they need to face during an online job interview in any European country. At the team meeting, students shared their findings with their peers, gave each other advice, recommended solutions to possible problems, rehearsed, and practiced a job interview scenario. As a final mission (Mission 5), students participated in a real online job interview with a recruiter. An international pool of recruiters, representing ten different nationalities from different companies in various business sectors in Europe, assisted the project and provided expert advice for our graduate students at the end of the interviews as well as a written feedback on the students' performances and areas for development. At the end of the project, students co-edited a final web magazine in which they reported on their project experience. This magazine was published[4] and shared with all

---

4. https://madmagz.com/fr/magazine/1691072

the different participants, as the tangible evidence of their participation in the project and of their contribution to the different missions.

In order to reach our objectives, it was important for us to facilitate the interactions between the students and to be selective in the choice of digital and online tools that the students would be using. Zoom was selected as the videoconference application. Slack was proposed as a very good application to help students organize themselves, coordinate teamwork, share resources, and chat. The tool Genial.ly enabled the students to create their online CVs and portfolios. Madmagz was the web application selected for the initial and the final web magazine. The team reports completed after each mission were co-edited in Google Docs. This provided a useful opportunity for the students in that they were keeping a personal digital record of all their productions (pitch, online CV, web magazines, team reports, online portfolio) during the project, which they can then decide to share and reuse when they submit job applications in relation to their future career.

4. Evaluation, assessment, and recognition

As far as evaluation is concerned, we thought that the assessment of the whole project was worthy of quite a substantial weighting in the final evaluation of students' course performance. As it was the first time we implemented our E+VE, we had to coordinate university calendars, adjust course curricula, grading methods, and respective constraints, i.e. mode of assessment, calculation of the final grade, university regulations. We agreed on co-assessing the team reports and written productions of our respective students. How we integrated this joint-assessment into our respective grading methods was up to each of us. The final online job interviews were assessed by the external recruiters and they provided written feedback on the participants' performances. Students had received precise instructions and an assessment document with all the important elements for improvement, for example: persuasive power, projected self-image of the student, ability to provide precise answers to interview questions, communication skills, and language proficiency. Student teams were also sent feedback after each of the five missions they carried out. The way they were graded differed on the basis of the integration of each mission's assessment in the global evaluation of the students.

At EPHEC Brussels, for example, the E+VE project was fully integrated in the global course assessment. Each of the five missions was supported by the grammar and lexical exercises which had been put online on the accompanying Moodle platform. Each mission was evaluated and commented upon in class when completed. One of the tasks EPHEC students had to do at the end of the project was to evaluate their own contribution and involvement. This activity brought stunning conclusions. Very often, the students had a realistic view of their potential, acquired skills, and could explain how they had personally measured their level of proficiency. This self-assessment score was also part of the final evaluation, which was worth five ECTS credits. The results were very good to excellent for a majority of students. Students were very enthusiastic and proud of their achievements, also because they could capitalize on all their online productions.

At PPCU, the assessment of the students' project performances made up 80% of their course evaluation. The remaining 20% came from individual and group language development activities and tasks that targeted students' preparations for the project. The course was worth three ECTS credits, most students achieved excellent or good results and only a few students actually received average grades. As our project was implemented under the E+VE project funded by the European Commission, the participants received an official E+VE digital badge for their successful completion of the project. The students who posted it on their professional networks expect recognition by the companies in their respective countries of origin.

5. Lessons learned and conclusion

We did not know what to expect from the first iteration of our virtual exchange when we decided to launch this project in October 2019. We had set goals and determined our joint online strategy, and we hoped that it would be worth all our efforts. In the course of the eight weeks, we saw that our students were able to really capitalize on their respective talents, take up the challenges, and enjoy working online. Both lecturers and students had to leave their comfort zones and operate in a field in which they also needed to manage the unknown (responsiveness, attendance, involvement). We all learned a lot, probably more than we expected.

The first message we tried to convey to students is that 'nothing is impossible' and we also maintained this attitude during the project. In the preparatory stage, the two lecturers often met and discussed the details of the project with the purpose of building trust and also making sure that the pedagogical objectives were fully understood by the two parties. It also gave us the opportunity to explain and reassure, as well as put words to teaching habits we no longer questioned in our respective institutions. We had managed to align our teaching approaches, course objectives, and learning processes before the project started.

The second point that we, instructors, learned is that it requires a lot of energy to get the students onboard. We placed the onus directly on our students and they appeared intimidated at first, thinking the challenge would be impossible to face. It took us some time (nearly two weeks) to assist them and provide them with the necessary tools (methodology, use of the different web applications, and sharing of the objectives of the first E+VE mission).

Finally, we had the opportunity to step out of the conventional teacher's role and follow a mentoring approach in our teaching (Arnesson & Albinsson, 2017; Lane, 2012). As the E+VE project started, our teaching attitude evolved. Instead of instructing students how to do things, we started guiding them through their missions by promoting students' autonomous learning (MacDougall, 2012). To do so, we analyzed their contributions, had group discussions, gave them feedback, and encouraged them to take responsibility for their team's dynamic. Many students reported having developed their management and problem-solving skills in a way they would not have expected.

The students were also encouraged to give feedback to us on this different approach in teaching business English classes. What one EPHEC student wrote in her final report is rather representative of the students' points of view:

> "This course has revealed itself as one of the most useful challenges that I ever faced in my university experience. [...] It has led me to a new kind of exercise that I would consider as 'introspective'. [...] We enjoyed talking about our personal experiences and developed our social skills. [...] My big challenge was the simulation of a job interview. [...] It helped me develop my digital and management skills. [...] I have discovered that helping others develop a common goal could bring a lot of satisfaction. [...] To sum up, I think the E+VE project has given us the possibility to strengthen our personalities and to reflect more about what kind of people we want to become in our future".

By reviewing and critically evaluating the project, we can conclude that there is space for improvement. First of all, we could have given students more transparent and self-explanatory instructions on the tasks and assignments to be completed and on the expectations we had. Despite the fact that we put all necessary information relating to the project in one place, including task descriptions, deliverables, deadlines, background materials, sample deliverables, and administrative instructions, it proved to be overwhelming for the students at the beginning of the project.

We could also have systematically provided students with the lexical support to help them acquire the terminology they needed for animated discussions. As the level of English differed from one student to the other, it could have given weaker students the opportunity to be more active. Furthermore, knowing that our objective was to put students in situations where they could use their creativity and be totally in charge of their learning process, we had not shown any templates of the expected final products to the students. Some students found it difficult to come up with their own ideas in terms of design and content of their final deliverables and felt that they did not receive enough guidance from the instructors.

Grading of students' individual and team work proved to be challenging, too. Students often expect grading to be only individual, whereas this project combines group evaluations and individual assessment. While we followed a co-assessment approach in the case of team reports and teamwork, individual grading was done by the instructor responsible. Students reported some discrepancies when receiving their final grades, as some students felt that they received lower grades than their team members, even though they evaluated their own performance higher than that of their peers. This may be due to their misperceptions of their own work or the difference in the two instructors' evaluations. Therefore, it is important to work out a common framework for the assessment and evaluation of students' performances for the next iterations of the project.

Is there anything else to learn from our experience? Probably, we can always rely on students to surprise us in a good way. They can certainly overcome unexpected challenges provided they receive clear explanations and guidance on how to reach their goals. We believe that teaching business English can be a vector to transform a language classroom into a virtual multicultural corporate working space in which students meet, discuss, evolve, take responsibility, and learn from one another. Another enthusiastic student wrote in her final report:

> "I'll certainly recommend the EVE project: it's a beautiful way to learn, know new cultures and also challenge yourself".

References

Arnesson, K., & Albinsson, G. (2017). Mentorship – a pedagogical method for integration of theory and practice in higher education. *Nordic Journal of Studies in Educational Policy*, *3*(3), 202-217. https://doi.org/10.1080/20020317.2017.1379346

Burke, H. (2019). *Living and working in Europe 2015–2018*. Eurofound. https://www.eurofound.europa.eu/publications/annual-report/2019/living-and-working-in-europe-2015-2018

Carretero, S., Punie, Y., Vuorikari, R., Cabrera, M., & O'Keeffe, W. (2018). *DigComp into action: get inspired, make it happen. A user guide to the European digital competence framework*. Joint Research Centre. https://publications.jrc.ec.europa.eu/repository/bitstream/JRC110624/dc_guide_may18.pdf

EPSC. (2019). *10 trends shaping the future of work in Europe*. European Political Strategy Centre. https://op.europa.eu/en/publication-detail/-/publication/e77a1580-0cf5-11ea-8c1f-01aa75ed71a1/language-en/format-PDF/source-121729338

Lane, H. C. (2012). Coaching and mentoring. In: N. M. Seel (ed.), *Encyclopedia of the sciences of learning*. Springer.

MacDougall, M. (2012). Autonomous learning and effective engagement. In: N. M. Seel (ed.), *Encyclopedia of the sciences of learning*. Springer.

7. Exploring foreign entrepreneurial ecosystems through virtual exchange

Nadia Cheikhrouhou[1] and Małgorzata Marchewka[2]

Abstract

This case study reports a Virtual Exchange (VE) between students at Cracow University of Economics (Poland) enrolled in business courses and students from the High Institute of Technological Studies of Béja (Tunisia) enrolled in an entrepreneurship course. The main aim of the project was to enhance students' awareness of similarities and differences between the Polish and the Tunisian entrepreneurial ecosystems. The goals also included improving language skills, Information and Communication Technology (ICT) literacy, teamwork, and increasing their self-confidence. The chapter describes the schedule of the project, tasks that students accomplished, and the technological and communication tools that were used. Finally, the study includes conclusions and suggestions for future initiatives.

Keywords: virtual exchange, business studies, entrepreneurial ecosystems, cultural intelligence, cross-cultural communication challenges.

1. Context

When it comes to business studies in general and entrepreneurship courses in particular, it is important for students to acquire knowledge about business practices in other countries. That is how they can broaden their horizons and

---

1. Higher Institute of Technological Studies of Béja, Béja,Tunisia; nadiachikhrouhou@yahoo.com; https://orcid.org/0000-0003-4849-3134

2. Cracow University of Economics, Cracow, Poland; marchewm@uek.krakow.pl; https://orcid.org/0000-0002-7633-001X

How to cite this case study: Cheikhrouhou, N., & Marchewka, M. (2020). Exploring foreign entrepreneurial ecosystems through virtual exchange. In F. Helm & A. Beaven (Eds), *Designing and implementing virtual exchange – a collection of case studies* (pp. 81-91). Research-publishing.net. https://doi.org/10.14705/rpnet.2020.45.1117

get inspired. Moreover, in the globalized and interconnected modern business world, it is of great importance that students develop their cultural intelligence to improve their employability skills.

Cultural intelligence is the capability of an individual to function effectively in situations characterized by cultural diversity (Ang, Van Dyne, Koh, & Ng, 2004). Thomas and Inkson (2017) defined it as "the capacity to interact effectively across cultures" (p. x). This is the context in which the VE project described here was developed, with the main aim of enhancing students' awareness of similarities and differences between the Entrepreneurial Ecosystems (EEs) of the two countries involved: Poland and Tunisia.

2. Aims and description of the project

The VE between Cracow University of Economics (Poland) and the High Institute of Technological Studies of Béja (Tunisia) took place from April 29th till June 13th, 2019.

Twenty-two students took part in this exchange, 11 students from Cracow and 11 students from Béja. The participation was voluntary for students from both sides to ensure that we worked with highly motivated students who are eager to cooperate with students from other countries. At the same time, participation would count toward their final grades.

The students from Cracow were both undergraduates and postgraduates studying management, international business, tourism, and recreation, while the students from Béja were undergraduates studying computer system networks, and the exchange was part of the entrepreneurship course.

As teachers, we both took part in the training course provided by Unicollaboration in the context of Erasmus+ VE, which helped us become familiar with the world of VE and join the VE community. We therefore decided to develop a VE project together, with the support of the trainers. While Gosia Marchewka wanted to do a VE to let her students experience work in an international virtual team, as usually they do not have such an opportunity during regular classes, Nadia Cheikhrouhou wanted to offer her students a cost-effective international experience which they lack in their studies. In fact, all the students in Béja are from Tunisia and have never experienced international mobility because of the absence of this opportunity in their institution.

As mentioned above, the main aim of the VE was to enable students to familiarize themselves with the EE in a different country to their own. That objective fits into the entrepreneurship course in Béja, since a part of this course is dedicated to exploring the EE in Tunisia. The VE was important because students cannot develop their critical thinking unless they know how foreign EEs function (in this case the Polish EE).

For students of Cracow University of Economics, the case was different as they were all participating in a variety of courses (with different learning goals). For them it was an extracurricular activity they could participate in for self-development.

It is also important to mention that, beyond achieving the above-mentioned learning goals, this VE aimed at improving students' employability skills. In the 2019 World Development report entitled *The changing nature of work*, the World Bank Group (2019) mentions that "three types of skills are increasingly important in labor markets: advanced cognitive skills such as complex problem-solving, socio-behavioral skills such as teamwork, and skill combinations that are predictive of adaptability such as reasoning and self-efficacy" (p. 3). That is important especially given that in Tunisia 28% of higher education graduates were unemployed in the year 2019 (National Institute of Statistics in Tunisia[3]), which is a relatively high rate.

By offering the students such an opportunity, we expected them to gain the following competencies required on the job market in both Poland and Tunisia:

---

3. http://www.ins.tn/en/themes/emploi#horizontalTab1

Case study 7

- enhanced language skills, reflected in students' ability to speak English during conference sessions and to write messages in English to project partners;

- enhanced ICT literacy, reflected in students' ability to post content, images, videos, and different files on a virtual platform called Padlet;

- enhanced teamwork skills reflected in students' abilities to work on a cross-cultural project: sharing tasks, coordinating efforts with project partners, cooperating, helping each other, and respecting the deadlines; and

- increased self-confidence reflected in students' ability to communicate in an intercultural environment and to build an international network.

3. Pedagogical design and tools

The VE between Béja and Cracow lasted one month and a half: it started at the end of April and ended by mid-June 2019.

All tasks and students' deliverables were posted on a private Padlet that was created by the teachers and shared with the participants.

Students were expected to accomplish five tasks.

- **Task 1**: Introducing themselves; posting a photo, and commenting and/or liking other posts. Of course, both instructors were the first to introduce themselves on Padlet and kick off the VE project.

- **Task 2**: Team building; the list of six teams (five teams of four students and one team of two students) was posted on Padlet by the instructors with the names and emails of each team member. The teams were formed heterogeneously in terms of gender and nationality to allow the maximum of diversity. Team members were asked to get in touch via email to set an appointment for a video-conference using a videoconferencing tool of their choice. During the video-conference they were supposed to get to know each other in a deeper way, choose a team name, and prepare a flower (teams of four) or a butterfly (team of two). In the center of the flower or the butterfly they were asked to put what the team had in common (personality traits, hobbies, interests…) then each student had to put what is unique about her or him and different from the others in the team, either on a petal (Figure 1) in the case of the flower, or on a wing in the case of the butterfly.

Figure 1. Example and instructions of team flower

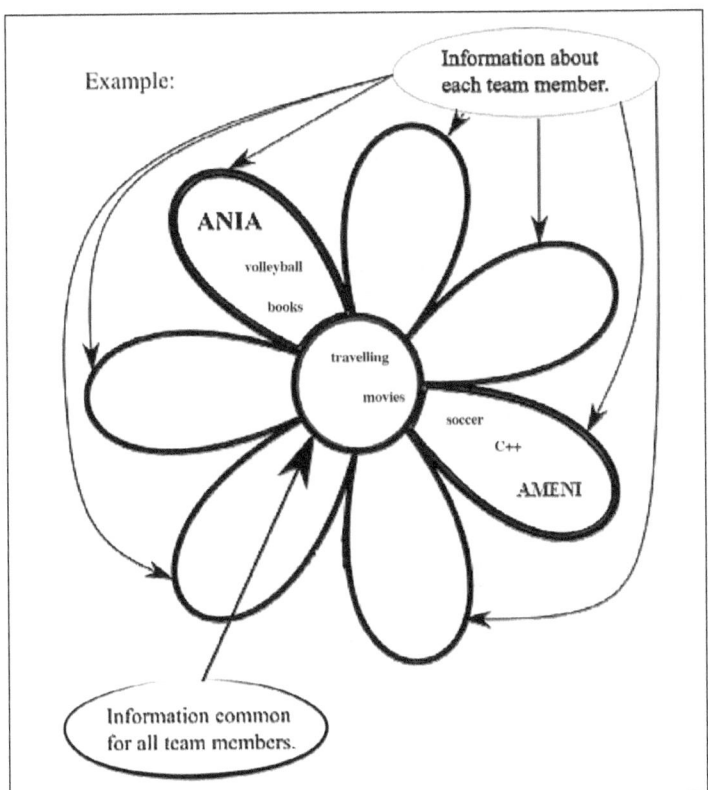

- **Task 3**: EE; each team had to work with the Isenberg model (Isenberg, 2010), which describes the EE of a country based on six interrelated aspects: policy, finance, culture, supports, human capital, and markets to discuss differences and similarities between the Polish and Tunisian EE.

- **Task 4**: Facilitated session; participating in a facilitated dialogue session. These are a form of intercultural conversation between the students in which a trained dialogue facilitator, provided by the Unicollaboration team, helps them overcome communication barriers and engage in a productive conversation. This facilitated session aimed to prepare them for the challenges of the next task related to decision making involving all voices and negotiating choices within an intercultural team.

- **Task 5**: Presentation of the results; preparing a poster or a video to summarize each team's findings about similarities and differences between Tunisian and Polish EE.

Table 1 below summarizes the learning goals of each task, the deliverables, the tools used to accomplish these tasks, and the targeted competencies to be acquired by students.

Table 1. Tasks, learning goals, deliverables, tools, and competencies

Tasks	Learning goals	Deliverables	Tools	Competencies
Students introducing themselves individually on Padlet	Breaking the ice between students	Introduction posts + Photos	Padlet	Presenting oneself in an international context

Students in groups share information about themselves	• The members of each group get to know one another in a deeper way • Establishing trust between the different team members that allows for collaboration in the next tasks	A team flower or butterfly with commonalities and differences between the different members of the team	• Team flower and butterfly templates • Videoconferencing tools: Skype, Zoom, Hangout, WhatsApp…. • Padlet	• Self-confidence • Networking • ICT competencies • Language competencies
Discussing similarities and differences between Polish and Tunisian EE	Students will be able to reflect on their own EE and compare it to that of another country	A screenshot of the videoconference	• Padlet • Isenberg's model • Videoconferencing tools	• Language competencies • ICT competencies • Critical thinking • Cross-cultural communication
Co-conceiving a poster or a video that summarizes the findings of the prior task	Enhancing students' cross-cultural teamwork and communication	A poster or a video	• Padlet • Videoconferencing tools • Online collaborative tools (Canva, Prezi, Google Docs…)	• Cross-cultural teamwork • Cross-cultural communication • Critical thinking • Problem-solving • ICT competencies • Language competencies

Case study 7

Participating in the facilitated dialogue session	Students share their thoughts and work toward mutual understanding despite cultural background differences	No deliverable but should have thought for example of a document with students' reflections on their facilitated session experience	• Zoom	• Cross-cultural communication. • Language competencies

Regarding General Data Protection Regulation (GDPR) and student privacy, when registering for the project, students were informed about the processing of their personal data to the extent necessary to participate in the project and were asked to give their consent.

4. Evaluation, assessment, and recognition

Polish students who successfully accomplished the project got one grade higher from the workshop part of one of the courses they attended.

Students in Béja were graded for their participation in the project and this grade contributed to 20% in their final mark for the entrepreneurship course. This percentage of 20% is attributed in the Tunisian system to projects accomplished by students in the frame of their different courses. The grade earned by the students took into consideration the quality of the poster assessed based on its appeal (design, layout, neatness), richness of its content, integration of graphics related to the topic, and presence of the different requirements assigned in the task. Commitment of the students during the whole project and their participation in the facilitated session were also taken into consideration in this grade. Moreover, students who successfully completed all the tasks earned Erasmus+ VE badges.

Tunisian students were happy with their badges, and intended to display them on their LinkedIn profiles and in CVs. They do believe that such a recognition is an added value to their CVs and they plan to mention this experience during their job interviews to stand out from the crowd. For the students in Poland, the badges are also of a great value in case of applying for international exchange programs at Cracow University of Economics since they gain extra points in their application process.

5. Lessons learned and conclusion

After the VE, both teachers had informal conversations with their students to reflect on this experience. According to Tunisian students, this exchange opened their eyes to cultural differences and how these impact the way people perceive things and the outer world. They experienced challenges of intercultural communication, and learned new practices typical of the education system in Poland. For example, they appreciated the fact that Polish students work after school, which is rare in the case of Tunisian students. Additionally, they were happy with the new relationships they built. The greatest disadvantage for them was the absence of Polish students during the facilitated session. Indeed, Tunisian students did their best to be present even though they were busy preparing the final projects of their different courses and therefore felt that these efforts were worthless, which caused their frustration. In addition, the absence of Polish students was perceived as a sign of disrespect to their Tunisian partners.

The overall benefits listed by the students in Poland were similar. They believed that the project was a good opportunity to learn what real life cross-cultural communication may be like. For many of them, delivering tasks on time was extremely important and some were stressed that they could not meet deadlines. In some cases, they were disappointed with the lack of response from their Tunisian teammates, as they were expecting prompt reactions and, since the notion of time is perceived differently across cultures, a prompt reaction could take longer for Tunisian students especially during the Ramadan month because they had extra chores like preparing special meals and going to the mosques after breaking the fast to pray for the Tarawih. This conflictual situation put their problem-solving competencies to the test and though both teachers had to intervene to clarify misunderstandings, it was a learning point for students: not to jump into conclusions and to set up ground rules from the beginning within teams to avoid conflicts.

Based on the feedback from students and a follow-up conversation between both instructors, we decided to implement our second VE, which is running at the time we are writing this case study, despite the very unusual circumstances due to the Coronavirus epidemic resulting in the reorganization of the work and social isolation.

We drew upon the first exchange to improve this experience for the students, implementing the following changes:

- students have more time for VE, and this year our project will last three months compared to the one month and a half of the first VE;

- tasks are as simple as possible, the value is in the process of collaboration, less is more;

- more tasks were implemented at the introductory stage to help in the development of the teams: this year, Tunisian and Polish students will be presenting their countries, regions, and institutions, as well as business etiquette, food, and important holidays/celebrations in their respective countries;

- different conflictual situations may occur, the difficulties encountered in the previous VE helped us discuss in advance with students how to avoid them and how to face them; and

- introduction of the e-portfolio provided by the Unicollaboration team: although we need to customize it, it is a useful form of assessment of the whole experience, as well as a record of the competencies gained by students throughout the project.

An additional benefit to organizing a VE for our students is the possibility of scientific cooperation. Working on the materials for students, we discovered topics that we are both interested in and we have expanded our cooperation at an academic level. Right now, we are working on the problems of EEs and their impact on start-ups.

References

Ang, S., Van Dyne, L., Koh, C., & Ng, K. Y. (2004). The measurement of cultural intelligence. *Paper presented at the 2004 Academy of Management Meetings Symposium on Cultural Intelligence in the 21st Century. New Orleans. L.A.*

Isenberg, D. (2010). The big idea: how to start an entrepreneurial revolution. *Harvard Business Review, June.* https://hbr.org/2010/06/the-big-idea-how-to-start-an-entrepreneurial-revolution

Thomas, D. C., & Inkson, K. C. (2017). *Cultural intelligence:surviving and thriving in the global village.* Berrett-Koehler Publishers.

World Bank Group. (2019). World development report "The changing nature of work". http://documents.worldbank.org/curated/en/816281518818814423/2019-WDR-Report.pdf

8 Virtual exchange for teaching EU economics: building enriching international learning experiences for European students

Rita Koris[1], Núria Hernández-Nanclares[2], and Francisco Javier Mato Díaz[3]

Abstract

This chapter presents a Transnational Virtual Exchange (VE) Project (TEP) developed in partnership between a Spanish and a Hungarian university. During this semester-long project, students worked in mixed virtual teams exploring selected topics related to the economics of the European Union. This report provides the details of the planning, design, and implementation of the project and reveals its Strengths, Weaknesses, Opportunities, and Threats (SWOT) from the students' perspectives. The in-depth SWOT analyses elaborate on students' disciplinary learning, 21st century skills development, engagement and motivation, use of digital tools, international online teamwork and collaboration, online communication, and intercultural competence.

Keywords: virtual exchange, transnational Erasmus+ virtual exchange project, technology-supported learning, EU economics, SWOT analysis.

---

1. Pázmány Péter Catholic University, Budapest, Hungary; koris.rita@btk.ppke.hu; https://orcid.org/0000-0003-1912-8744

2. University of Oviedo, Oviedo, Spain; nhernan@uniovi.es; https://orcid.org/0000-0002-6143-8378

3. University of Oviedo, Oviedo, Spain; jmato@uniovi.es; https://orcid.org/0000-0002-4356-6296

How to cite this case study: Koris, R., Hernández-Nanclares, N., & Mato Díaz, F. J. (2020). Virtual exchange for teaching EU economics: building enriching international learning experiences for European students. In F. Helm & A. Beaven (Eds), *Designing and implementing virtual exchange – a collection of case studies* (pp. 93-103). Research-publishing.net. https://doi.org/10.14705/rpnet.2020.45.1118

Case study 8

1. Context

The UNIOVI-PPCU[4] VE project was born out of a partnership formed between two professors teaching the 'Economics of Spain and the European Union' course at the School of Economics and Business at the University of Oviedo in Spain and a professor running the 'English for European Union Contexts' course at the Institute of International Studies and Political Science at the Pázmány Péter Catholic University in Hungary. The professors were brought together by the Erasmus+ Virtual Exchange (E+VE) initiative and decided to design a TEP focusing on the shared disciplinary area of EU economics involving second-year Bachelor of Arts students studying at the two universities. The motivation for setting up this project was threefold: (1) to engage students in meaningful discussion on key topics and current issues of the EU with international peers from other EU member states; (2) to broaden students' horizons by sharing diverse perspectives of tackling common problems in the EU; and (3) to enrich the students' learning with international project experiences and provide an opportunity for skills development. VE initiatives and practices are now gaining ground in European Higher Education (HE) with the aim of extending local teaching and learning contexts, introducing new methods to teaching and learning, adopting a multidisciplinary approach to stimulating students' academic performance, deepening their disciplinary knowledge, and developing their transversal skills (Helm, 2015; O'Dowd & Lewis, 2016). While these aims go hand in hand with the new trends in European HE (EPSC, 2017), they also play an important role in increasing students' future career prospects, and therefore narrowing the gap between education and work (Burke, 2019).

The first iteration of our project was implemented in the autumn semester of the 2018/2019 academic year after a three-month-long design phase between June and August 2018. During this preparation phase, we dedicated time to planning the project logistics, designing the student assignments, setting up the project working environment, and preparing all project documentation, background

---

4. UNIOVI stands for University of Oviedo (Spain); PPCU stands for Pázmány Péter Catholic University (Hungary)

materials, and handouts for the students. This was a very important step to take as there were fundamental differences in our two course curricula in terms of course objectives, content, learning approaches, teaching practices, term holidays, the number of weekly classes, grading and assessment of students' performances, and the number of credits. The fact that our courses had to be aligned to cater for the goals of the collaboration experience, yet leave enough space for pursuing the individual objectives of our own courses, posed great challenges for the design and the implementation process of our project. For the second iteration of the project, which ran in the autumn semester of the 2019/2020 academic year, we decided to make some adjustments to the original agenda and project outline. These decisions are explained in the last section of this chapter.

2. Aims and description of the project

Due to the interdisciplinary nature of our TEP project, we still kept the individual objectives of the two courses, while also setting the shared goals and learning outcomes of the virtual collaboration. The main objectives of the 'Economics of Spain and the European Union' course at UNIOVI were to allow students to explore concepts and theories related to EU economics and develop a coherent discourse to describe, interpret, and discuss the Spanish and EU economy by using new technologies as a means of communication and information search, working in groups to apply and integrate knowledge. This course followed the English as Medium of Instruction (EMI) approach and the 'English for European Union Contexts' course at PPCU applied a Content and Language Integrated Learning (CLIL) design, set out to introduce students to the key EU terminology in English through topics related to the EU institutions, procedures, and policies. PPCU students enrolled on this course had a high level of proficiency in English, ranging from upper-intermediate to advanced levels[5]. These two different linguistic approaches determined the Lingua Franca spirit of the exchange and highlighted the importance

---

5. Equivalent to the Common European Framework of Reference for languages (CEFR) from B2 to C1

of the preparatory phase of the project in which the professors were able to go beyond the limits of their own course objectives in terms of content and language. They found shared aims focusing the exchange on innovative teaching practices and competences (Dearden & Macaro, 2016; Guarda & Helm, 2017), which included offering the Spanish and Hungarian students the opportunity to (1) gain international experience, (2) engage in disciplinary research and academic activities, (3) practise and develop 21st century skills (i.e. collaboration, intercultural communication, critical thinking, creativity), and (4) actively use their English language communication competences.

3. Pedagogical design and tools

Throughout this 14-week-long collaboration project, students worked in mixed teams of four students each (two Spanish and two Hungarian students) on a series of shared authentic assignments and project tasks (Dee Fink, 2003). It was fortunate that the Spanish and Hungarian academic years coincided, so the students at both universities started the project at the same time. The first weeks of the project were called a preliminary phase and were devoted to: (1) the introduction and orientation of the students on the project objectives, tasks and activities, tools, final deliverables, assessment, and grading; (2) the formation of student teams; (3) the engagement in ice-breaker and team-building activities; (4) the assignment of research topics to teams; and (5) the presentation of the online tools for collaboration.

The aim of this preliminary phase was to encourage students to socialise with their team members, to build trust, and to start a conversation within the team. One of the students' tasks in the preliminary phase was to organise a synchronous online meeting with their team with the agenda of finding a name and a logo for it. These had to be related to the content of the courses, i.e. to the EU, its social, political, economic, or institutional framework. After these team-building activities, we assigned key topics to the teams to work on collaboratively during the project. We initially offered the following four main topics: (1) the EU's history, philosophy, and integration process; (2) the

EU's internal market; (3) the EU's foreign trade; and (4) the Euro as a common currency in the Eurozone. During the design of the project, we created separate presentations to introduce each of the topics[6]. Each team watched the presentations online, ranked the four main topics according to the team's preference, and wrote a detailed justification for their choice. The professors then assigned the topics to the teams making sure that the teams' preferences, claims, and arguments were taken into account.

The first phase of the project started with an analysis of the given topic including its background, key facts, institutions, policies, and the related issues. The analytic activities started in the form of textbook reviews and individual research. First, each student had to find a piece of news related to the team's topic, write a brief summary of the article, and share and discuss it online within their team. Second, each team reviewed op-ed articles[7] and more analytical papers selected by the professors with the aim of developing a deeper insight into the issues concerning their topic of research. The students also shared their written reviews of the articles online with their team members. The findings of their overall background analysis were then discussed separately with the whole group in their respective classes, providing opportunities for face-to-face feedback from their peers and guidance from the professors.

The second phase of the project was dedicated to the development of the final project deliverables based on all the team members' findings in the previous phase. The teams had to narrow down their topic and identify a specific issue that would become the focus of their final video presentation. In the presentations, they had to summarise their previous research findings, state their issue or problem, as well as their research questions, provide a critical analysis, and suggest possible alternatives for the solution to the problem. The video presentations were then uploaded to a video-sharing platform and were evaluated by the students following pre-set assessment criteria. At project close, we had an

---

6. Two examples of the topic presentations can be found here: https://spark.adobe.com/page/BQNQzzE1cYTnd/ and https://spark.adobe.com/page/53qqZS96EZLUT/

7. op-ed, short for 'opposite editorial page' expressing the opinion of an author usually outside the publication's editorial board

in-class discussion with the students on their achievements, performances, and learning experiences.

At the start of the project, the students signed a General Data Protection Regulation (GDPR) consent form and agreed to use and share their email addresses within the two cohorts for communication purposes. During the project, we asked the students to use a third-party platform called Moxtra to manage their collaboration activities and communication with their team members and professors. Besides Moxtra, we used various online tools such as Google Docs, Forms, and applications for video and presentation design (e.g. SparkAdobe). For the online meeting, each project team used Zoom as a videoconferencing tool.

4. Evaluation, assessment, and recognition

Students' academic performances and achievements in the project were assessed and graded separately at the two universities. The teams' deliverables, however, were co-reviewed and co-evaluated by all three professors and feedback to student groups was given accordingly. As the form of assessment, the equivalence of project participation to the percentage of the grade, and the number of credits to be earned differed at the two universities, the professors had decided to grade and assess their own students' performances only. Both the Spanish and the Hungarian participants who completed the project successfully were given official E+VE digital badges as a proof of their online collaboration experience and as an acknowledgement of the skills they had developed. The course credits and the evaluation scheme of the two universities is summarised in Table 1.

Table 1. Credits and evaluation scheme at the two universities

	UNIOVI	PPCU
Course module	9 ECTS	2 ECTS
Students project performance	40%	80%
Non-project related performance (exam)	60%	20%

5. Lessons learnt

At the end of the project, we randomly selected participants from both Spanish and Hungarian student groups and asked them to provide feedback on their project experience in the form of a SWOT analysis and identify the strengths, weaknesses, opportunities, and threats related to the project in which they had participated. The SWOT analysis allowed students to assess the critical elements of the project and provide a thorough, in-depth exploration into the advantages and the challenges they encountered in the educational context (Leiber, Stensaker, & Harvey, 2018; Romero-Gutierrez, Jimenez-Liso, & Martinez-Chico, 2016). We wanted to collect information from students with the aim of creating a critical analysis of these factors from the students' perspectives and draw conclusions for the future iterations of the project. The results and discussion of the students' SWOT analyses are summarised here following the four main components of the framework.

5.1. Strengths

Both the Spanish and the Hungarian students claimed that the project was a new experience for them and online collaboration represented an innovative approach to learning which made the course different than other university courses and took them out of their comfort zone. Students' motivation was high for completing the project successfully. Another strength of the VE was that it promoted the use of various online tools and applications, which they became familiar with and began to use more confidently. Students also appreciated the variety of project tasks they had to carry out. They thought that these activities gave them the opportunity to hone their academic skills, collaboration skills, use their creativity, and practise their English language communication skills. According to respondents, our VE promoted openness and communication with students from other countries.

5.2. Weaknesses

Among the weaknesses of the project, some students highlighted the lack of effective teamwork and communication among some of the Spanish and

Hungarian team members, which affected the quality of their collaboration negatively. Others were more successful in managing their teams, but reported that unequal distribution of project tasks and activities among the team members was evident. In the opinion of one of the respondents, the students at the two universities were doing different majors, therefore their subject knowledge and understanding of the issues involved varied. Some of the groups could not work on their first preferred topic and students believed that this had a negative effect on their level of motivation and project engagement as they lost interest in the assigned topic. Also, students felt that they had to invest more time and effort into the completion of the project than they would have needed to in a regular course. The execution of some of the tasks required more time than planned by the professors, so the interim deadlines of certain tasks had to be extended and rescheduled.

For the next iterations of the project, we decided to include more ice-breaking activities at the beginning of the project with the aim of building better rapport among the team members, ensuring more effective teamwork and better task management. As for solving the problem of the varying expertise of the student groups, in the second year we asked them to approach the same topic from two different angles complementing each other by focusing on their own discipline and specific perspective. Furthermore, we changed our practice and allowed student teams to select their preferred research topic, rather than assigning the topics to the teams. We believe that it helped maintain students' high initial motivation and interest in the project. For the sake of keeping the deadlines, we revisited our course schedules and reduced the number of tasks, so that enough time is now allocated to the completion of each deliverable.

5.3. Opportunities

Engaging in a meaningful intercultural exchange with students from another European country was one of the opportunities of the project. Students appreciated the opportunity of getting to know other cultural perspectives, especially how issues about certain areas of the EU are perceived by students in another member state. Also, our online collaboration project fulfilled its potential not only to develop students' subject knowledge in the area of the EU's economy, but also their creativity, teamwork, leadership, and organisational skills. Some students highlighted that their digital skills greatly improved and they were given the opportunity to practise online communication in English.

5.4. Threats

In their reflection, students believed that the threats to the success of the project were the instances of misunderstanding and miscommunication among the team members and the difficulties of managing these situations. Another issue for some teams was student drop-outs leaving some teams with fewer members to work with or even without international partners to collaborate with. Students also believed that their concurring university obligations of other courses sometimes made it difficult to meet the deadlines of the project, thus hampering their successful completion of the project as well as the course.

To avoid external threats during the implementation of the project, we tried to set up contingency plans in case of student drop-outs. Also, in future iterations we increased the number of students assigned to each team with the aim of reducing the damage of any potential drop-outs and reducing the students' workload.

6. Conclusion

This chapter presents an example of a TEP that offers students a virtual international experience using new approaches to learning and providing opportunities for online collaboration, which would not be possible in standard university course settings. Working in teams with university students of another country opens doors to new perspectives and contributes to the development of students' 21st century skills, which would be limited in a local national environment. Nonetheless, this case study also highlights some complex and subtle elements that educators have to take into account when planning this type of exchange.

Initially, one of the main drivers to set up a TEP is to find a suitable partner who runs a very similar module with the same disciplinary content and approach. In our experience, it is very difficult to find a partner module in the same discipline at other foreign universities that fully match our own course. An interdisciplinary approach to the TEP provides a more enriching experience and gives way to a more sophisticated and elaborated design. Curricular differences allow for shared learning goals along with the course-specific objectives and direct the focus on skills and competences beyond the subject content specific knowledge, thus requiring innovative ways of teaching. We believe that matching content modules that are taught in English (following an EMI approach) with modules of English for specific purposes (applying a CLIL approach) is an ideal combination to construct shared knowledge embedded into English communicative competence. Therefore, we would encourage university educators who are seeking TEP partners to look beyond their specific content and disciplinary area and explore other bordering realms to establish interdisciplinary partnerships.

The main ramification of this recommendation is that it requires a considerable preliminary effort put into project planning and preparation in advance, involving multiple discussions, coordination, as well as agreements and compromises. Also, trust and partnership need to be built within the teaching team to ensure close cooperation. Clear statement of expectations, equal work distribution, and recognition of individual contributions are essential to lead the project, and consequently to form a community of practice that maintains the partnership and results in multiple iterations of the TEP (Martin, 2005; Wenger, 1998).

References

Burke, H. (2019). *Living and working in Europe 2015–2018*. Eurofound. https://www.eurofound.europa.eu/publications/annual-report/2019/living-and-working-in-europe-2015-2018

Dearden, J., & Macaro, E. (2016). Higher education teachers' attitudes towards English medium instruction: a three-country comparison. *Studies in Second Language Learning and Teaching*, *6*(3), 455-486. https://doi.org/10.14746/sllt.2016.6.3.5

Dee Fink, L. (2003). *Creating significant learning experiences: an integrated approach to designing college courses*. John Wiley & Sons.

EPSC. (2017). *10 trends transforming education as we know it*. European Political Strategy Centre. https://op.europa.eu/en/publication-detail/-/publication/227c6186-10d0-11ea-8c1f-01aa75ed71a1

Guarda, M., & Helm, F. (2017). 'I have discovered new teaching pathways': the link between language shift and teaching practice. *International Journal of Bilingual Education and Bilingualism, 20*(7), 897-913. https://doi.org/10.1080/13670050.2015.1125848

Helm, F. (2015). The practices and challenges of telecollaboration in higher education in Europe. *Language Learning & Technology, 19*(2), 197-217. http://llt.msu.edu/issues/june2015/helm.pdf

Leiber, T., Stensaker, B., & Harvey, L. C. (2018). Bridging theory and practice of impact evaluation of quality management in higher education institutions: a SWOT analysis. *European Journal of Higher Education, 8*(3), 351-365. https://doi.org/10.1080/13538322.2015.1111007

Martin, D. (2005). Communities of practice and learning communities. In D. Barton & K. Tusting (Eds), *Beyond communities of practice: language power and social context* (pp. 139-157). Cambridge University Press. https://doi.org/10.1017/cbo9780511610554

O'Dowd, R., & Lewis, T. (2016). (Eds). *Online intercultural exchange: policy, pedagogy, practice*. Routledge.

Romero-Gutierrez, M., Jimenez-Liso, M. R., & Martinez-Chico, M. (2016). SWOT analysis to evaluate the programme of a joint online/onsite master's degree in environmental education through the students' perceptions. *Evaluation and program planning, 54*, 41-49. https://doi.org/10.1016/j.evalprogplan.2015.10.001

Wenger, E. (1998). *Communities of practice*. Cambridge University Press.

9 E+VE-SFI: developing spoken interaction in a foreign language

Margarita Vinagre[1], Ciara R. Wigham[2], and Marta Giralt[3]

Abstract

E+VE-SFI (Erasmus+ Virtual Exchange – Spain, France, Ireland) is a higher-education VE between students from Universidad Autónoma de Madrid (UAM), Université Clermont Auvergne (UCA), and the University of Limerick (UL). Its primary aim is to develop the speaking skills of undergraduates enrolled in foreign language programmes. Running over a six-week period, students interact in pairs via videoconferencing to carry out a series of tasks using either the foreign language (UAM-UL) or English as a lingua franca (UAM-UCA). Finally, students participate in an online session mediated by E+VE facilitators whose purpose is to increase their intercultural awareness in preparation for their study abroad experience.

Keywords: oral skills, virtual exchange, intercultural competence, preparation for study abroad.

1. Context

The European Commission recently launched E+VE, a project that aims to explore the effects that virtual exchange can have in enhancing youth's

---

1. Universidad Autónoma de Madrid, Madrid, Spain; margarita.vinagre@uam.es; https://orcid.org/0000-0002-4370-8880

2. Université Clermont Auvergne, Clermont-Ferrand, France; ciara.wigham@uca.fr; https://orcid.org/0000-0001-9704-1906

3. University of Limerick, Limerick, Ireland; marta.giralt@ul.ie; https://orcid.org/0000-0002-1629-7641

How to cite this case study: Vinagre, M., Wigham, C. R., & Giralt, M. (2020). E+VE-SFI: developing spoken interaction in a foreign language. In F. Helm & A. Beaven (Eds), *Designing and implementing virtual exchange – a collection of case studies* (pp. 105-115). Research-publishing.net. https://doi.org/10.14705/rpnet.2020.45.1119

intercultural dialogue and awareness and in building their 21st Century skills[4]. In order to contribute to this initiative, a Transnational Exchange Project (TEP) was organised between university students in SFI. The aim of the E+VE-SFI exchange is to engage students in transnational partnerships to develop their foreign language spoken interaction and cultural awareness. Over six weeks, the students complete synchronous tasks using videoconferencing tools (*Skype* or *Zoom*) and discuss cultural topics included in their respective syllabi. This telecollaborative initiative has successfully run since September 2018 and engaged students from the three institutions described below.

The students from UAM are first year undergraduates from the programmes in Modern Languages and English Studies. They are learners of English who are enrolled in an oral skills English module (three contact hours per week over six weeks). The students take a placement test at the beginning of the academic year and their level of competence in the foreign language is between a B2 and C1 in the Common European Framework of Reference for languages (CEFR – Council of Europe, 2001).

The students from UCA are first year undergraduates from the Applied Foreign Languages degree programme. The TEP is part of a spoken English module (two contact hours per week over a ten-week semester). Before enrolling in the course, the students complete the open-access SELF (*Système d'Évaluation en Langues à visée Formative*) placement test (Innovalangues, 2014) and, following results, the level is set at CEFR C1.

The students from UL are second year students from the Applied Languages and Arts programmes. The exchange is part of their Spanish oral and aural lab (one contact hour per week over a 12-week semester), which is a compulsory element of their Spanish module. The level of the learners is set at CEFR B1+/-B2.

---

4. https://europa.eu/youth/EU_en

2. Aims and description of the E+VE-SFI exchange

The primary aim of the TEP is to engage undergraduates enrolled in the foreign language programmes to develop speaking and interaction skills. A secondary aim is to develop intercultural skills and cultural awareness to better prepare students for physical mobility periods which are compulsory components of the degree programmes at UCA (students spend the sixth semester of their Bachelor's degree at a partner institution abroad) and UL (students spend Semester 4 on work placements abroad and Semester 5 on study abroad). This practice is also encouraged within the Modern Languages and English Studies programme at UAM, where an important number of students spend Year 3 abroad.

The six-week exchange engages participating students in partnerships to carry out five tasks that involve introducing themselves using *Padlet*, three oral tasks in which they discuss in pairs, via *Zoom* or *Skype*, specific cultural topics included in the syllabus for their respective courses, and a self-reflection video. The cultural topics are first discussed in class with the teacher and classmates and then outside the classroom with the partner in order to explore their cultural differences and whether these are reflected in their partners' and their own perceptions of the same topics. Finally, in the self-reflection video the students elaborate on the different aspects they have learnt and the competences they perceive they improved throughout the experience. In addition to these tasks, the students participate in a facilitated dialogue session mediated by E+VE facilitators (see Table 1).

Table 1. Summary of the tasks

	Task 1	Task 2: Discussion	Task 3: Discussion	Task 4: Discussion	Task 5	
UAM-UCA	Introductions	Tourism	Technology and social media	Employment	Self-reflection video	Mediated session
UAM-UL	Introductions	Tourism	Technology and social media	Music, literature and cinema	Self-reflection video	Mediated session

For all participants, the practice of the foreign language is one of the most important elements of the TEP as it provides a unique opportunity to practise the language orally with peer learners in an authentic and interactional manner. As the three universities implement the exchange in their oral skills modules, the TEP fits effectively into the courses as a component.

3. Pedagogical design of the TEP

Given the different semester lengths, dates, and holiday periods, it was decided to run the TEP over a six-week period during which the teaching periods at the three institutions overlap. This does not prevent the partner teachers from conducting preparatory or evaluation activities in-class before or after this period.

Given the large number of students (n=90) involved in each TEP instantiation, students are paired randomly and, in some cases, triads are also organised if needed. The Spanish partner organises this and, where possible, places students who are also studying French as a third language in the UAM-UCA exchange. In this exchange, English as a lingua franca is used by the participants while both English and Spanish are used by participants in the UAM-UL exchange.

After the students are partnered, they participate in an asynchronous getting-to-know-you activity by contributing a post in which they introduce themselves to their TEP partners on *Padlet*. They are instructed not to stick to 'regular' introductions (e.g. age, hometown, hobbies) but encouraged to include photos, interesting facts about themselves, a description of their personality, or to share their favourite place/book/film/joke. They are also asked to share some information about their degree programme and their experience of the University semester so far. This allows each student to search for their partner and read their introduction before they meet for the first time. After this activity, the students must arrange a date and time with their partner in order to carry out the first task. During the TEP, each dyad carries out three 20-minute tasks via videoconferencing which take place outside the face-to-face lessons.

This is the minimum time required and some students have been known to have conversations with their partner of up to an hour. As mentioned above, to align with the different course content at the three institutions, the topics of technology and social media, employment and qualifications, and tourism are discussed in the UAM-UCA exchange, while the UAM-UL exchange explores cinema, books, and music instead of employment. In order to gather students' data for assessment and research purposes, a consent form was designed so that ethical considerations and General Data Protection Regulation (GDPR) compliance is ensured at all times. After the students sign these forms, they are asked to record the screencasts of their interactions. Students that use *Skype* for their exchanges generally use *Skype*'s built-in video recorder to generate the screencasts or rely on free trial versions of recording software such as *Camtasia* and *Evaer*. Students who use *Zoom* benefit from the built-in recording function.

In order to prepare the discussions, the partner teachers provide prompting questions on the selected topics (see supplementary materials, Appendix 1). For the bilingual exchanges, students are encouraged to speak half the time in one language and then switch to the other language.

The connection between the online synchronous interactions and the face-to-face sessions differs depending on the institution. For example, at UAM, a focus is placed on activities that help prepare students for the interactions with reference to the thematic content and topic-related vocabulary. In addition to language and vocabulary development, the students also analyse their recordings individually, looking for improvements in their communicative skills following a grid provided by the teacher. At UCA, the students also evaluate their language level by, for example, identifying examples of complex structures, phrasal verbs, or idiomatic expressions they used as well as words or phrases they used inappropriately. At UL, the topics discussed in the exchanges are practised in the face-to-face lab lessons focusing on developing aural skills through listening exercises. Face-to-face sessions at all institutions are used to debrief on the interactions and any linguistic and/or intercultural observations as well as any technical or organisational difficulties.

Prior to the final partner interaction, a mediated session run by E+VE facilitators is conducted in larger groups (15 students) via *Zoom* with students from the three institutions. For the UAM-UCA exchange, the sessions are conducted in English, while for the UAM-UL exchange bilingual sessions in English and Spanish are organised. The partner teachers decided that it would be beneficial for the students to explore cultural identity issues during this session, and suggested they could base their discussion on the 2014 TED talk by Taiye Selasi (2017), 'Don't ask me where I'm from, ask me where I'm a local'.

4. Assessment, evaluation, and recognition of the exchange

As already mentioned, each institution's language course is hybridised to allow full integration of the TEP within the learning objectives and summative evaluation components as well as recognition via ECTS credits.

To assess the students, the three partner teachers have aligned their summative evaluations so that all students have similar tasks as well as specific grade weights attached to them, in the hope of encouraging engagement in the TEP (see Table 2).

Table 2. Course assessment for each of the institutions

	UAM	UCA	UL
Number of ECTS credits	50% component of a 6 credit module	50% component of a 3 credit module	25% component of a 6 credit module
Screencast of best interaction	40%	40%	50%
Video self-assessment and feedback on exchange	30%	20%	50%
Other	30% topic-related vocabulary for in-class discussion	40% self-assessment task based on screen casts of interactions	n/a

As regards the tasks, all students are required to submit the screencast of their best interaction (or the two best) and the five-minute self-assessment video elaborating on different aspects of the TEP and on what they have learnt with their partners. A list of prompts is provided to guide the students, e.g. *In what ways do you think this project has helped you to learn Spanish/English and to interact in Spanish/English*; *In what way do you think this project has helped you to develop intercultural skills?*; *Out of the different tasks, which task did you enjoy and why?*; *Which task did you not enjoy and why?* (see supplementary materials, Appendix 2 for the complete list of prompt questions).

The E+VE coordinators also ask students for feedback on the TEP through a post-exchange questionnaire. Although only 29 out of 90 participants responded and therefore the sample is not representative, the feedback was highly positive with the vast majority of students agreeing that they would be interested in having further opportunities to engage in virtual exchange in the future.

Regarding the primary aim of the TEP to develop L2 speaking and interaction skills, 24 out of 29 students agreed or strongly agreed that the TEP had helped them improve their foreign language skills and 23 out of 29 students felt the exchange had helped them develop skills to communicate in a culturally diverse setting. Concerning the secondary aim, the development of intercultural skills to better prepare students for physical mobility, 27 out of 29 students described what they had learnt about people from other cultures as positive or very positive; 28 out of 29 students felt that they had developed knowledge about the relationship between and across different societies; and 26 out of 29 students expressed that the TEP had increased their interest in taking part in an educational programme abroad. Although the questionnaire results offer only a partial view of the TEP, and the data is self-declarative, this initial feedback is certainly encouraging.

For future iterations, we are considering asking students to complete this questionnaire in-class and also making its completion a prerequisite to be awarded the E+VE Open Digital Badge. Students are currently awarded this if they submit all three interaction tasks and participate in the mediated session.

While being actively involved in TEPs within their courses, all three partner teachers are also advocating for recognition within their institutions of VE as an innovative and effective learning approach. Such an approach should become fully integrated into the institutions' curricula as a fully recognised educational practice rather than a voluntary activity based on the goodwill and enthusiasm of a few motivated practitioners. In order to contribute to this goal, the following initiatives have been taken.

At UAM, TEP implementation as an innovative pedagogy that facilitates virtual mobility has recently been integrated in *CIVIS* (https://civis.eu/en), an alliance of eight European universities[5] labelled Erasmus+ by the European Commission in 2019. This European Civic University brings together a community of over 384,000 students and 55,000 staff members, including 30,000 academics and researchers. On a national level, UAM secured funding for a three-year National Research Agency project to analyse and assess the effects that integrating virtual exchange as an innovative teaching method has on the development of key competences for lifelong learning and employability of students in English as a Medium of Instruction (EMI) classrooms. Data from the TEP will be explored within the *VELCOME* research project (Oskoz & Vinagre, 2020; Vinagre & Corral, 2019), which engages over 20 researchers in five countries.

At UCA, as of September 2020, the TEP will form part of the University-wide innovative pedagogy project (*Skills linked to Internationalisation at Home*) alongside the CLAVIER project (MacKinnon, Ensor, Kleban, & Trégoat, 2020 this volume). The project, in which the International Office is a partner, will examine the skills students develop during projects that promote 'Internalisation at Home', defined as "the purposeful integration of international and intercultural dimensions into the formal and informal curriculum for all students within domestic learning environments" (Beelen & Jones, 2015, p. 69). The aim is to promote and better highlight these skills, which are currently not clearly visible, for UCA's 2021-2025 skills-based degree programme.

---

5. Autónoma University of Madrid, Spain; Aix-Marseille University, France; National and Capodistrian University of Athens, Greece; Free University of Brussels, Belgium; University of Bucharest, Romania; La Sapienza University of Rome, Italy; University of Stockholm, Sweden and Eberhard Karls University of Tübingen, Germany.

At UL, the implementation of VEs in teaching practices occurs mainly within the School of Modern Languages and Applied Linguistics, where several initiatives have been launched in the last few years (Batardière et al., 2019; Giralt, 2020 this volume; Giralt & Jeanneau, 2016). At the same time, the International Office Division provides support to all these initiatives and it is envisaging the expansion of VEs across the university as a means to prepare students for their mobility programme.

On these grounds, positioning our telecollaboration practices as a TEP within the E+VE initiative has been instrumental in helping us to gain recognition within our own institutions and we hope it will help us to develop links with partners working in similar initiatives within our own institutions as well as upscale our practices.

5. Lessons learnt and conclusion

Since the start of the TEP among the three universities, a very positive and encouraging response has been received from the students. It is essential that the VEs are integrated in the curriculum and that participation in the TEPs translates into credits awarded and external recognition, in this case, digital badges recognised by the European Commission. For our TEP, we would also like to better promote the award of these open badges. For example, at UCA, the students in the third semester have a teaching unit on writing CVs, which includes the Europass CV. Links with this course's teacher could be established in order to include the addition of open badges to the CV as part of the course aims.

With hindsight, for future TEPs we may consider subdividing the students into smaller groups and creating online notice boards or forums for each group to facilitate access to their partners' background information. This could be achieved, for example, by organising students into the groups in which they will later meet for the mediated session, or adding another facilitated session at the beginning of the project, thus allowing students not only to get to know their partner but also the other students in the group.

Overall, as practitioners we are very satisfied with the TEP and our students also appreciate the effort since, in addition to the positive findings mentioned above, they reported an increase in self-confidence and self-reliance when communicating in the foreign language.

6. Supplementary materials

https://research-publishing.box.com/s/e3t9gkwpl6nirvuux4ugh9nfy5yz2xtq

References

Batardière, M.-T., Giralt, M., Jeanneau, C., Le-Baron-Earle, F., & O'Regan, V. (2019). Promoting intercultural awareness among European university students via pre-mobility virtual exchanges. *Journal of Virtual Exchange, 2*, 1-6. https://doi.org/10.14705/rpnet.2019.jve.4

Beelen, J., & Jones, E. (2015). Redefining internationalization at home. In A. Curaj, L. Matei, R. Pricopie, J. Salmi, & P. Scott (Eds), *The European higher education area*. Springer.

Council of Europe (2001). *Common European framework of reference for languages: learning, teaching, assessment*. Cambridge University Press.

Giralt, M. (2020). Communication across cultures: when the virtual meets the classroom. In F. Helm & A. Beaven (Eds), *Designing and implementing virtual exchange – a collection of case studies* (pp. 191-203). Research-publishing.net. https://doi.org/10.14705/rpnet.2020.45.1126

Giralt, M., & Jeanneau, C. (2016). Preparing higher education language students to their period abroad through telecollaboration: the I-TELL project. *AISHE-J: The All Ireland Journal of Teaching and Learning in Higher Education, 8*(2). http://ojs.aishe.org/index.php/aishe-j/article/view/278/

Innovalangues. (2014). *Système d'évaluation en langues à visée formative (SELF)*. Projet IDEFI Innovalangues: Université Grenoble Alpes.

MacKinnon, T., Ensor, S., Klebin, & Trégoat, C. (2020). Recognising participation in virtual exchange: open badges and the CLAVIER contribution. In F. Helm & A. Beaven (Eds), *Designing and implementing virtual exchange – a collection of case studies* (pp. 141-152). Research-publishing.net. https://doi.org/10.14705/rpnet.2020.45.1122

Oskoz, A., & Vinagre, M. (2020). *Understanding attitude in intercultural virtual communication.* CALICO Special Volume. Series: Advances in CALL Research and Practice. Equinox.

Selasi, T. (2017). *Don't ask where I'm from, ask where I'm a local.* TEDGlobal 2014. https://www.ted.com/talks/taiye_selasi_don_t_ask_where_i_m_from_ask_where_i_m_a_local

Vinagre, M., & Corral, A. (2019). Tracing the development of intercultural competence in telecollaborative interaction: an analysis of evaluative language in eTandem exchanges. In C. Tardieu & C. Horgues (Eds), *Redefining tandem language and culture learning in higher education* (pp. 95-112). Routledge. https://doi.org/10.4324/9780429505898-7

10. Task-enhanced virtual exchange between University of Sfax, Tunisia, and Hacettepe University, Turkey

Asma Moalla[1], Nadia Abid[2], and Ufuk Balaman[3]

Abstract

This chapter presents a case study of an online task-enhanced Virtual Exchange (VE) project that involved 19 English students at Hacettepe University, Turkey, and 19 students of English at Sfax University, Tunisia. The objective behind the VE was to provide students with opportunities for intercultural and interactional development through the performance of collaborative intercultural tasks. At the end of the project, students' performances were assessed and graded, and the project was evaluated by Tunisian students, by means of narratives. The case study concludes with recommendations to be taken into consideration for future VE projects.

Keywords: virtual exchange, task-enhanced project, intercultural tasks, Skype, intercultural communicative competence, collaboration.

1. Context

The VE project described in this chapter took place under the umbrella of the Erasmus+ VE program and involved two groups of students based in

---

1. Faculty of Arts and Humanities of Sfax, Sfax, Tunisia; asma.moalla130@gmail.com; https://orcid.org/0000-0001-9521-2716

2. Faculty of Arts and Humanities of Sfax, Sfax, Tunisia; nadia.abid@flshs.usf.tn; https://orcid.org/0000-0002-6293-1121

3. Hacettepe University, Ankara, Turkey; ubalaman@gmail.com; https://orcid.org/0000-0001-5092-9414

How to cite this case study: Moalla, A., Abid, N., & Balaman, U. (2020). Task-enhanced virtual exchange between University of Sfax, Tunisia, and Hacettepe University, Turkey. In F. Helm & A. Beaven (Eds), *Designing and implementing virtual exchange – a collection of case studies* (pp. 117-126). Research-publishing.net. https://doi.org/10.14705/rpnet.2020.45.1120

Case study 10

Turkey and Tunisia. The Tunisian group included 19 second year students majoring in English and taking an intercultural communication course at the Faculty of Arts and Humanities, Sfax, Tunisia. The Turkish group also consisted of 19 students taking the advanced speaking class at Hacettepe University, Turkey. The project designers' participation in the project was motivated by their interest in providing Tunisian and Turkish students with a practical experience of working collaboratively on virtual intercultural tasks in an authentic context for intercultural learning. Added to that, the teachers wanted to introduce their students to new ways of learning based on the use of video-mediated communication tools. The teachers were also interested in exchanging teaching practices and techniques to benefit from a better quality of learning and teaching.

2. Aims and description of the project

The VE project was based on the performance of intercultural tasks where participants collaborated and communicated to seek and exchange cultural information (Dooly & O'Dowd, 2010; Lewis, 2017; O'Dowd & Lewis, 2016). It aimed to promote participants' intercultural learning and development of intercultural communicative competence. More specifically, the project sought to improve students' intercultural communication skills which required gaining knowledge of the culture and attitudes of openness, empathy, and respect.

To achieve these objectives, a task-based approach was used (Balaman, 2018; Hauck, 2010; Hauck & Youngs, 2008; Kurek & Müller-Hartmann, 2017; Müller-Hartmann & Kurek, 2016; O'Dowd & Ware, 2009). The task performance started by giving participants the necessary instructions and materials. Collaboration and interaction were emphasized to achieve the interactional and intercultural purposes of the tasks such as informed decision making (taking decisions about an issue after doing some research about it), categorizing and classifying cultural information, discussing cultural norms from different perspectives, applying intercultural skills such as comparing cultural aspects, and managing misunderstandings in interactions. After receiving and understanding the instructions for the tasks, partners started discussing, sharing, classifying, collaborating as well as using different language functions and conversation mechanisms.

3. Tasks and tools

The VE started in April 2019 and lasted for one month. Each student in Sfax, Tunisia was paired with a partner based in Hacettepe University, Turkey. The first meeting consisted of an ice breaking activity, and was followed by a further five meetings during which they completed ten tasks (two tasks per meeting). The tasks were designed by another group of Turkish students taking the "Instructional Technology and Materials Development" class at Hacettepe University. These students had been asked to design interactional tasks as part of their pre-service teacher training assignments[4] (cf. Balaman, Ekin, & Badem-Korkmaz, in review). The tasks were meant to be performed by Tunisian students and their Turkish partners. Part of the pre-implementation procedure included an email that was sent to all participants containing details about recording their performance of the tasks, an instruction video, and further documents setting out general arrangements for communicating with their partners. Instructions included the suggested duration of the tasks, which were to be completed within a recommended 20 minutes and should in any case not exceed 40 minutes.

It is to be noted that participants performed the tasks at home outside ordinary class time using English as the medium of communication. The following is an example of a task designed for the project: it consisted in having partners collaborate in making choices and taking informed decisions after looking for cultural information on the net. Participants had to imagine that they had to visit the maximum number of places in Cairo during 14 hours. They were given a list of places they could visit and a timeline on which they had to put the places they would visit and the time they would spend there. The first and the last places were given to them. Finally, partners had to decide on the other places and put

---

4. The task design procedures are beyond the scope of the current study.

them on the timeline after searching the internet for information about those places and the time the visit would take.

4. Assessment and recognition

The Tunisian students were taking an intercultural communication course which was based on engaging in different VE projects – including an exchange with a French university the previous semester. The VE project with Hacettepe University was based on the program of the advanced speaking course at Hacettepe, which aimed to improve the students' interactional and intercultural competencies mainly by engaging in the VE project.

At the end of the project, the Tunisian students were assessed and graded on the basis of the interactional and intercultural skills they used with their partners. Each pair's interactions were recorded and the students' development of interactional skills were tracked and compared over the period of the exchange (Balaman, 2018; Balaman & Sert, 2017; Sert & Balaman, 2018). The criteria adopted for the assessment included maintaining smooth interactions with the other, discovering the other culture, and reflecting on one's own culture, avoiding communication breakdowns, readjusting and revisiting one's own attitudes, and creating new ones (Moalla, 2015). The Tunisian students were awarded grades based on local institutional assessment requirements while the Turkish students were assessed on end of project self-reflection reports on each of the VE tasks and overall changes in their interactional practices based on screen-recordings of each meeting. All students were granted online badges in recognition of their participation in the VE.

5. Evaluation of the exchange

The Turkish students' evaluation of their experiences was limited to self-reflections toward their interactional gains, and is not within the scope of the current study. The Tunisian students were asked to write a detailed narrative about the challenges they faced, the way they handled them, and the lessons they learned.

From the outset, the Tunisian students were excited to embark on VE because of the Turkish series broadcast on Tunisian TV. The presumed familiarity with the Turkish culture prepared students for motivating interactions as they were curious to discover whether what they knew about Turkey was right or wrong.

The Tunisian students reported that they found the exchange "mind-provoking", "fulfilling", "unforgettable", and "priceless". The analysis of students' narratives revealed their attitudes toward the video-mediated interactions (via Skype), the topics they discussed, the tasks they performed, and the relationships they built.

Skype proved to be beneficial as a tool of instruction and interaction because it provided participants' with flexibility of time and place as well as multiple opportunities for intercultural development. One Tunisian student, for example, explained: "the best thing was that we could work from any place at any time". Another student reported: "we had the possibility to choose which time to talk without pressure or a supervisor". Participants expressed preferences for Skype as it enabled them to see their partners' reactions and interpret them in the right way: "there is always something special about getting to see people's reactions for yourself and not just interpreting their feelings throughout text messages".

Additionally, students appreciated working in pairs because they had more space and time to engage in more enriching conversations and to collaboratively join their efforts in completing the tasks. From the students' perspectives, the tasks provided them with a secure context for learning as they were clear, well-structured, and guided by teachers. The topics discussed could promote culture learning for they were varied and motivating. Using one student's own words:

> "these tasks were really meaningful and they succeeded to reveal the main cultural features of both Tunisia and Turkey. For instance, I still remember that Kebabs is one [sic] of the favourite dishes in Turkey as well as the refreshments such as the Turkish coffee or the Turkish tea".

Case study 10

In their accounts on the exchange, most participants focused on the human dimension and relationship building. They asserted that the exchange helped them make friends and maintain contacts with their partners after the end of the exchange. They have even invited their partners to visit their own country. Some students managed to develop a more universal view of human relationships. One participant believed that the exchange could help rethink and strengthen the relationship between people and cultures across the globe. He argued:

> "it is fairly safe to say that intercultural communication was a unique experience because it re-established the relationships between different people from different countries; especially that globalisation today is creating a real gap between nations".

Despite the generally positive attitudes toward the project, participants evoked some limitations. They believed that the design of the exchange relied on the performance of tasks and gave little time for personal interaction. While some students reported that the tasks were clear and motivating, one participant found the tasks to be poorly designed and did not meet her expectations.

6. Lessons learned

As a result of the video-mediated interactions, students became more aware of the differences and similarities between the two cultures:

> "with these activities, we noticed the similarities and differences between the two cultures for example the attitude of drinking tea many times during the day, the similar recipes of food, and believing in the evil eye in both countries".

Moreover, participants recognized that they learned about themselves and their partners at the same time:

> "there were moments when I was puzzled and I was positioned in an emergent situation where I had to explain something in my culture that I myself do not know anything about".

Finally, participants became more aware that human behavior, thoughts, and beliefs were culture-bound and that 'cultural conditioning' could hinder communication:

> "also, we are always stuck in our own cultural conditioning. We have always been ingrained since our childhood by certain values, certain assumptions, worldviews and behavior patterns. This could create problems for us when we are coming to different cultural environments".

In terms of communication skills, participants reported learning how to handle emerging situations of intercultural misunderstanding by explaining and clarifying its underlying causes:

> "what is important is how to handle a situation like this and how to explain to the other ..., and if we want the conversation to run smoothly, then, the best way is to explain in order to make them understand".

Some participants came to realize that the attitudes of respect and tolerance were necessary to manage challenging situations and build relationships:

> "also respect has to be the first stone in the building of intercultural communication".

One of the key outcomes of the exchange was the change in the participants' attitudes toward their partners' culture and their attempts to challenge the stereotypes they had from the Turkish TV series:

> "this experience had a great impact on me. First, it changed my opinions towards the Turkish cultures that I got them [sic] from media and series".

They learned to understand and tolerate their partners' perspectives and abandon ethnocentric attitudes:

> "first of all, this experience helped me a lot to avoid ethnocentrism which is to think that our culture is superior to other cultures in background, attitudes and values. It also allowed me to break down stereotypes and have more respect and acceptance towards others".

7. Final recommendations and conclusion

One of the students' achievements from the exchange is building strong ties with each other despite the limited duration of the exchange (Moalla, 2015). Having two meetings a week during a month made their timetables tight, which put some pressure on them in terms of time and efforts. Having one meeting a week over a 14 week semester could produce better results in terms of relationship building and development of intercultural and interactional skills. Not limiting students to the 20 minutes of the task could have also brought about better results. Tunisian students reported that they stayed focused on the task to abide by the time limits set for them, which made them avoid initiating new conversations. The conversations they had after the task was performed were reportedly more meaningful and spontaneous and led to the emergence of interactional skills that did not feature during the completion of tasks. The time constraint, therefore, seemed to hinder opportunities for further gains.

The flexibility of the use of Skype encouraged interactions and gave participants freedom to choose the time and place convenient to both. Skype could have been supplemented by other tools including emails and learning management systems (e.g. Moodle) as a potential solution for some of the problems encountered regarding VE procedures in the current project and for incorporating a lived sense of a community of practice in future implementations.

The tasks have a high potential to promote intercultural skills such as the ability to compare cultures and seek cultural information (Dooly & O'Dowd,

2010; Lewis, 2017; O'Dowd & Lewis, 2016). The mere exposure to culture, however, may not help students develop the skill of interaction (Byram, 1997); especially managing situations of misunderstanding due to cultural differences. The topics discussed including exchange of cultural information may lead to enriching students' knowledge of the other culture but not to the development of interactional skills. Selecting authentic video-recorded situations of misunderstanding from the participants' interactions or from everyday social interactions could be beneficial, especially if the partners are asked to identify the problems and the underlying causes.

The topics and tasks designed for the project were mainly addressed to tourists such as describing tourist attraction places, looking for information about food, artistic choices etc. Such types of cultural information can be useful for a tourist who needs some knowledge before traveling to a particular destination. It, however, might not be enough for people who travel for other reasons, including work, education, business, and medical care. Communicating with people from other cultures requires knowledge of the conventions and norms of social interactions and relations. The topics suggested in this project, furthermore, do not reflect real life as lived by Turkish and Tunisian people. Raising awareness of differences in body language, norms of social interaction, social life, gender roles, and relationships could better prepare students for future intercultural communication.

This case study reported on the objectives, design, and assessment of a VE project carried out between the Faculty of Arts and Humanities of Sfax, Tunisia, and the Department of English Language Teaching, Hacettepe University, Turkey. The data obtained revealed that the use of Skype, as an interactional tool, offered students flexibility of place and time and the opportunity to interact directly with real people. Additionally, participants' collaborative efforts to perform the tasks led to maintaining and strengthening their relationships. The discussion and negotiation of intercultural tasks helped students come up with accommodating strategies to maintain smooth and coherent conversations and to handle communication breakdowns. The dyadic nature of the interactions allowed students to revisit and adjust their attitudes and judgments, and led to the emergence of a new, shared identity.

References

Balaman, U. (2018). Task-induced development of hinting behaviors in online L2 task-oriented interaction. *Language Learning & Technology, 22*(2), 95-115. https://doi.org/10125/44640

Balaman, U., Ekin, S., & Badem-Korkmaz, F. (in review). *The interactional story of a task : design, feedback, implementation, and reflection.*

Balaman, U., & Sert, O. (2017). Development of L2 interactional resources for online collaborative task accomplishment. *Computer Assisted Language Learning, 30*(7), 601-630. https://doi.org/10.1080/09588221.2017.1334667

Byram, M. (1997). *Teaching and assessing intercultural communicative competence.* Multilingual Matters.

Dooly, M., & O'Dowd, R. (2010). (Eds). *Telecollaboration in education.* Peter Lang. https://www.peterlang.com/view/serial/TE

Hauck, M. (2010). The enactment of task design in telecollaboration 2.0. In M. Thomas & H. Reinders (Eds), *Task-based language learning and teaching with technology* (pp. 197-217). Continuum. https://doi.org/10.5040/9781474212366.ch-010

Hauck, M., & Youngs, B. L. (2008). Telecollaboration in multimodal environments: the impact on task design and learner interaction. *Computer Assisted Language Learning, 21*(2), 87-124. https://doi.org/10.1080/09588220801943510

Kurek, M., & Müller-Hartmann, A. (2017). Task design for telecollaborative exchanges: in search of new criteria. *System, 64,* 7-20. https://doi.org/10.1016/j.system.2016.12.004

Lewis, T. (2017). Introduction to system special issue on telecollaboration. *System, 64,* 1-6.

Moalla, A. (2015). Intercultural strategies to co-construct and interpret humor. *International Journal of Applied Linguistics, 25*(3), 366-385. https://doi.org/10.1111/ijal.12074

Müller-Hartmann, A., & Kurek, M. (2016). Virtual group formation and the process of task design in online intercultural exchanges. In R. O'Dowd & T. Lewis (Eds), *Online intercultural exchange* (pp. 145-163). Routledge.

O'Dowd, R., & Lewis, T. (2016). (Eds). *Online intercultural exchange: policy, pedagogy, practice.* Routledge.

O'Dowd, R., & Ware, P. (2009). Critical issues in telecollaborative task design. *Computer Assisted Language Learning, 22*(2), 173-188. https://doi.org/10.1080/09588220902778369

Sert, O., & Balaman, U. (2018). Orientations to negotiated language and task rules in online L2 interaction. *ReCALL, 30*(3), 355-374. https://doi.org/10.1017/S0958344017000325

11. How a multilingual project can foster and enhance international mobility

Lisa Griggio[1] and Sara Pittarello[2]

Abstract

This case study refers to the eTandem pre-mobility project coordinated by the Padova University Language Centre running twice a year since 2015 for approximately eight weeks. The project matches up local university students with incoming international students, thus boosting integration between the two groups and increasing internationalisation at home. One-to-one and many-to-many interactions are organised, the latter with the support of trained facilitators, who launch asynchronous (in an online multilingual community) and synchronous, intercultural, theme-based learning activities to be discussed every week. Students' linguistic, intercultural, and digital competences, as well as autonomy, are enhanced throughout the project, making them better prepared for their mobility.

Keywords: virtual and physical exchange, pre-mobility exchange, international mobility, soft skills, multilingual, multicultural, etandem, online community.

---

1. University of Padova, Padova, Italy; lisa.griggio@unipd.it

2. Freelance interpreter and expert in EU HE projects, Padova, Italy; sara.pittarello@unicollaboration.org

How to cite this case study: Griggio, L., & Pittarello, S. (2020). How a multilingual project can foster and enhance international mobility. In F. Helm & A. Beaven (Eds), *Designing and implementing virtual exchange – a collection of case studies* (pp. 127-139). Research-publishing.net. https://doi.org/10.14705/rpnet.2020.45.1121

© 2020 Lisa Griggio and Sara Pittarello (CC BY)

Case study 11

1. Context

1.1. Who is involved

The eTandem project was developed by the Language Centre of the University of Padova, in collaboration with the International Office (IO) in 2015 as a virtual exchange between incoming international students and domestic students interested in a language and intercultural exchange. It runs twice a year and with every iteration following a review of feedback received, slight adjustments are made. The number of participants has grown every year, and the most recent edition (ninth) involved 68 Italian and 75 international students.

Domestic students come from a range of degree courses. A substantial number are majoring in languages and literature and their participation in the project is recognised with three ECTS. Another substantial group (recruited through the IO) are future 'outgoing' students, who will be going on an Erasmus or other mobility project in the future and are interested in practising their language and/or learning more about the country and university system where they are going.

The very first edition saw Italian and English used as *linguae francae* in the exchange between peers. Additional languages such as Spanish, French, German, and Portuguese have been added in the following iterations thus contributing to the multilingualism called for in European language policy[3].

1.2. Project rationale – why it takes place

The eTandem project was conceived to respond to several needs. First of all, it was pivotal for the University Language Centre to meet the requests of domestic students interested in the already existing face-to-face tandem learning (Formentin, Griggio, & Whigham, 2004) but who could not be paired up with

---

3. With the adoption of the Barcelona objective (16 March 2002), which recommended the teaching to all of "at least two foreign languages from a very early age", multilingualism has become key in the European policy: "As part of its efforts to promote mobility and intercultural understanding, the EU has designated language learning as an important priority… Multilingualism, in the EU's view, is an important element in Europe's competitiveness. One of the objectives of the EU's language policy is therefore that every European citizen should master two other languages in addition to their mother tongue" (https://www.consilium.europa.eu/uedocs/cms_data/docs/pressdata/en/ec/71025.pdf).

international students because there were never enough international students to meet the demand.

Secondly, the initiative can contribute to deepening the participants' linguistic and cultural knowledge as well as their digital competence, thus enhancing soft skills. As universities prepare young people to become not only active global citizens but also effective members of the global workplace, increasing emphasis is being placed on soft skills in enabling them to operate effectively in work contexts which are both highly globalised and digitalised[4].

Thirdly, the project is also a way to boost 'internationalisation at home' and abroad. For those students who cannot or do not want to go abroad, eTandem provides an international dimension, i.e. experience in virtually communicating with people from different countries, gaining intercultural skills, creating networks, and improving their language competences and global competence (European Commission, 2009). However, the project also enhances mobility abroad as it triggers an emulation process among those students who have not applied for an international exchange programme yet.

2. Nuts and bolts

2.1. Communication modes and matching

The eTandem project foresees two communication modes, in a double line of interaction (see Figure 1):

- **many-to-many** through the e-community, where Italian, French, Spanish, Portuguese, German, and English are used as *linguae francae*, with facilitated dialogue sessions in mixed groups of eight to 12 students; and

---

4. The OECD (2018) suggests that "[e]ducating for global competence can boost employability" (p. 7). Global competence is "the capacity to examine local, global and intercultural issues, to understand and appreciate the perspectives and worldviews of others, to engage in open, appropriate and effective interactions with people from different cultures, and to act for collective well-being and sustainable development" (OECD, 2018, p.7).

- **one-to-one**, where the time should be equally split between Italian and other target languages, for both students to benefit from the language exchange. To this end, the e-moderators match pairs of students prior to the project start and remind them to meet up regularly. Because the number of participants for each group is not always equal, not only dyads but also triads are formed in certain cases. Students are matched according to different criteria: their destination/country of origin, study area, and language chosen.

Figure 1. Outline of interactions in eTandem

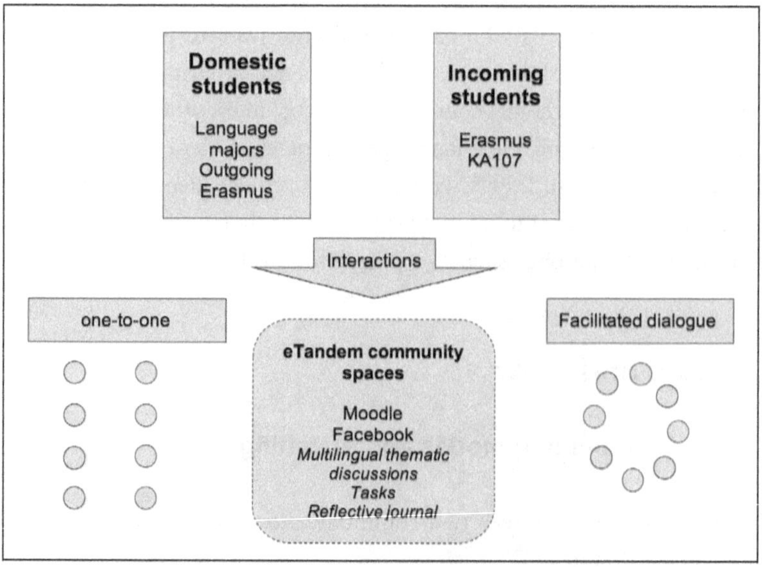

2.2. Tools

In the one-to-one interaction, students are free to choose the interaction language and tools (WhatsApp, Instagram, Facebook, Messenger, Skype, Zoom, etc.).

The online multilingual community has instead been hosted on two separate platforms simultaneously: an institutional one (Moodle) and an informal one

(Facebook). Although not all students enrol on both platforms, since neither is compulsory, they have been invited to join at least one in order to contribute to the e-community.

While Moodle was chosen by the eTandem team for its widespread use at Padova University and the opportunity to create a closed and safe environment, Facebook was instead chosen to make the informal language learning happen and create an enriching intercultural context. Although students are not obliged to become friends, through Facebook they can learn different attitudes, beliefs, and behaviours of their Italian and international peers[5] (Griggio, 2018).

2.3. Activities

The many-to-many interaction is favoured by a pattern of topics provided by the e-moderators. In the first week, students enter the online platform(s) and time is devoted to social and technological familiarisation. The project also includes theme-based asynchronous activities on a weekly basis, from the second to the tenth week, which guide learners through the topics discussed in the e-community. Prompts are launched every week, starting with a Motivation Monday activity, followed by further sub-themed activities throughout the rest of the week. Students, however, are left free to contribute even after the end of the week to whatever discussion they liked.

Students are encouraged to write weekly diaries of language and culture in Moodle, so as to keep a record of what they cover during one-to-one interactions and what they think about the intercultural issues addressed in the e-community. There is no specific format to be followed, as these diaries are mainly aimed at free writing and self-reflection. This type of activity serves as a tool to reflect on and evaluate thoughts, ideas, feelings, skills employed, and students' own learning process, closely following and recording their progress. The 'writing space' in Moodle contributes to enhancing students'

---

5. Moreover, Facebook being an open platform, its access can give students an everlasting possibility to belong to the closed e-community and they could carry on the exchange again, even beyond the end of the project, with different participants, simply by using the prompts, rules and resources provided. Despite the characteristic openness of social networks, a safe and protected virtual place has been ensured.

self-awareness, but also helps tutors to monitor the project development, in particular the constant interaction between students in the dyads/triads, while also enabling a continuous adjustment of the project to students' needs, competences, and suggestions. Moreover, a final reflection paper and feedback questionnaires are required at the end of the project.

In addition to the asynchronous activities, synchronous sessions, facilitated by Erasmus+ Virtual Exchange (E+VE) trained facilitators, have also recently been offered on Zoom, dealing with various topics.

2.4. Topics

Tutors propose and moderate debates on both safe and more controversial themes, like reading, traditions, stereotypes and superstitions, differences between cultures (body language, gestures, and tips), culture shock, cultural intelligence, food, and many others. More controversial topics include the role of media, climate change, veganism, social inequalities (job and gender, gender and pay gap), technology and education, humans *versus* robots, and social inclusion[6].

Any argument introduced in the social community area can be dealt with in the dyadic interactions as well as more personal themes such as families, hobbies, and interests.

3. Aims of the project

From a linguistic perspective, the first aim is that students learn and/or practice the languages of study in the one-to-one exchange, and the various *linguae francae* in the online multilingual and multicultural community. Plurilingualism

---

6. The topics discussed are pretty much in line with the UNESCO Sustainable Development Goals: "[t]hese are the blueprint to achieve a better and more sustainable future for all. They address the global challenges we face, including those related to poverty, inequality, climate change, environmental degradation, peace and justice"(https://www.un.org/sustainabledevelopment/sustainable-development-goals/).

and inclusive multilingualism[7] are key for the project, first of all because a better knowledge of more than one foreign language is needed to compete worldwide, second because of the high level of intercomprehension among romance languages, which are widely used in the students' exchanges. The focus is on the content rather than on the linguistic form (fluency *versus* accuracy) thus favouring spontaneity in the exchanges (Griggio, 2018)[8].

Secondly, the eTandem project gradually fosters students' cultural and intercultural awareness, by enhancing their curiosity towards otherness and familiarising them with different cultures while at the same time also being asked to deepen their knowledge of their own culture. This all requires the development of active listening and interaction strategies with foreign e-partners, but also the ability to relativise one's own values.

As far as the social level is concerned, boosting the integration of international students with those of the host country is a key aim. International students have the opportunity to be introduced to students who know the Italian university system and culture and can benefit from some language practice before their departure (Griggio, 2018, p. 91).

With reference to the technological and digital aim, students are encouraged to learn '*savoir faire*' and '*savoir être*' online (Griggio, 2012), participating in an e-community and safeguarding their web reputation. Through specific activities and resources, participants learn not to overexpose themselves online and how digital tattooing[9] may spoil their digital identity and hinder some future employment opportunities. Thus, participating students not only experience

---

7. Multilingualism is defined as the ability to use several languages, either by an individual speaker or by a community of speakers, either actively (speaking, writing) or passively (listening, reading). In other words, a mutual interaction of languages according to the user's mind, experience, and social experiences (Council of Europe, 2001, p. 168). Plurilingualism, the concept promoted by the Council of Europe in its Common European Framework of Reference for languages (CEFR), is the attempt to use one's linguistic knowledge and skills to communicate with others in many different situations. It means the ability to use language effectively and being connected in a multinational and multicultural community (Council of Europe, 2001, p. 168).

8. The ability to communicate in various languages is one of the fundamental requirements in the labour market, as confirmed by the European Council Recommendation of 2018 (https://eur-lex.europa.eu/legal-content/EN/TXT/PDF/?uri=CELEX:32018H0604(01)&from=EN).

9. A tattoo is permanent, much like the information posted online: photos shared, comments written, videos liked. Even if they are deleted, they may still be out there – saved and shared by others, or even kept by the site or app itself.

opportunities and potential risks linked to social networks, but also how to live and participate in an online community (Griggio, 2018, p. 91).

4. Evaluation, assessment, and recognition

The project was awarded the European Language Label[10] in Italy in 2016. Following the e-tutor's participation in training and the signing of a Memorandum of Understanding, the project has also been recognised as an E+VE.

Three ECTS are awarded to the language and literature majors, provided that they successfully complete the project, as this has been formalised as optional activity within their curriculum. Other participants are not awarded credits as they take part on a voluntary basis. A certificate of attendance is nevertheless issued to all students when they successfully complete the activities required: (1) writing at least four (out of six) language and culture diaries, (2) contributing to at least six eTandem community discussions, (3) writing a short final essay in the language of study, (4) participating in at least one online session, and (5) completing a questionnaire at the end of the project.

Since 2019, students fulfilling the requirements described above have also been awarded E+VE open badges. Students are not fully confident with how to use and display them so potential ways of displaying them have been illustrated (e.g. using them to enrich the CV, or displaying them on their social media profiles) in a final synchronous session.

At the end of each edition, students are asked to fill in a feedback questionnaire aimed to explore students' participation, motivation, and perspectives related to different areas: technological and digital, content, linguistic and metalinguistic, cultural, psychological, and social. Data analysis indicates that the majority

---

10. "The European Language Label is an award encouraging the development of new techniques and initiatives in the field of language teaching and learning, as well as the enhancement of intercultural awareness across Europe. The Label is awarded annually or biannually to the most innovative language learning initiatives in each Erasmus+ programme country participating in the scheme. The Label covers all sectors of education and training" (https://ec.europa.eu/education/policies/multilingualism/european-language-initiatives_en).

of students found Facebook, Instagram, and WhatsApp to be the most useful tools for interacting. From a cultural perspective, it emerges that all but few participants considered the project very or quite useful. Almost all respondents said they intended to stay in contact with their eTandem partner once in Padova and that they felt mentally and emotionally more prepared to study abroad, while other Italian students felt more encouraged to apply for an Erasmus scholarship after this experience. Linguistically, they developed informal lexicon and written and oral skills both in the languages used as *linguae francae* and their target language, and perceived the benefit of peer-to-peer correction as high (Griggio & Rózsavölgyi, forthcoming). English (33%) was used as much as Italian (31%) and other languages (36%), and learners appreciated the multilingual environment. Last but not least, most of them felt less inhibited when speaking a foreign language, and said they had cultivated curiosity towards 'diversity' and developed active listening[11].

5. Lessons learnt and conclusion

Several lessons have been learnt through these nine editions. Crucial to the project success is the students' motivation, which has been encouraged by:

- letting them choose the topics they preferred to deal with first and proposing topical themes that are relevant both at a global and local level;

- the multilingual community space which allowed for communication beyond the dyads and enabled students to provide their contributions openly;

- avoiding to correct mistakes publicly; corrections were given directly by their peers in a private setting only;

---

11. More recent detailed results will be published in Griggio and Rózsavölgyi (forthcoming): eTandem: analisi di un progetto di pre-mobilità presso il CLA dell'Università di Padova.

- issuing E+VE open badges: the number of students who completed their learning path has almost doubled compared to previous editions (18 participants in the eighth edition *versus* 31 in the ninth edition);

- providing task based activities (Appel & Gilabert, 2002) on a regular basis;

- setting up online synchronous sessions in addition to asynchronous communication, which students have highly appreciated, as demonstrated by feedback collected through final questionnaires and meetings;

- leaving students free to choose the tools for one-to-one interactions; and

- leaving learners free to choose the languages they prefer to interact in with their e-peers.

5.1. Benefits

The project has proven to be highly beneficial at various levels. First of all, it is strategic at Higher Education Institution level as it promotes internationalisation at home as well as study abroad: both the initiative's timing (it is a pre-mobility project) and the composition of the Italian group (encompassing students of different disciplines and, notably, language students to further strengthen its multilingual aspect) were planned and chosen carefully. Not only does the project mentally and emotionally prepare students to study abroad, but it also makes those who have not won a scholarship yet, eager to emulate their fellows and thus willing to apply for an international exchange programme.

Second, it links virtual exchange to physical mobility, thus building a bridge in temporal and linguistic terms: "students can visit their virtual space before, during and after their physical exchange" (Griggio, 2018, p.108). Moreover, after their arrival in Padova, international students can finally meet in person with their Italian partner to continue a face-to-face relationship (face-to-face tandem project). Students show real empathy by providing mutual help and solidarity as well: Italian students help the international ones around the city and take care of some matters such as finding a house, saying where to purchase sim cards, or introducing them to nice places to hang out. During the lockdown due to Covid-19, the eTandem was for many of the international participants the only opportunity they had for contact with domestic students. This was particularly valued by those who had remained in Padova as they could be supported in their understanding of local news and regulations.

5.2. Challenges

Implementing such a project also presents some drawbacks, such as being very demanding and time consuming for the eTandem team to pair students, manage high numbers of emails, look for alternative fellows whenever students are 'abandoned' by their partners as some dyads/pairs may not work properly due to different expectations, time zones, or commitment incompatibilities.

Secondly, for students to be able to speak freely, a community of trust must be created (Helm, 2013), where all actors can feel safe to address sensitive topics and let students come out of their comfort zone, which is not easy in the very beginning. There is a need for well trained, multilingual e-tutors, able to be flexible, creative, prompt to intervene, and be as neutral as possible.

Third, there is a strong need to involve counterparts from other institutions and countries to balance students' participation. Although both Italian and international students enrol on a voluntary basis, Italian students have proven to be more proactive if compared to their e-partners, partly due to the ECTS they receive and strong local coordination.

5.3. Future steps

The project team is constantly working on enhancing the project even further and adapting it to student's changed needs and expectations. The first enhancement would be to form a parallel network of international university e-tutors or

Case study 11

teachers willing to implement such an initiative in their own institutions, so as to increase the integration of Padova University outgoing students. By working on both sides (or on many sides, as would be the case if other universities were involved), foreign learners would also be encouraged to be more proactive and receptive in developing their multilingual and intercultural competences (Griggio, 2018).

Another future step would be to train potential future foreign e-tutors or teachers, in order to equip them with techniques, strategies, and a tool kit of activities, tricks, and tips to carry out intercultural discussions. Based on students' feedback, the eTandem team is also evaluating to increase the number of synchronous sessions, and structure them in a way that both internal and external tutors are envisaged.

To conclude, the high project potential in terms of development of transversal competences, internationalisation at home and critical thinking would inevitably be very beneficial for other university stakeholders. That is why extending the project implementation to administrative staff would be a desired outcome in the near future (Griggio & Pittarello, forthcoming).

References

Appel, C., & Gilabert, R. (2002). Motivation and task performance in a task-based web-based tandem project. *ReCALL, 14*(1), 16-31. https://doi.org/10.1017/s0958344002000319

Council of Europe. (2001). *The common European framework of reference for languages: learning, teaching and assessment*. Cambridge University Press.

European Commission. (2009). *Green paper : promoting the learning mobility of young people*. https://op.europa.eu/en/publication-detail/-/publication/54058424-b822-4f3e-89b0-fcdd323961db/language-en

Formentin, R., Griggio, D., & Whigham, C. (2004). Face-to-face tandem learning. In C. Taylor Torsello, A. Pasinato & N. Whitteridge (Eds), *L'apprendimento linguistico al CLA: experience innovative e riflessioni per il futuro* (pp. 43-56). CLEUP.

Griggio, L. (2012). Parle avec moi: training in digital and linguistic competence in a French course hosted in a wiki platform. *Procedia-Social and Behavioral Sciences, 34,* 73-78. https://doi.org/10.1016/j.sbspro.2012.02.016

Griggio, L. (2018). Linking virtual and physical mobility: a success story of a multilingual and multicultural exchange. *Sustainable Multilingualism, 12*(1), 88-112. https://doi.org/10.2478/sm-2018-0004

Griggio, L., & Pittarello, S. (forthcoming). *Participants' perceptions and perspectives of intercultural and social inclusion in an awarded telecollaboration project.* Routledge Focus Collection: Mobile Assisted Language Learning Across Educational Contexts.

Griggio, L., & Rózsavölgyi, E. (forthcoming). *eTandem: analisi di un progetto di pre-mobilità presso il CLA dell'Università di Padova.* LinguaInAzione-ILSA Italiano L2 - Rivista digitale semestrale per l'insegnamento dell'Italiano L2/LS.

Helm, F. (2013). A dialogic model for telecollaboration. *Bellaterra Journal of Teaching & Learning Language & Literature, 6*(2), 28-48. https://doi.org/10.5565/rev/jtl3.522

OECD. (2018). *Preparing our youth for an inclusive and sustainable world.* The OECD PISA - global competence framework. https://www.oecd.org/education/Global-competency-for-an-inclusive-world.pdf

12. Recognising participation in virtual exchange: open badges and the CLAVIER contribution

Teresa MacKinnon[1], Simon Ensor[2], Marcin Kleban[3], and Claude Trégoat[4]

Abstract

The CLAVIER (Connected Learning And Virtual Intercultural Exchange Research) network grew rhizomatically as a result of open practice (Blyth, 2019), which is central to the CLAVIER approach. Informed by the field of Computer-Mediated Communication (CMC), the network has provided a safe space to experiment with the development and implementation of open badges to support sustained participation in Virtual Exchanges (VEs). This case study describes the rationale for CLAVIER's open badge framework and its links with the Erasmus+ VE (E+VE) badges.

Keywords: virtual exchange, open badges, micro-credentials, telecollaboration, computer-mediated communication.

---

1. University of Warwick, Coventry, United Kingdom; t.mackinnon@warwick.ac.uk; https://orcid.org/0000-0002-1701-3727

2. Université Clermont Auvergne, Clermont-Ferrand, France; simon.ensor@univ-bpclermont.fr; https://orcid.org/0000-0001-7219-5772

3. Jagiellonian University, Kraków, Poland; marcin.kleban@uj.edu.pl; https://orcid.org/0000-0002-3985-392X

4. University of Warwick, Coventry, United Kingdom; c.s.i.tregoat@warwick.ac.uk; https://orcid.org/0000-0002-2313-6870

How to cite this case study: MacKinnon, T., Ensor, S., Kleban, M., & Trégoat, C. (2020). Recognising participation in virtual exchange: open badges and the CLAVIER contribution. In F. Helm & A. Beaven (Eds), *Designing and implementing virtual exchange – a collection of case studies* (pp. 141-152). Research-publishing.net. https://doi.org/10.14705/rpnet.2020.45.1122

Case study 12

1. Context

The CLAVIER network emerged from a serendipitous person to person connection online in 2011 and has developed into a large scale VE with many 'threads' connecting both students and practitioners in discussions, co-creation, and physical exchange. The initial interaction followed by connections made on the social media platform Twitter resulted in a decision to connect the classrooms of language learners in Warwick, UK, and Clermont Ferrand, France, through computer-mediated activities (MacKinnon, 2016). CLAVIER has at its hub a core group of founding partners working in higher education institutions in the UK, France, and Poland. The students are undergraduates and postgraduates from a range of disciplines, wishing to enhance their language proficiency for diverse academic, professional, or personal reasons. They include specialist graduate students from Poland who are preparing to teach languages. In this chapter we will explain how the piloting and implementation of open badges in CLAVIER was connected to their use in E+VE.

The guiding principles of the exchanges were that:

- interactions would be computer-mediated;

- the tutor's role would be light, supportive, a 'more knowledgeable other'.

The resulting VE activities crossed the boundaries between formal and informal learning (Ensor, Kleban, & Rodrigues, 2017). Key elements contributing to the rhizomatic growth of this network include the openness (Blyth, 2019) central to the CLAVIER approach. Students and staff work together to design tasks and sequences of tasks appropriate to the learner context that provide progression in both language and CMC skills. Many tasks require the use of open channels such as social media sites.

Over time, due in no small part to the Open Educational Practice (OEP) of the lead practitioners, CLAVIER grew into a wider network of practitioners interested in the potential of CMC for international professional development. OEP, as described by Cronin (2017) is "complex, personal, and contextual; it is also continually negotiated" (p. 1). The use of social media platforms such as Twitter, Facebook, and Google coupled with hashtags (e.g. #warcler #clerwar) to aggregate conversations and amplify activities to a wider audience helped to support this growth. Physical exchanges supported by E+ teaching staff mobility funding have enabled the founding practitioners to better understand their respective contexts, and to facilitate the development of both online and offline activities.

Staff and student visits have strengthened the network. Engaging in the normalisation of such open practices has contributed in unexpected ways to the Continuing Professional Development (CPD) of the practitioners concerned and resonates with the findings of Daniels (2019), "contributing in nuanced ways to participants' CPD in terms of skills development, knowledge building, and language literacy. This seems to be occurring through individual and social practices" (p. 168).

2. Aims and description of CLAVIER

CLAVIER practitioners, mainly language educators, share a network of contacts and classes. They define the terms of their own class's VE collaboratively with suitable partner class/es whilst collaborating through the CLAVIER network. This means that each practitioner can benefit from a range of shared ideas yet still tailor tasks, tools, and assessments to best suit their context. This balance of infrastructure (shared tools such as Google Drive and communal spaces including an official Facebook page) and flexibility in terms of timing and task design allows individuals to participate in their own way, increasing their agency. We know that the attitude of practitioners towards any given learning intervention is crucial to student engagement (Guichon & Hauck, 2011). CLAVIER's approach is one of a collective (Thomas & Seeley-Brown, 2011) whereby strength results from participation, forming a virtuous circle for both staff and students. The network provides informal

CALL (Computer Assisted Language Learning) preparation for practitioners who feel they have not been well prepared for the use of technology in their teaching by formal qualifications (Kessler, 2007, p. 179).

The significance of recognition of participation was acknowledged early on in CLAVIER. In 2015, CLAVIER began to issue open badges in order to valorise the work of students, having investigated badge use as signifiers of participation (Hauck & MacKinnon, 2016). Open badges contributed to the infrastructure supporting the objectives of our collective.

3. Nuts and bolts of badges in CLAVIER

Open badges are online representations of skills, interests, and achievements which are verified through credible organisations. The system is based on an open standard and earners can display multiple badges from different issuers to tell the complete story of their achievements – both online and off. Badges can be displayed wherever earners want them on the web, and share them for employment, education, or lifelong learning (adapted from the badge wiki https://badge.wiki/wiki/What_Are_Open_Badges%3F#cite_note-1).

Badge design requires identification of the key learning moments along the route to more significant skill development (Hauck & MacKinnon, 2016).

Badges can be awarded through a push mechanism, which is to say that those who have earned a badge will receive an email via the platform confirming that they have met the criteria for issue. When a badge platform is integrated within a Virtual Learning Environment (VLE) it is possible to set such issuing events remotely so that the criteria, once recognised as met by the VLE, result in the automated issue of badges. It is also possible to set up a 'pull' mechanism for badge issueing whereby the badge earner has to provide evidence through the platform, for example through the submission of a link to a recording, file, or e-portfolio. The issuing event takes place via email notification when the evidence is accepted by an authorised user such as the lead tutor. CLAVIER has used both approaches.

The founders of the CLAVIER exchange had been investigating badges for some years. In 2014 we set up a CLAVIER connector badge on the badge list platform and claimed the badge for ourselves using evidence of our activity in the CLAVIER community. This experiment helped us to understand the importance of using a badge as a signifier of community. Providing evidence of one's activity online in order to claim a badge can be a powerful way to learn how to manage one's online presence.

Subsequently CLAVIER began to award badges to students as recognition for participation in different activities, for example an engagement badge for sharing information and participating in conversations in certain communities (see Table 1).

As one of the VEs described in O'Dowd and Lewis's (2016) collection on Online Intercultural Exchange , CLAVIER was pleased to support the E+VE initiative when it started in 2018. We agreed to align the CLAVIER VEs to the goals of the E+VE initiative so they could be classed as TEPs (Transnational Exchange Projects). In other words, CLAVIER leaders completed training and decided to 'TEPify' CLAVIER's core VEs. This involved the following steps:

- ensuring that all students registered with E+VE, completing a pre-VE survey, giving consent for research into their experience;

- recording student participation in set VE tasks;

- encouraging student participation in online facilitated dialogue sessions, offering a further experience of a different form of VE; and

- signing a memorandum of understanding between participating partner institutions.

Case study 12

Participating in the initiative meant that students of our TEPs could earn an E+VE participant badge. We recognise this as a valuable way for students to communicate their experience. The E+VE badge has a wider significance than the CLAVIER badges because the graphics after 2019 carry the European flag, and the metadata in the badge links to a competences framework[5]. This relationship between our CLAVIER initiative and the E+VE development helped to underline the importance of VE activity to our institutions, offering the endorsement of a transnational body, the European Commission. CLAVIER badges continued to provide recognition of the steps at micro-level needed to participate in CLAVIER VEs, with the E+VE TEP Participant badge offering student recognition of an extended commitment and a possible pathway to further engagement in the wider European initiative.

Table 1. Examples of badges from Clavier and E+VE

Badge Graphics Examples from CLAVIER and E+VE	Criteria
You're hired!	**YOU'RE HIRED!** Students have to: • select an advert for a job or an internship, and write a CV and a cover letter; • make contact with their partner, access their material, and negotiate an online meeting to interview each other through videoconferencing (e.g. Zoom) for the job they are applying for; and • submit a reflection on this process. In order to be awarded this badge: • Document your interaction through CLAVIER with recordings/screenshots and submit with your reflection.

---

5. https://badge.wiki/wiki/What_Are_Open_Badges%3F#cite_note-1, https://europa.eu/youth/node/69178_en

	**OIE5** Engagement badge You have shared information with the Echange Warwick Clermont community[6] and participated in a conversation about how you engage in a community in order to improve the lives of others. #CMC, #OIE You need to provide screenshots or links to show that you have created a post to the EWC Engagement filter and a reply to at least two other posts on the same filter.
	**TEP PARTICIPANT** E+VE is a ground-breaking project enabling youth in Europe and the Southern Mediterranean to engage in meaningful intercultural experiences online, as part of their formal or non-formal education. Awarded for participation in a VE organised by TEP trained practitioner/s. Participation in this activity builds competencies[7] in: digital competence A, intercultural competence A, transversal skills A; plurilingualism A, cooperation skills A, empathy and sensitivity A, knowledge and critical understanding of self in the world A, and tolerance of ambiguity A. See E+VE competency framework for details: https://europa.eu/youth/node/69178_en The owner of this badge has taken part in a TEP. The project was designed and implemented by a trained TEP coordinator. The awardee has completed the required assessments. The TEP lasted a minimum of four weeks and comprised both asynchronous and synchronous online communication and collaboration with transnational peers.

---

6. Name of a google plus community created for interaction.

7. E+ Competences Framework https://europa.eu/youth/erasmusvirtual/erasmus-virtual-exchange-competences-framework_en

4. Evaluation, assessment, and recognition

Central to the assessment in CLAVIER is the use of web-based tools such as e-portfolios and blogs according to the course requirements locally. At the University of Warwick, this has included the use of an e-portfolio tool (Mahara) integrated within the VLE. In Clermont, the students use a Google Drive to collect and share their activities with their tutors. In Krakow, students are encouraged to blog their experiences publically. The requirement to collect, curate, and reflect upon their participation in VEs can contribute to the course assessment which in turn encourages student engagement.

The use of badges as visual signifiers provides a way of connecting VE participants and practitioners online. Once awarded, badges can be incorporated into an individual's online presence. Open badge passports provide a mechanism for continued engagement with VE activities. In CLAVIER, we are keen to show students that learning is not just about achieving recognition from one institution, as valuable as that may be. We aim to engage our students in a lifelong process of learning, helping them to appreciate the importance of self-directed learning in shaping their development. Our practitioners bear witness to the transformational effects of engagement with VE on their own practice as evidenced in our retelling of our lived experience (MacKinnon, 2019).

However, this shift from students as consumers of assessment to students as owners of their own progress requires a different mindset. Clearly, as open badges are relatively new to most students, there is a process of acceptance reliant on clear communication from tutors. There is critical alignment between participants' growing confidence in the virtual domain and earning a badge in recognition of that expertise. This process encourages the badge owner to take an active role in curating and declaring their expertise and can potentially provide possibilities for discovering new paths of study and extending networks. Students are encouraged to open their own open badge passport account to manage and display their badges. This approach has also been adopted in E+VE. The challenges experienced within CLAVIER have been replicated in the wider E+VE context that involves multiple delivery partners working as a consortium. These challenges are explained in the following section.

5. Lessons learnt and conclusion

Several challenging themes emerge from experiences of CLAVIER (Ensor et al., 2017) and they have much in common with those found by others working in this area. As noted in their editorial referring to the article by Ensor et al. (2017), Potolia and Stratilaki (2017) point to the complexity of telecollaborative practice: "[i]t is precisely this difficulty that leads the authors to stress the importance of telecollaboration as a means to bring about a profound transformation of education in order to prepare for the education of tomorrow" (n.p.). The CLAVIER challenges include:

- the importance of flexibility and dynamic adjustments during VEs;
- the challenge of establishing sustained engagement without compulsion;
- the unexpected developments and connections arising from the growing network; and
- the transformational nature of persisting with VE on the lives and work of the practitioners.

5.1. Lessons from issuing badges

Over time, the tools used for CLAVIER VEs have changed and the technical infrastructure has been impacted by decisions that were beyond the influence of the practitioners. Our willingness to work in the open online through OEP has meant that we have been able to continue despite this. The practitioners have built a shared understanding of the importance of putting the learning experience at the heart of the VE. The technology is a mediator but it does not dictate what can be achieved. The badge design and implementation process has required fundamental engagement with the detail of the intended learning as part of task design. Tasks can progress from information exchange, comparison, and analysis to collaborative co-creation, and this framework[8] for badging supports the task design.

As revealed in the badge investigations into CLAVIER (Hauck & MacKinnon, 2016), there is a tension between the necessary bureaucracy of badge award (verification of evidence for example) and the positive effects of the immediacy of badge award. To some extent the integration of a badge platform within a shared VLE can help to address this as the VLE offers automation of the award process based around completion of given criteria such as assignment submission or grade thresholds. The process of reviewing student engagement with the VE, quantified by the badge collection, is a constant feedback loop enabling practitioners to critically appraise their interventions.

5.2. Lessons from collecting badges

Using open badges in CLAVIER and engaging in OEP has enabled us as practitioners to overcome some of the challenges of VE. We have worked as a team to deal with the need for dynamic change over time. The badges are visual motivational tools which, when explained clearly to students, can produce further opportunities and routes to their development. When collecting their open badges, students also have to face decisions around their open practice. They have to decide which badges to share, where, and how to share them. Those decisions will be complex, personal, and contextual. They have to build their own digital resilience.

The shift from student as assessee to student as curator of their learning is an important one in a challenging job market where new roles are emerging.

---

8. https://www.justframeworks.com/#!/frameworks/53db2e9a-0bf4-e411-8f25-d067e5ec4c65

Students sometimes have to hunt for the badge award email that may be filtered by their email programme. They have to engage with their digital professional identity. In so doing they can significantly increase their understanding of the digital environment which increasingly dominates their lives.

VE is not well understood within the formal learning framework of higher education. Institutional use of technology tends to focus on provision for registered students and rarely offers the flexibility of a space which can be shared across institutions and beyond into informal learning settings. As such, VE is a hybrid activity but one based upon the importance of interconnection in a world where we are ever more interdependent. The socio-political context of higher education institutions demands market driven competition between institutions as they jostle for higher places in the rankings in order to attract ever more students. This pressure runs counter to the focus on collaborative learning which is at the heart of VE. Using open badges enables practitioners and students to work together to establish what they value, presenting a clear set of identifiers around the activities and interactions which underlie their learning. It reconnects them to the purpose of education. Open badge use provides the means to achieving the sort of paradigm shift referred to by Blyth (2019) in his foreword on openness in and beyond the language classroom.

6. Supplementary materials

https://research-publishing.box.com/s/f2kcaywgw2jclyeqsp02wz5e44io1x41

References

Blyth, C. S. (2019). Foreword. In A. Comas-Quinn, A. Beaven & B. Sawhill (Eds), *New case studies of openness in and beyond the language classroom* (pp. xvii-xviii). Research-publishing.net. https://doi.org/10.14705/rpnet.2019.37.961

Cronin, C. (2017). Openness and praxis: exploring the use of open educational practices in higher education. *IRRODL, 18*(5), 15-34. https://doi.org/10.19173/irrodl.v18i5.3096

Daniels, P. (2019). Open practices as a catalyst for language teachers' professional development. In In A. Comas-Quinn, A. Beaven & B. Sawhill (Eds), *New case studies of openness in and beyond the language classroom* (pp. 159-171). Research-publishing.net. https://doi.org/10.14705/rpnet.2019.37.973

Ensor, S., Kleban, M., & Rodrigues, C. (2017). Telecollaboration: foreign language teachers (re)defining their role. *Alsic, 20*(2). https://doi.org/10.4000/alsic.3140

Guichon, N., & Hauck, M. (2011). Teacher education research in CALL and CMC; more in demand than ever. *ReCALL, 23*(3), 187-199. https://doi.org/10.1017/s0958344011000139

Hauck, M., & MacKinnon, T. (2016). A new approach to assessing online intercultural exchange: soft certification of participant engagement. In R. O'Dowd & T. Lewis (Eds), *Online intercultural exchange: policy, pedagogy, practice* (pp. 209-231). Routledge. https://doi.org/10.4324/9781315678931

Kessler, G. (2007). Formal and informal CALL preparation and teacher attitude toward technology. *Computer Assisted Language Learning, 20*(2), 173-188. https://doi.org/10.1080/09588220701331394

MacKinnon, T. (2016). The Clavier Network. In R. O'Dowd & T. Lewis (Eds), *Online intercultural exchange: policy, pedagogy, practice* (pp. 235-240). Routledge. https://doi.org/10.4324/9781315678931

MacKinnon, T. (2019). Lived experience of connected practice: Clavier. In A.Turula, M. Kurek & T. Lewis (Eds), *Telecollaboration and virtual exchange across disciplines: in service of social inclusion and global citizenship* (pp 105-110). Research-Publishing.net. https://doi.org/10.14705/rpnet.2019.35.946

O'Dowd, R., & Lewis, T. (2016). (Eds). *Online intercultural exchange: policy, pegagogy, practice*. Routledge. https://doi.org/10.4324/9781315678931

Potolia, A., & Stratilaki, S. (2017). Editorial. *Alsic, 20*(2). http://journals.openedition.org/alsic/3228

Thomas, D., & Seeley-Brown, J. (2011). *A new culture of learning: cultivating the imagination for a world of constant change*. CreateSpace Independent Publishing Platform.

Section 2.
Ready-made

3. The Sharing Perspectives Foundation: a case study in blended mobility

Sophie C. Millner[1]

Abstract

This case study explores the Sharing Perspectives Foundation's (SPF) blended mobility course: *Europe on the Edge*, which included a 10-week Virtual Exchange (VE) followed by a 1-week physical mobility held in Brussels. Engaging 131 students from 30 different nationalities and partnering with 10 European universities, this 2015 intercultural exchange aimed to give students from diverse backgrounds the space to completely rethink what it meant to be a citizen in contemporary Europe. The 1-week event in Brussels at the end of the course for a selected group of 15 students created an opportunity for physical mobility and makes this an interesting case study for analysing the value of blended mobility.

Keywords: blended mobility, virtual exchange, facilitated dialogue, interactive online course, Erasmus+.

1. Context

SPF has developed a model of VE based on three key elements: facilitated dialogue, expert material, and interactive assignments. Our model coheres with the framework of VE defined by the Virtual Exchange Coalition as technology-enabled, sustained, people-to-people education programmes. This means that our VEs take place on an internet-based platform; the exchanges are facilitated

---

1. The Sharing Perspectives Foundation, Amsterdam, Netherlands; sophie@sharingperspectivesfoundation.com; https://orcid.org/0000-0002-0542-4844

How to cite this case study: Millner, S. C. (2020). The Sharing Perspectives Foundation: a case study in blended mobility. In F. Helm & A. Beaven (Eds), *Designing and implementing virtual exchange – a collection of case studies* (pp. 155-166). Research-publishing.net. https://doi.org/10.14705/rpnet.2020.45.1123

Case study 13

and continue over a number of weeks rather than being one-off encounters, and, fundamentally, they focus on meaningful encounters between young people.

These meaningful encounters between people are the motivation for our courses and it is for this reason that facilitated dialogue is used to create relationships. This element is fundamental to our model of VE and we share this with Soliya, a US based organisation who pioneered this educational practice. This focus on facilitated dialogue makes both SPF and Soliya's model distinctive.

Over the years, we have adapted and defined our model along the principle of inclusivity to take into account both the greatly increased numbers and to accommodate the growing diversity of participants in terms of countries, backgrounds, and needs. During the development of our courses, we have also explored the value of additional activities. However, at the foundation of all our courses there remains the same three key elements: facilitated dialogue, expert material, and interactive assignments.

This case study analyses our 2015 flagship VE, *Europe on the Edge*, which provided the foundation for our more recent *Cultural Encounters* series. One of the additional activities we explored for this earlier course was an event in Brussels that brought together a select group of participants to share a week of meetings with policy makers. This physical mobility following on from the VE created a *blended learning* experience.

2. Aims

The overarching objective of this one-year European Commission funded project was to bring together youth from across Europe in order to foster their sense of European identity and encourage democratic participation of youth at a union level.

The intended learning outcomes of the VE *Europe on the Edge: Redefine Politics for the 21st Century* were to give young people from diverse backgrounds the opportunity to completely rethink, from a youth perspective, what it means to be a citizen in contemporary Europe. In the context of growing youth disengangement from politics, students were encouraged to critically reflect on the norms surrounding European citizenship which are historically based on being white, able-bodied, heterosexual, and male. We invited academics and experts to also challenge these norms and created a course that discussed topics from race and unconscious white bias to immigration, environmental responsibility, the role of the media, and youth activation.

3. SPF model

Funded by the Education, Audiovisual, and Culture Executive Agency (EACEA) Europe for Citizens programme, *Europe on the Edge: Redefining Politics for the 21st Century* was our flagship 10-week course for MA level students which ran from October to December 2015. As in all the courses designed by SPF, it is based on the model of three core elements: facilitated dialogue, expert material, and interactive assignments.

Ten universities[2] partnered with SPF during this course and at this time we had not expanded to include youth organisations. Partnership with SPF meant engaging around 10 to 20 students in the course as well as contributing their academic expertise to the course by producing one video lecture in close collaboration with the SPF team. Whilst only European universities were partners for this exchange, we were still able to accept individuals applying independently from other universities in any region and of any age range. This, we believe, only enhanced the diversity and thus the learning experience. Students came from a range of subjects but mainly within political sciences, social sciences, and humanities such as international relations, languages, and business.

---

2. Vesalius College, Belgium; Tartu University, Estonia; Helsinki University, Finland; Osnabrück University, Germany; Aristotle University of Thessaloniki, Greece; Corvinus University, Hungary; Trinity College Dublin, Ireland; Padova University, Italy; Utrecht University, Netherlands; AGH University of Science and Technology, Poland.

Our partner universities tailored the integration of the course to their needs. For some, this meant accrediting the VE as a stand-alone course and offering up to 10 ECTS by requiring an additional paper marked within the university. Other universities offered this course as a 5 ECTS optional or elective alongside the students' compulsory modules. For a few universities, this was an extracurricular course without credits.

Europe on the Edge included a VE and a physical mobility phase. Below are outlined the activities that students engaged in for each phase.

3.1. Expert materials

These took the form of video lectures by academics from our partner institutions as well as specialist practitioners on the theme of the course. In this case, students were critically exploring citizenship and each week they would watch three or four films of around 20 minutes each. The video lectures were produced as interview-style presentations by academics, activists, film-makers, and grassroots organisations who, after working with the SPF team to design the presentation, were then self-filmed by the presenters[3].

3.2. Facilitated dialogue

The students each attended a weekly, two-hour long, facilitated dialogue session. They met the same small group of students hosted by the same facilitator each week online for the duration of the ten-week course. The facilitator guided the students to explore their perspectives and understand the beliefs, values, and experiences that shape their understanding. In this way, the facilitated sessions were different to taught seminars as the facilitator was not there to impart knowledge but rather to ensure that every student engages equally, to create a safe space and to pose thought-provoking questions to keep the discussion flowing.

---

3. Europe on the Edge Video lecture playlist (2015) https://www.youtube.com/playlist?list=PL2bVdbBmPHDe6OQt_dIVdDRdkix6rQyO6

This method of facilitated dialogue allows for a deepening of understanding and development of trust, honesty, and empathy as the course progresses. The length of the course follows the group-process theory which explains different phases that the group passes through in order for participants to feel comfortable enough to articulate their perspectives.

3.3. Interactive assignments

These included video-lecture comments, a short presentation, and European-wide primary research.

3.4. Video-lecture comments

Students were asked to write a short comment on each video lecture and prepare a question to put to their group. This short task served to ensure that they watched the videos as well as encouraging them to reflect on the content. This meant that students came to their group session feeling prepared and helped create a more fruitful dialogue.

3.5. Presentation

Students were asked to prepare one short presentation of around 10 to 15 minutes based on one of the week's topics which they delivered to the rest of the group. Working in pairs, this task required cross-cultural collaboration and a chance to get to know another member of the group more closely outside the classroom setting.

3.6. Research

All participants also jointly conducted a European-wide primary research project into the perceptions of European citizenship among youth across different national and socioeconomic boundaries. Through the research we created unique, real time results and there was a sense of being part of a big research project together that would have been unattainable as individuals. Students also learnt valuable skills in primary and quantitative research, analysis, and interpretation of data.

3.7. Paper as a final assignment

Students were asked to write a paper of 3,000 to 4,000 words expanding on one of the topics of the course. This was marked and second marked by the SPF team after the end of the course and the grades helped inform the selection process for the Brussels event.

3.8. Physical mobility

Brussels: Physical mobility was a requirement as part of the EACEA *Europe for Citizens* funded programme with the aim being to increase students' democratic understanding and participation at European Union level. The *Europe on the Edge* course thus culminated in a week-long summit held in Brussels for some of the highest graded participants who had the opportunity to take the results of the research directly to the doors of EU officials. This physical event in Brussels also allowed a select group of the participants to meet in person, thus creating a 'blended mobility'.

SPF set up interactive meetings where students shared and discussed the findings of the research with policy makers and practitioners. In small groups, students took the lead to present and disseminate the findings of the data generated from the primary research project and took the opportunity to pose questions directly to politicians, media, and local non-government organisations. Reporting on the day, students also filmed and created a video diary reflecting on their experiences in small groups[4]. We were also conscious to provide spaces for students to get to know each other as people over the five days, so, as well as a full schedule of meetings, each evening included time to eat and socialise together.

---

4. Brussels Summit Europe on the Edge videoblog (2016) https://www.youtube.com/playlist?list=PL2bVdbBmPHDdqR8 W4AmQLGS5sWMQw3v2s

4. Lessons learnt

4.1. Virtual exchange

The aim of our VEs is to help youth from diverse social and cultural backgrounds to develop their transversal skills which the course creates opportunities for students to practise. Our skills-oriented and active learning approach (EUA, 2019) is reflected across all areas of the course from the active participation in the facilitated dialogue sessions to the interactive assignments.

The assignments included were therefore primarily assessed through students' engagement in a task rather than on the results of that task. This model of assessment based on regular active participation rather than a final verbal or written task is starting to emerge within the traditional model for educational assessment.

We evaluated and adapted a few assignments following this course. We decided that the paper neither enhanced the skills-based learning outcomes nor our inclusive values since some students were more accustomed to writing papers than others. Furthermore, rather than all activities being contained within the timeframe of the VE it left students with an outstanding assignment.

Although the viewing data showed us that students watched the videos, most did not view the video in its entirety. Therefore, in subsequent iterations of the VE, we employed a professional film company to produce academic quality films that captured the material in a much shorter time frame of around 5 minutes each and providing participants with a total of only 20 minutes of weekly viewing.

The large scale research was also adapted into a more dialogue based project. This laid less emphasis on individuals to access their networks, as not all students had such wide circles to draw on. It also required a great effort on the part of the research team to turn the data into an accessible format for the students in such a short space of time.

Case study 13

More generally, we learnt that where the course is strongly integrated, for example as a compulsory course with ECTS, then the completion rates and learning outcomes are high. The completion rates are higher due to the monitoring by their educator and the motivation of passing an accredited course. In terms of learning outcomes, where the course is optional and students are self-selecting, the course tends to attract students who already have some experience of intercultural settings. By contrast, a compulsory course engages all students including those with little or no intercultural experience. For the latter, the learning curve for skill development is greater than for those self-selecting students whose initial skills level is higher.

4.2. Physical mobility

In our later VEs, we decided not to include the Brussels event, dropping the blended mobility in order to focus exclusively on the VE. Students were selected based on their final grades so the physical mobility element served as a motivating factor to perform well during the course. However, the event was selective rather than inclusive, favouring students who performed well in the traditionally academic final paper. Furthermore, it was open only to 15 of the 131 students who participated in the entire programme. For these reasons, as we scaled up the course, we decided to dedicate all our resources to the VE element that was accessible to all the students.

Cost was a significant factor in this decision as the Brussels event represented a minimum of 15% of the overall budget for the programme whilst only benefitting around 10% of the participants. To take 15 students and 4 staff to Brussels we had to budget for flights, hotel, travel passes around Brussels, and cover all meals. The one-week event cost at least two times the budget per participant of the ten-week VE. It also required a dedicated member of staff to organise it over a number of months.

It is important to link the cost of a physical exchange to the learning objectives of the programme. In this case, the objective was to give young people from diverse backgrounds the opportunity to completely rethink, from a youth perspective, what it meant to be a citizen in contemporary Europe. This was primarily done through a designed series of virtual interactions between a large group of diverse European youth. A limited number of participants were then selected to also travel to Brussels. Whilst the Brussels event definitely contributed to the learning objective and allowed the participants a peek into 'Brussels', this was only the case for a limited number of participants. So, whilst having a high impact on a small number of participants, it had no impact on the other 116 participants in the programme. Had we brought all participants to Brussels, the cost of that one week would have been double of all costs for the entire programme we developed.

Four years on, students from the Brussels Summit were invited to reflect on their experience. The feedback created a picture in which participants were left with a positive experience of intercultural exchange that has "definitely had an impact on my life" (Said, Hungary) creating "amazing memories" (Joanna, Greece), and "wonderful human experience for our futures", the "physical meeting was an honour for me" (Gloria, Italy). "The physical exchange was a really positive added benefit which complemented the VE experience" (Gemma, UK).

In terms of the meetings supporting their studies of politics and European institutions, students explained: "I felt involved in a student-centred experience based on boosting independence and critical thinking" (Gloria, Italy). "I treasure the insights and inspiration I gained from the refugees in Molenbeek" (Joanna, Greece); and the EU institutions which had once been "perceived as distant and detached from one's everyday life. To actually be there brings somehow everything back to the world of the real and the concrete" (Federico, Italy).

They spoke of their experience as informing the direction of their work life and studies: "Thanks to this programme I could understand how to mediate different perspectives, diversity and interests, which is important in workplace and job activities such as mine" (Gloria, Italy). In reference to undertaking an online MA, "I've been thinking about the sharing perspectives class as a basis for my decisions" (Gemma, UK).

Case study 13

Aboveall, they highlighted the relationship building. Although the VE was described as "a humbling and eye-opening experience" (Joanna, Greece), it was by necessity always defined by a framework of roles, topics, and time. By contrast, interactions in Brussels spilled out unhindered by the framework of the virtual classroom, enabling them to engage in "in-depth conversations spanning over several hours where we could discuss things that we were not necessarily able to bring up during our one-hour online learning sessions" (Said, Hungary). This time spent physically together helped participants "connect on a much deeper level" (Gemma, UK) and in those five days (and nights) forged "lasting friendships" (Joanna, Greece). The physical encounters "gave me many more nuances about the persons themselves as well as about their opinions, thoughts, and views" (Federico, Italy), which they largely put down to the spontaneous, informal, and natural encounters that a physical mobility offers. It would be interesting to understand whether the ease with which these relationships strengthen, happens so effectively because they have shared a prior intense and challenging virtual experience, nevertheless, in summary, "consolidating the VE experience in person, in my opinion, helped cement this commitment to and passion for cross-cultural dialogue" (Joanna, Greece).

5. Transversal skills

SPF courses are VEs with young people from diverse backgrounds and as such students are learning about new cultures. This means that the most important learning is not the academic knowledge but rather the skills to be able to interact and communicate with confidence, honesty, and empathy in an intercultural setting, namely transversal and intercultural communication skills.

Our evaluation of the learning outcomes is therefore focused on the transversal skills that students develop and strengthen over the period of the course. As our courses are primarily cultural exchanges, we looked to the Erasmus+ mobility evaluation as a starting point. Students were evaluated on their transversal skills at the beginning and end of the course using an elaborative self-assessment survey of 50 questions. Besides evaluating the satisfaction of the participation, participants' prior international and intercultural experience and their attitudes towards politics (the theme of the programme), the survey also evaluated cross-cultural competencies and six personality traits. The evaluated traits were: self-esteem, curiosity, decisiveness, tolerance of ambiguity, self-efficacy, and resilience. These traits were selected because similar traits were evaluated in the Erasmus Impact study of 2014. The evaluation methodology was developed by SPF but is based on extensive academic research on these different traits.

The findings from this course were modest but statistically significant. Given the course lasted a period of only ten weeks, this indicated a strong potential for skill development. The skills with significant increases included self-efficacy which increased by 3.11% and curiosity by 4.40% (Van der Velden, Millner, & Van der Heijden, 2016).

In terms of the physical mobility, it would be useful to have evaluated the students again after the Brussels event to see if any transversal skills had changed. However, with such a small sample this would need to have been replicated over a number of courses before results could be of value. There was no formal evaluation done but we might infer that given the intensity of the intercultural experience and the activities set up (including public speaking and team work), the participants may well have consolidated some of the skills they developed during the VE. Nevertheless, it would have been unlikely to have rendered any significant increase in transversal skills over only a week. Further research would need to be done on this.

6. Conclusion

This case study outlined and critically reviewed the blended mobility model we used for our 2015 *Europe on the Edge* course which was composed of a ten-week VE followed by a one-week physical mobility.

We recorded a significant increase in transversal skills during the VE and, although it was not formally measured, testimonies and observations indicated that those students who joined the physical mobility consolidated the skills and understanding developed during the VE as well as strengthening friendships.

Given the disproportionate costs and its selective rather than inclusive criteria, we weighed up the value and impact of the physical mobility on students and, following evaluation, we retained and refined the three core elements of our SPF VE model: facilitated dialogue, expert material, and interactive assignments, but removed the physical mobility phase in order to focus our resources on an inclusive and accessible VE. This current model of VE has been implemented in various forms through the Erasmus+ Virtual Exchange initiative and the impact on participant learning is significant[5].

What is clear, is that the physical mobility was an opportunity that left a lasting, positive impact but was not afforded to all the students. It is our assessment, therefore, that when designing a blended mobility, adding a VE phase strengthens a physical mobility, whereas a *selective* physical mobility added to a VE detracts resources and is not inclusive.

References

EUA. (2019). *Learning & teaching paper #5. Promoting active learning in universities: thematic peer group report.* European University Association. https://eua.eu/downloads/publications/eua%20tpg%20report%205-%20promoting%20active%20learning%20in%20universities.pdf

Helm, F., & Van der Velden, B. (2019). *Erasmus+ virtual exchange – Intercultural learning experiences : 2018 impact report.* Publication Office of the European Union. https://op.europa.eu/en/publication-detail/-/publication/a6996e63-a9d2-11e9-9d01-01aa75ed71a1

Van der Velden, B., Millner, S., & Van der Heijden, C. (2016). Comparing the development of transversal skills between virtual and physical exchanges. In S. Jager, M. Kurek & B. O'Rourke (Eds), *New directions in telecollaborative research and practice: selected papers from the second conference on telecollaboration in higher education* (pp. 217-224). Research-publishing.net. https://doi.org/10.14705/rpnet.2016.telecollab2016.510

---

5. The SPF model is the iOOC model of virtual exchange (activity 4) and impact of this activity has been reported in the Impact Report (Helm & Van der Velden, 2019).

4. Erasmus+ Virtual Exchange for internationalisation in besieged areas: a case study of the Islamic University of Gaza

Amani Al Mqadma[1] and Ahmed Al Karriri[2]

Abstract

The Islamic University of Gaza (IUG) has participated in the Erasmus+ Virtual Exchange (E+VE) programme since the beginning of 2019. The international relations office, the body responsible for managing the programme at IUG, noticed that there was a positive change in participants' knowledge and perceptions about VE and its role in enhancing their academic competencies and soft skills during the spring and autumn 2019 terms. As a result, IUG conducted an in-depth study to explore the role of a VE programme at the university in enhancing the students' cultural understanding, cross-cultural communication, and collaboration while engaging in project based learning.

Keywords: Erasmus+, virtual exchange, cultural understanding, cross-cultural communication, project based learning.

1. Context

The Gaza Strip is the southern part of the Palestinian Territories and is located in the heart of the Middle East, directly on the Eastern coast of the

---

1. Islamic University of Gaza, Gaza City, Palestine; aelmgadma@iugaza.edu.ps; https://orcid.org/0000-0002-1255-3986

2. Islamic University of Gaza, Gaza City, Palestine; aakarriri@iugaza.edu.ps; https://orcid.org/0000-0002-1511-716X

How to cite this case study: Al Mqadma, A., & Al Karriri, A. (2020). Erasmus+ Virtual Exchange for internationalisation in besieged areas: a case study of the Islamic University of Gaza. In F. Helm & A. Beaven (Eds), *Designing and implementing virtual exchange – a collection of case studies* (pp. 167-178). Research-publishing.net. https://doi.org/10.14705/rpnet.2020.45.1124

Mediterranean sea. It has a 51 km border with Israel and an 11 km one with Egypt. Following the political situation in the Gaza Strip in 2006, a siege was imposed on this territory, affecting all developmental, educational, economic, and international activities. As a result of the blockage, people were not able to mobilise outside the Gaza Strip due to border closure (OCHA, 2020). Therefore, Palestinians in the Gaza Strip missed many scholarship opportunities, exchange opportunities, international project meetings, and conferences (Bowler, 2018). However, educational institutions in the Gaza Strip have deployed information technology and VE to break the isolation of their students and staff by enabling them to participate in different international, educational, cultural, and research activities. This utilisation of VE has supported the universities' internationalisation efforts as a synergy for physical exchange (Oliva et al., 2017). In this way, learners and professors are exchanging their thoughts, acquiring international competencies, and paving the way for future collaboration in education and research, in addition to increasing cultural understanding (Oliva et al., 2017). VE can be viewed as 'low-cost internationalisation' (Michou & Bottin-Rousseau, 2018). Moreover, the trend of universities using VE has created a new type of internationalisation, namely internationalisation at a distance (Mittelmeier, Rienties, Gunter, & Raghuram, 2020).

IUG seeks to internationalise its courses through constructive engagement in online initiatives, which are an ideal way of providing students with an international mindset (Michou & Bottin-Rousseau, 2018; Oliva et al., 2017). Therefore, through its international relations office and different departments, IUG has engaged in virtual activities such as having guest lecturers, organising online workshops, and conducting online examinations of master and doctoral students. Moreover, one of the projects that focuses on students' intercultural exchange is the one done in partnership with the University of Glasgow in Britain. IUG has conducted five rounds of the programme English for Academic Study Telecollaboration (EAST), since 2015. The EAST programme aims at strengthening communication and interaction among the enrolled students by using English. In this five-week programme, each year, the Glasgow students learn about the problems of Gaza, working within mixed groups to develop suitable solutions for the problems with ultimate benefit from international practices (IUG, 2010-2019).

All examples mentioned are evidence of the importance that IUG has placed on VE as a great opportunity to develop student skills such as effective communication and collaboration, critical and independent thinking, providing constructive feedback, digital literacies, and intercultural awareness. Through these initiatives, IUG also mitigates the risks of the current isolation of the students and staff in the Gaza Strip through virtual exposure to international experience.

IUG has a privileged relationship with Erasmus+ programmes as a participant in many projects and as a partner with other universities in different disciplines. Based on that relationship, IUG was introduced to the E+VE programmes: during 2018, it offered the VE courses to all IUG students as extracurricular activities to improve their personal and academic competencies and introduce them to international students in an interactive space.

Institutionalisation of VE at IUG took two forms, starting from the strategic level and moving to the operational level. At the strategic level, IUG has recognised the significance and contribution of VE and the E+VE initiative to the university's internationalisation efforts. Therefore, its participation and engagement in VE activities is considered a central strategic action that is intended to continue until 2024 (IUG, 2020a).

At the operational level, based on the strategic direction towards E+VE for internationalisation, IUG has started to concentrate on E+VE and has assigned an employee to coordinate IUG's participation. Moreover, some departments integrate the E+VE courses within their courses (for example, the English and the business administration departments for undergraduate students). Many factors motivated IUG to participate in VE:

- effective engagement of IUG students with global issues, allowing them to experience these issues on a personal level;

Case study 14

- orientation for physical mobility, as most of our students have not travelled before, so VE is a great chance for them to be introduced to the wider world;

- a very good place to invest in its invaluable asset, human capital, and enriching the soft skills of students and preparing them to be well-qualified in the 21st century; and

- acceptance of others, as different perspectives are discussed through VE courses, which means a good chance to be more accepting and forgiving.

2. Aims and description of the E+VE implemented

Based on the international relations semiannual report (IUG, 2020b), IUG participated in two E+VE ready-made programmes provided by Sharing Perspectives Foundation[3] and Soliya[4]. Within these two programmes, IUG participated in four courses during the first semester 2019-2020 (Table 1).

Table 1. IUG participation in E+VE courses per programme

VE Programme	VE Course	Course at IUG	No. of students who participated at IUG	Language	Duration
Sharing Perspectives Foundation	Cultural Encounters/ Newcomers and Nationalism	Syntax and Semantics and Shakespeare	33	English	10 weeks

---

3. https://sharingperspectivesfoundation.com/

4. https://www.soliya.net/

Sharing Perspectives Foundation	Cultural Encounters: Perspectives on Populism	Introduction to Literary Appreciation	42	English	6 weeks
Sharing Perspectives Foundation	Technology and Society Connections Across Frontiers	Introduction to Entrepreneurship	40	Arabic	6 weeks
Soliya	Identity and Cross-Cultural Communication in Digital World	Discourse Analysis	80	English	5 weeks

These E+VE courses have different names, but they have common learning outcomes for the students, namely fostering the intercultural exchange among the students in addition to developing transversal skills among them such as empathy, self-esteem, curiosity, and the confidence to communicate in cross-cultural settings (Sharing Perspectives, n.d.; Soliya, n.d.). These aims crosscut all the course learning outcomes and aims at IUG. However, the idea behind the participation is to strengthen these skills among the students through the course's different concepts. For example, the IUG course titled 'Discourse analysis' benefited from the E+VE course titled 'Identity and cross-cultural communication in the digital world' to strengthen IUG students' skills in discussion and analysis of a common cultural issue.

The engagement process in the E+VE activities is a collective effort between the international relations department and the different departments and professors at the university. In more details, the process can be described in the following phases.

- **Phase one**: promotion and networking

As soon as the international relations officer received the announcement for the VE courses, the memorandum of understanding for joining the projects were signed by the university's legal representative. Then, the E+VE coordinator, who is a staff member at the international relations department, contacted potential professors to

Case study 14

engage in the project courses based on the course description at IUG. In addition, the language of the courses and the students' levels of language proficiency were key selection criteria, because IUG students' English language proficiency varied from one student to another and from one discipline to another, i.e. students from disciplines that use English as a medium of instruction have higher English proficiency than students in courses that use Arabic for teaching and assessment. As a result of this promotion and networking, three different professors were interested in the courses as part of their coursework during the 2019 academic year, two from the English art department, and one from business administration.

- **Phase two**: student enrolment and orientation

The professors announced the E+VE courses for the students during lectures where they briefly described the course, the learning objectives, and the evaluation criteria. As it was the first experience for the professors in the E+VE courses, the students' participation in these courses was optional, with a bonus for those who could complete the E+VE course requirements successfully; nevertheless, the students showed great interest in these courses.

Once each professor had a list of interested students, they sent the list to the E+VE coordinator who contacted the students to start the registration process. All registration instructions in addition to the course brochure were sent to the students via email. As a last step, the international relations office organised an orientation session for the students to introduce them to the E+VE programme and answer their questions.

During the registration process, the E+VE coordinator at the international relations office provided students with the required support and assistance to complete the registration process.

- **Phase three**: monitoring and evaluation

Once the students started their participation, the E+VE coordinator at IUG was responsible for receiving and monitoring the weekly achievement reports of the students sent by the organising foundation. These reports were sent to the professors to inform them about the students' performance in these courses. Additionally, international relations officers usually asked for students' feedback and impressions during the start and middle of the E+VE course. Furthermore, at the end of the course, the E+VE coordinator sent the students' evaluations he had received from the organisers to the professors to be included in the course's overall marks for the students.

IUG students participated in the E+VE courses, however, IUG did not design or offer specific E+VE courses. The student's participation in the courses were implemented in a way that each student joined the E+VE sessions using his/her own computer with good internet connection, and internet browsing application. In particular, the four courses in which IUG students participated had an online group meeting each week, and prior to this meeting each student was asked to watch the week's videos[5] and write a comment on them. Each online group consisted of eight to ten students and one facilitator.

During the group meetings, the facilitators encouraged participants to engage in thought-provoking conversations that allowed them to clearly express their ideas, experiences, and arguments about the topic under discussion. Furthermore, at the end of the sessions, all participants reflected on what they learnt during the session.

3. Evaluation, assessment, and recognition

IUG started the integration between its accredited courses and E+VE courses gradually at the beginning of 2019. Thus, IUG is progressively developing the mechanisms and follow-up procedures for VE programmes from its end. The IUG professors who were involved in E+VE assessed their students based on the final assessment and evaluation sheets that were received from the programme

---

5. https://sharingperspectivesfoundation.com/programme/newcomers-and-nationalism-2/video-lectures/

monitors. Students received additional credits based on specific criteria ranging from one to five by the end of the course.

Moreover, an evaluation form was prepared and distributed using Google Forms among the participants after the end of the courses. The aim of this form was to identify the benefits of the E+VE courses from the perspectives of the students. The form constituted two main parts: a questionnaire and a qualitative statement.

The questionnaire consisted of five questions that concentrated on the anticipated learning outcomes of the E+VE courses, namely: communication skills, cultural exchange, and using technology in learning. The satisfaction level ranged from one (total disagreement with the statement) to five (total agreement with the statement).

A total of 30 participants from IUG filled in the evaluation form: these students were the participants from one course provided in 2019 and 2020. At the end of the questionnaire, the participants were asked to provide a statement about the E+VE courses. The results are summarised in Table 2.

Table 2. E+VE courses impact evaluation on IUG students

	Impact on Students	Level of Acceptance
1	Satisfaction level	88%
2	The programme helped me to improve my communication skills	85%
3	The programme enhanced my ability to work in a culturally diverse place	82%
4	The programme helped me to build new relationships with new peers from other countries	71%
5	The programme helped me to improve my digital competencies	68%
6	Average	78.8%

Based on the students' opinions, E+VE courses helped them the most to improve their communication skills and secondly to cope with international and culturally diverse contexts. This means that the E+VE courses achieved their anticipated outcomes.

Furthermore, the participants provided feedback about the courses. Overall, they were happy with the experience, but they mentioned the following main constraints they encountered during the sessions:

- technical problems due to connection drops and the challenges of re-entering the group meeting;

- some participants within the group were not very committed to the start time of the group meeting, and late arrivals limited the discussion; and

- the composition of the group sometimes did not consider the geographical distribution, so that some IUG students found themselves in a group that was dominantly from their class or school.

The following opinion is from one of the IUG participants in the VE programme.

> "This VE programme have [sic] filled my expectations and even more. I have attended the previous three meetings and I am totally satisfied with how the whole discussion is organised. Beside that, I found this a great opportunity to share my thoughts with various minds from different countries, it actually makes me feel like I am traveling. Moreover, it allowed me to break the barrier of communicating about social and political issues in English language. I think that this experience will add a lot to my personality and to my personal career. I am glad that I have been introduced to such an opportunity by my university. I wish them to work more on similar programs to give the students a path towards active communication and to build a bridge of knowledge between different civilisations" (SH.O).

Whereas another participant commented the below.

> "As a student in the English department, I always feel that I need to interact with international students so that I can be able to practise my English language with native speakers. However, living in

Case study 14

> Gaza under the siege makes it unrealistically hard for me to leave the Gaza strip, which in turn reduces my chance of interacting with students from all over the world. Therefore, when I heard about this programme and knew that it will allow me to meet with and speak to international students in order to discuss different political and social issues that have an impact on our generation; I was so excited and keen to join this programme. Since it has always been my dream to leave Gaza Strip and travel around the world to discover more about other cultures and work on my language skills... As a matter of fact, it was wonderful to experience the feeling that I am traveling around the world. In my sessions, I had six friends from different countries so for me it was a journey to six countries. However, my experience was not limited to only getting to know about different cultures, but it also involved interesting discussions concerning many different issues. Living in Palestine under strict laws makes [it] really hard for young people to express their own political views... Therefore, I will always be grateful to my university which provided me with such a unique opportunity" (D.O.).

Additionally, we have received a testimonial from one teacher of the Discourse analysis course.

> "Allow me first to thank you for giving my students in the Discourse analysis course the opportunity to participate in this virtual connect programme that was a valuable addition to the knowledge and skills the participating students were expected to gain in the course. Much emphasis in the course I teach is on cross-cultural understanding and communication and on realising the role of language/discourse in bringing about effective intra- and intercultural communication. I think this is a primary aim of the connect programme, and therefore, the feedback I got from those participating students underscored the importance of such a programme in giving them further opportunities and the ability and confidence to share ideas, express themselves, and talk to people from various cultural backgrounds. This is precisely

what I have aspired and worked to equip my students with. I am very satisfied with the way the VE was conducted and the progress made by the participants. I would certainly be keen on having another round of connect programme for my next batch of students. I equally recommend increasing the number of participating students in the programme and the number of weekly sessions to cover more topics and issues" (Dr M.A.).

4. Lessons learnt and conclusion

The E+VE courses have promoted IUG's efforts and strategic direction to provide its students with international competences and experiences. E+VE connects them to their counterparts, creating a virtual platform of communication and discussion, which plays a vital role in mutual understanding of common issues academically, socially, and politically.

Furthermore, the E+VE integration at IUG provided a rich experience and, with the global presence of a paradigm shift from teaching to learning, IUG finds the VE programme an invaluable chance to contribute in such a smooth transformation. This experience is considered as a great step in improving the perspective towards future teaching practices at IUG.

Some of the things IUG recommends from its own experience in the VE programme in order to make VE a more effective educational tool:

- to reflect on what the students learnt from their online sessions in their classrooms and share it in public spaces, such things would happen when teachers are getting actively engaged as facilitators, direct supervisors, or contributors in designing the VE courses to be aligned with their academic ones; and

- to organise E+VE courses that have more specific academic content and are part of the curriculum, in which the students can utilise the different context to address some cases in their curriculum. i.e. project based learning.

As IUG is committed to internationalisation and virtual internationalisation as a way to break the siege imposed, the international relations department is planning to start designing VE courses for the international students.

References

Bowler, H. (2018). *The suffocation of Gaza Strip: the protracted closure of the Rafah Crossing and its impact on building a successful and self-sustaining society*. Palestinian Return Centre.

IUG. (2010-2019). *Annual reports*. IUG.

IUG. (2020a). *IUG strategic plan 2020-2024*. IUG.

IUG. (2020b). *International relations semiannual report*. IUG.

Michou, V., & Bottin-Rousseau, S. (2018). Student's virtual erasmus exchange program. Blended and online learning. In G. Ubachs & F. Joosten-Adriaanse (Eds), *Blended and online learning "changing the educational landscape"* (pp. 260-263). The Online, Open and Flexible Higher Education Conference.

Mittelmeier, J., Rienties, B., Gunter, A., & Raghuram, P. (2020). Conceptualizing internationalization at a distance: a "third category" of university internationalization. *Journal of Studies in International Education*. https://doi.org/10.1177/1028315320906176

OCHA. (2020, Feb). *Gaza blockade*. https://www.ochaopt.org/theme/gaza-blockade

Oliva, M. A., Murata, K., Pérez-Portabella, A., Romero, M. S., Coronas, T. T., Clavero, G. M., & Fernández Ortiz, R. (2017). *URV international virtual campus: development of competences via the virtual internationalization of education*. URV.

Sharing Perspectives. (n.d.). *Erasmus+ Virtual Exchange programmes*. https://sharingperspectivesfoundation.com/

Soliya. (n.d.). *Connect Program*. https://www.soliya.net/programs/connect-program

15. Implementing E+VE at the University of Bordeaux within English for specific purposes courses

Laüra Hoskins[1] and Alexandra Reynolds[2]

Abstract

This case study reports on an Erasmus+ Virtual Exchange (E+VE) course at the University of Bordeaux. VE enables students to develop communication skills in an English as a Lingua Franca (ELF) environment (Helm, 2016; Kohn & Hoffstaedter, 2017). The present study reports on student language and content learning experiences through E+VE, where L2 users of English interacted with a more culturally diverse group of peers than they would likely meet in their local area. Our students' perspectives echo the E+VE impact report (Helm & Van Der Velden, 2019) and place a particular emphasis on English language learning outcomes.

Keywords: English as a lingua franca, English for specific purposes, intercultural communication, internationalisation at home, virtual exchange.

1. Context

This case study reports on the implementation of E+VE at the University of Bordeaux within the context of English for Specific Purposes (ESP) courses. The University of Bordeaux is a multidisciplinary university organised into

---

1. University of Bordeaux, Bordeaux, France; laura.hoskins@u-bordeaux.fr

2. University of Bordeaux, Bordeaux, France; alexandra.reynolds@u-bordeaux.fr; https://orcid.org/0000-0001-9758-5735

How to cite this case study: Hoskins, L., & Reynolds, A. (2020). Implementing E+VE at the University of Bordeaux within English for specific purposes courses. In F. Helm & A. Beaven (Eds), *Designing and implementing virtual exchange – a collection of case studies* (pp. 179-190). Research-publishing.net. https://doi.org/10.14705/rpnet.2020.45.1125

Case study 15

different disciplinary colleges. Students in this study were enrolled in a range of undergraduate and postgraduate programmes (ISCED[3] Levels 6 and 7) at the College of Health Sciences, the College of Human Sciences, and the College of Science and Technology. In all these programmes, the study of English as a second language is compulsory. None of the students involved in this study were majoring in English or language studies. At an institutional level, the university is engaged in a process of pedagogical transformation and there is a strong strategic drive towards the internationalisation of the curriculum and internationalisation at home.

The needs of learners following ESP courses are however diverse, with the majority of undergraduates entering our university with an A2 or B1 level of English[4] and only a minority entering with a B2 level or above. For this minority of students with a higher than average level, the challenge is to offer them meaningful interactions in English and learning opportunities that allow them to go beyond the language skills they have already acquired. From 2018 to 2019, 120 of these students reading biology, chemistry, dentistry, education, physics, psychology, public health, and sociology were therefore encouraged to participate in E+VE's pilot scheme. They followed Sharing Perspectives Foundation's (SPF) flagship course *Cultural Encounters* instead of attending their mainstream English course with their local peers.

We discovered E+VE through a connection with SPF in January 2018, when we received a call for participants to join the first *Cultural Encounters* interactive Open Online Course (iOOC) exploring the theme of European refuge/s. In each edition of this iOOC, participants explore a current affairs topic through an original lecture series, reflective writing, and a community engagement video project, and, crucially, weekly online meetings with a diverse peer group. These *facilitated dialogue sessions* are the cornerstone of the iOOC experience. Led

---

3. International Standard Classification of Education

4. Levels described by Common European Framework of Reference for languages (CEFR, https://www.coe.int/en/web/common-european-framework-reference-languages/). On the global scale, A2 refers to an upper basic user of English and B1 to a lower independent user of English. A B2 level refers to an upper independent user of English and is the target level for school leavers (https://www.coe.int/web/common-european-framework-reference-languages/table-1-cefr-3.3-common-reference-levels-global-scale).

by trained facilitators, facilitated dialogue engages diverse groups in meaningful interaction to achieve an intercultural understanding of complex and controversial issues such as migration, nationalism, and populism. The opportunity for our students to explore both topical and meaningful content through facilitated dialogue appealed to us. We therefore sought ways of integrating *Cultural Encounters* into our current offer.

For the first pilot, we decided to offer the programme to C1/C2 level second-year sociology students (about 5% of a cohort of 230) instead of following the mainstream English course. Three of these students took up the offer. We also offered it as an option to C1/C2 level first-year biology students (one student) and as an optional course to second-year psychology students.

The initial return from these five students was overwhelmingly positive, motivating us to extend the reach of the programme to a further 115 students. A workshop on international collaboration through VE at our university and dissemination of the initial pilot through the university's language network helped us engage a small number of language teachers, who in their own sectors promoted E+VE to students and faculty. From Year 2, the offer of E+VE was widened in some sectors to recruit students with a B2 level or above or who expressed a strong motivation to join the exchange to the programme.

2. Aims and description of the project

In all the ESP sectors where E+VE was offered, there was a strong motivation to give students an opportunity to interact in ELF settings while at the same time gaining intercultural learning (Helm, 2016; Kohn, 2018; O'Dowd, 2018). Communicating in ELF contexts is one of the major learning outcomes targeted by our English programmes because many of our students are destined to professions where English will be used at home or internationally. However, the majority of our ESP programmes have a tradition of being strongly anchored in the disciplines the students major in, with a focus on disciplinary literacy –

communicating in the academic and professional contexts of the students' area of study. Intercultural Learning Outcomes (ILOs) have not always been made explicit, though they are now part of a wider institutional strategy. As ESP curriculum designers, we have given ILOs greater attention in recent years, working from a perspective of global citizenship education (O'Dowd, 2019). E+VE aligned, therefore, with our own intended ILOs and satisfied the personal goals of advanced students of English who were looking to broaden their perspectives by learning about and discussing topics not related to their course of study.

From 2018 the exchange was promoted across the health sciences, human sciences, and science and technology. The authors of this study acted as local language teacher coordinators in their respective communities by disseminating information about the exchange and about how to mentor students through the enrolment process at the start of term. Given national and institutional accreditation constraints, the exchange could not be offered as a standalone accredited course in its own right. Students were therefore recruited to follow the exchange instead of following their mainstream English course.

At the start of each term, mailings were sent out to students via the institutional learning platform (Moodle) by their own English course coordinators and classroom teachers, who had received this information from the local coordinators. Some teachers also identified students interested in the exchange during a first classroom session. In parallel, information sessions were held at university language centres by the local E+VE coordinators, during which the requirements for validating English course credits (three ECTS) through participation in the exchange were also explained to the students. Students who passed the E+VE course (60% pass mark) would also pass their English course. Their grade could be raised depending on the quality of the English used by students in their reflection journals, which they had to submit to their own teachers for assessment, or lowered if students did not pass the exchange. From Year 2, and with the signing of a memorandum of understanding, we were able to factor the scores given by SPF into the grading of our students. In some cases, where ESP courses had both a continuous assessment component and a final exam component, students were still required to sit the final exam for their English course, which was unrelated therefore to the exchange.

Students were recruited mostly based on their level of English, identified through placement tests at the start of term. In some cases however, students' test scores did not indicate an above average level of English, but they expressed a strong personal motivation to engage in the exchange. It was therefore agreed that they could follow the programme. We noticed that students seemed to come into the exchange for different reasons. Some students were looking to be "more intellectually challenged" than they felt they would be in their English course, while others had less ambitious motivations and were looking to tailor their schedules by being exempt from coming to face-to-face sessions at university. Many of them wanted to develop their English skills further than they felt they could in a mainstream English class.

3. Activities and tools

Once students had signed up for the exchange, and as they were exempt from face-to-face sessions, we did not follow their progress on a week-by-week basis. SPF took care of organising them into seminar groups according to their algorithms.

A few weeks into each exchange, we would 'check in' with the students by mail, but it was often at the end of the exchange, when they submitted their reflection journals, that we gained insights into their experiences. General Data Protection Regulation (GDPR) prevented SPF from sharing student submissions with us. We worked round this by asking students to submit their reflection journals directly to their English course coordinators.

From the spring term 2020 we sought to implement a more structured system that allowed teachers to better follow progress on a week-to-week basis. A space dedicated to E+VE was set up on the institutional Moodle platforms where students could upload their reflective journal, (the same one they submit to SPF), after their weekly online facilitated dialogue sessions. This enabled teachers to mentor them more closely.

These reflective journals have helped us to gain insights into our students' experiences of the exchange. They have also incited us to widen the reach of the exchange through outreach with colleagues in other departments. Finally, the journals helped cement the engagement of our language colleagues, who, on reading their students' writing for assessment purposes, were able to discover the positive feedback expressed by students.

4. Evaluation, assessment, and recognition

E+VE was evaluated before, during, and after the programme using a variety of complementary methods. The objective was to evaluate E+VE throughout the duration of the programme. This was to ensure the wellbeing of the students and address any issues, in close association with our SPF correspondents, as quickly as possible. Our evaluation methods enabled us to monitor and ensure our students enjoyed and benefited from the E+VE programme.

The E+VE programme was evaluated using pre and post online questionnaires. The analysis of the diaries by the Bordeaux research team provided a micro representation of a wider parallel study of learner diaries during VE (Helm & Baroni, 2020). The diaries were qualitatively analysed for emergent themes which gave us greater access to the participants' experiences of E+VE.

Five one-hour interviews were held with individual students for further in-depth analysis of their E+VE experience. One focus group was held with 15 E+VE participants during Year 2 when they were halfway through the programme. Student participation was monitored throughout the programme by an attendance and assignment register which the SPF managers shared with us. This sharing of information, through a memorandum of understanding, enabled us to monitor whether the students were attending the E+VE programme and whether they were handing in their assignments.

The evaluation of the participants' experiences in terms of intercultural and language learning outcomes was key to this study. This was because the students were learning about content (namely nationalism, populism, and immigration) which was not associated with their major discipline. Our focus was on what the students gained in terms of transferable communications skills which could then be applied to their scientific disciplines and beyond. As the exchange replaced the students' home English module, we were also interested whether the exchange had initiated any English language learning gains.

Perceived[5] English language progression was assessed through the analysis of the questionnaire responses, the diary entries, and the interviews held with the students. This includes changes in confidence and stance as much as progression in identifiable language markers. On the whole, the students perceived a progression in their English communicative skills, the most identifiable areas of self-perceived language progression were as follows.

4.1. English language improvement

The students reported that their English improved thanks to participating in E+VE. Listening was referred to as the skill which improved the most through E+VE, especially adjusting to and understanding different accents. The students also referred to learning new vocabulary (i.e. 'patriotism' and 'nationalism'). The group appeared to agree that reading and writing did not improve as much as speaking and listening (despite the journal and chat function).

4.2. Difference of English language learning environment

The students highlighted many differences between the ESP classroom and the E+VE exchange. The E+VE 'classroom' was described as more convenient as most of the participants participated from home.

---

5. In terms of actual language improvement, the study revealed that the students, tested with the ELAO test (Efficient Language Assessment Online), and did not jump from one CEFR level to another during the ten-week course. According to Cambridge Assessment English (2020), a jump to a higher level can only be expected after 200 hours of guided learning.

> "At home you can do research on the side and you are more comfortable and relaxed".

The students believed that E+VE required more involvement and preparation prior to the facilitated dialogue than English classes did. E+VE also differed to ESP because the participants could speak with peers without the presence of a 'teacher'.

> "In E+VE, we don't have the feeling that we are tested. It is like a discussion with anyone. We are talking about actual subjects, important subjects".

The students were generally very positive about the exchange, with 85.5% of the Bordeaux participants reporting that they were satisfied to very satisfied with the E+VE programme[6]. In the second year of the E+VE pilot, we were able to better assess this result by providing the students with a pre-course questionnaire to assess their expectations before they participated in the exchange. The students' expectations were focused on the exchange part of the programme first, and on the content second. Judging by the positive feedback concerning the exchange as a whole, these expectations were met.

Through the combined analysis of the questionnaire responses, diary entries, and interviews, the main student criticisms of the exchange were as follows.

4.3. Connection interruptions (technical issues)

The main criticism that the students voiced were related to technical issues that resulted in the breakdown of communication during webinars.

---

[6]. The results of the questionnaire data were stable over both pilot years. Year 1 (2018-19), 86% of respondents were satisfied to very satisfied with the E+VE programme. Year 2 (2019-20), 85 % of respondents were satisfied to very satisfied with the E+VE programme.

"It is a good program, but the main point is the technological problems. The human experience is great with deep conversation, but slowed down by technology" (Focus group, 13.11.2019).

The students made recommendations about improving technical aspects of E+VE webinars. The students would have liked to have had more opportunities to carry on chatting after the facilitation by leaving the portal open to chat among themselves (without the facilitators) for an extra 30 minutes. This was something occasionally made possible by the facilitators and was appreciated by the group. In terms of content input, (when preparing for the webinars), the students preferred the videos to reading articles, which echoed our own experience of student attitudes to video and text resources at Bordeaux University.

4.4. Dealing with the topic of 'culture'

Students sometimes struggled with the exchange themes, and felt less prepared and knowledgeable about the topic of politics and 'culture' in general.

> "It was a bit heavy on the politics. It was hard participating in debates sometimes. I usually find it hard. Not because I'm shy but because I sometimes I didn't [sic] really have an opinion on things – I agreed".
>
> "E+VE is not related to science, and it is kind of hard for us to learn about culture".
>
> "It is difficult to answer questions about culture, I couldn't even discuss it in my own language".

The sense of difference, and often the status of privilege felt by the Bordeaux students was not necessarily negative, as these aspects needed to be understood in relation to cultural perspectives, as highlighted by the student feedback below:

> "In Europe the connection is good but in Algeria and Syria the connection is really bad".

"You feel lucky when compared to the others in Syria".

"The conversations go towards the differences and the different backgrounds of the participants. The cultural difference is key, we have lots of questions about that".

5. Lessons learnt and conclusion

Overall, our strategy for implementing E+VE within the context of ESP courses has met with success and students have generally expressed positive attitudes towards the exchange. However, the substitution of the E+VE participation grade for the Bordeaux students' English grade was in some cases problematic for several reasons.

Firstly, there is an issue with alignment. Our students validate a set of competences through E+VE that are not fully in line with those targeted by their ESP course. For example, *Cultural Encounters* does not have English language learning outcomes. A minimum recommended CEFR level of English competence (equivalent to B2) to participate in E+VE would be useful to all future participants who are L2 speakers of English.

In addition, our current system for implementing E+VE means that it is not an accredited course in its own right, available to all Bordeaux University students. This raises the issue of equity, as not all students are given the same opportunities. Furthermore, this system may result in the more *internationalised* students[7] opting *out* of English classes because they are more proficient in English and motivated by intercultural exchange than their domestic peers. This in turn could reduce the *internationalisation at home* experience for domestic students by reducing the diversity and authenticity of communicating in the English language class.

---

7. By 'internationalised student' we mean students who may fall into the following categories: bilingual language skills, mixed nationality, and/or previous experience with living or studying abroad.

In the spirit of internationalisation at home, it would be preferable for E+VE and non-E+VE students to meet and work together, possibly during the E+VE video project. Some of the E+VE participants did decide to interview local peers from the University of Bordeaux, but this could be further formalised. Some of the E+VE participants reported feeling isolated from their local peers. We have subsequently encouraged new E+VE participants to choose a local E+VE student delegate[8] so that they help each other through social media spaces. Finally, further thought needs to be given to how intercultural perspectives can best fit in with the disciplines at our university.

We would recommend other educators initially experiment with a small cohort of students because the management and monitoring of the exchange group can be time consuming. Understanding the terms and conditions of E+VE is key to student success. If the students do not attend facilitated dialogue sessions or hand in the assignments, both the students and educators find themselves having to justify why they have failed. This can lead to lengthy email exchanges and meetings.

Overall, the students who chose to take part in the programme were very satisfied with the programme. Many may wish to carry on with VE and may not wish to return to 'home English classes'. This is something educators may have to consider if they are not able to maintain participation in E+VE. Once the students have had a taste of exchanging with other students in English through E+VE, they may view home classroom interactions as 'inauthentic' (Kohn & Hoffstaedter, 2017, Pinner, 2016, Van Lier, 2014).

References

Cambridge Assessment English. (2020). *Guided learning hours*. Cambridge English Support Site. http://support.cambridgeenglish.org/hc/en-gb/articles/202838506

---

[8]. A local E+VE student delegate represents the local community of E+VE participants to signal issues and questions to their Bordeaux coordinators (for example technical issues). The local delegate also hosts social media pages for Bordeaux University E+VE participants

Helm, F. (2016). Facilitated dialogue in online intercultural exchange. In R. O'Dowd & T. Lewis (Eds), *Online intercultural exchange: policy, pedagogy, practice*. Routledge. https://doi.org/10.4324/9781315678931

Helm, F., & Baroni, A. (2020). Researching emotions and attitude through student teachers' reflections on virtual exchange. In A. Oskoz & M. Vinagre Laranjeira (Eds), *Understanding attitude in intercultural virtual communication*. Equinox Publishing Ltd.

Helm, F., & Van Der Velden, B. (2019, July 18). *Erasmus+ virtual exchange: intercultural learning experiences : 2018 impact report*. https://op.europa.eu:443/en/publication-detail/-/publication/a6996e63-a9d2-11e9-9d01-01aa75ed71a1

Kohn, K. (2018). Towards the reconciliation of ELF and EFL: theoretical issues and pedagogical challenges. In N. C. Sifakis & N. Tsantila (Eds), *English as a lingua franca in EFL contexts*. Multilingual Matters. https://doi.org/10.21832/9781788921770-005

Kohn, K., & Hoffstaedter, P. (2017). Learner agency and non-native speaker identity in pedagogical lingua franca conversations:insights from intercultural telecollaboration in foreign language education. *Computer Assisted Language Learning, 30*(5), 351-367. https://doi.org/10.1080/09588221.2017.1304966

O'Dowd, R. (2018). From telecollaboration to virtual exchange: state-of-the-art and the role of UNICollaboration in moving forward. *Journal of Virtual Exchange, 1*, 1-23. https://doi.org/10.14705/rpnet.2018.jve.1

O'Dowd, R. (2019). A transnational model of virtual exchange for global citizenship education. *Language Teaching*, 1-14. https://doi.org/10.1017/S0261444819000077

Pinner, R. S. (2016). Reconceptualising authenticity for English as a global language. *Multilingual Matters, 208*, 29-95.

Van Lier, L. (2014). *Interaction in the language curriculum: awareness, autonomy and authenticity*. Routledge. https://doi.org/10.4324/9781315843223

16. Communication across cultures: when the virtual meets the classroom

Marta Giralt[1]

Abstract

This chapter showcases the implementation of an E+VE (Erasmus+ Virtual Exchange) project in a 'broadening module' (elective content-specific modules offered across the university curricula) at the University of Limerick (UL), entitled 'Communication Across Cultures'. The pedagogical approach follows a blended learning model where face-to-face lectures are combined with the *Cultural Encounters* programme series of iOOCs (interactive Open Online Courses) offered by E+VE. This pedagogical practice has received positive feedback due to the practical appropriateness and effectiveness of the VE to the module, and has also been successful in terms of intercultural awareness and learning, in addition to the development of intercultural competence and communication skills.

Keywords: intercultural communication, Erasmus+ Virtual Exchanges, internationalisation, intercultural learning, intercultural awareness.

1. Context of implementation

The broadening module 'Communication across cultures', one of the elective content-specific modules offered across the university curricula, strongly aligns

---

1. University of Limerick, Limerick, Ireland; marta.giralt@ul.ie; https://orcid.org/0000-0002-1629-7641

How to cite this case study: Giralt, M. (2020). Communication across cultures: when the virtual meets the classroom. In F. Helm & A. Beaven (Eds), *Designing and implementing virtual exchange – a collection of case studies* (pp. 191-203). Research-publishing.net. https://doi.org/10.14705/rpnet.2020.45.1126

with the UL (n.d.) strategic goal of internationalisation which, among other objectives, aims at "embedding global perspectives into the curriculum [and] fostering cross-cultural competencies" (p. 24). This module offers students

> "an opportunity to engage in learning about language and intercultural communication. In our increasingly multicultural and multilingual society, communities and organisations are faced with a number of difficult challenges as they strive to provide a respectful, safe and harmonious environment for all. It is crucial that students have opportunities to understand and appreciate their own culture and make connections to appreciate the cultures and experiences of others"[2].

When we first started the design of 'Communication across cultures' in 2017, it was decided that a VE element would be part of the course in order to include both a practical and an experiential learning (Kolb, 2014) dimension. The idea was to build upon our knowledge and expertise in telecollaborative practices with language students in the school of Modern Languages and Applied Linguistics (MLAL) at UL (Batardière et al., 2019; Giralt & Jeanneau, 2016). Some language modules in Spanish, German, and French within MLAL include online tandem learning practices as part of the curriculum to prepare students linguistically and interculturally for their period abroad. What began as an individual and anecdotal practice is becoming an established part of our language modules, developing expertise among our staff on VEs and bringing awareness of the benefits of such pedagogical practices.

Coincidentally, at the time of developing the aforementioned module, the European initiative E+VE[3] was launched, providing the possibility of integrating ready-made options such as iOOCs into university courses. Therefore, we decided to follow a blended learning model and extend face-to-face lectures with one such interactive online course. This approach to VEs is a 'service-provider approach', where a non-profit organisation provides academic content, online

---

2. https://www.ul.ie/international/sites/default/files/user_media/Autumn%202020%20Module%20Booklet.pdf

3. https://europa.eu/youth/erasmusvirtual_en

discussions, and engagement in collaborative research through the medium of English as a *lingua franca* (O'Dowd, 2018). The aim of 'service-provider approach' VEs is to promote intercultural awareness and develop employability skills such as critical thinking, cross-cultural communication, team-work, collaboration, and digital literacies.

The UL students participating in the VE represent different disciplines (social sciences, languages, economics, and politics) and nationalities (Irish students and Erasmus international students from Europe and outside Europe). The first programme that our students took part in was being offered in 2018 by the non-profit organisation Sharing Perspectives Foundation (SPF)[4], one of the E+VE consortium partners, and was entitled: 'European refuge/es: cultivating diversity together'. Since then, UL students have participated in subsequent courses offered by SPF: 'Newcomers and nationalism: exploring the challenges of belonging in diverse societies' and 'Perspectives on populism'. It may be noted that the titles of the E+VE programmes in the *Cultural Encounters* strand give a firm idea of the topics and contents covered therein. By bringing together young people in Europe and the southern Mediterranean area, the *Cultural Encounters* courses initiate, stimulate, and facilitate international and intercultural dialogue and collaboration to foster skills, knowledge and open attitudes among students, in this case through VEs.

In this chapter we will be using the terms course, programme, seminar, and VE to refer to different things. Some clarifying definitions may be useful to be able to distinguish the different components of our case study. Course and programme refer to the courses that SPF offers within E+VE. Module is used in the context of the courses that UL offers to their students, in our case, referring to the broadening module 'Communication across cultures'. The term VE is used when talking about the online cultural exchanges that take place among the students and the weekly seminar is the two hour mediated session which the participants in the E+VE programme need to attend.

---

4. https://sharingperspectivesfoundation.com/

2. Aims and description of the VE

The 'Communication across cultures' module brings the concept of intercultural learning (Bennett, 2009) alive into the students experience making them critically aware of the crucial role that language and culture have in intercultural communication.

To this end, the module aims at developing the students' intercultural awareness as "a conscious understanding of the role of culturally based forms, practices, and frames of understanding and an ability to put these conceptions into practice in a flexible and context specific manner in real time communication" (Baker, 2012, p. 73).

Our module "explores views of identity, culture, and intercultural communication including the role of language. Students reflect on their own cultural identities and how these might have informed their interpretations of the 'other'"[5]. The second part of the module is the practical part where the students participate in the programme offered by SPF. This provides them with opportunities to achieve some of the learning outcomes, i.e. demonstrate and practise skills of intercultural communicative competence (Fantini, 2019), cultural and intercultural awareness, and deepen their understanding of people from different cultural backgrounds in real life situations. Both aims of the module fit effectively with the programme that SPF offers.

Following this framework, the module is taught using a blended learning approach, which combines traditional face-to-face lectures with online delivery (see Table 1). The *Cultural Encounters* programme is the online learning component, which has a VE component that allows students to actively engage in communication with students of other cultures. The module aims at equipping students with the know-how for engaging with real world intercultural problems, encouraging them to be socially responsible citizens and making a positive difference.

---

5. https://www.ul.ie/international/sites/default/files/user_media/Autumn%202020%20Module%20Booklet.pdf

Table 1. Summary of the face-to-face component and the online delivery component

FACE-TO-FACE	ONLINE DELIVERY/VE
Total duration: 12 weeks	Total duration: ten weeks
Delivered: Lecturer	Delivered: SPF
Two hour lecture per week	Two hour online mediated sessions plus other activities
Objectives and learning outcomes	**Objectives and learning outcomes**
• Problematise definitions of culture and language in intercultural communication, especially in global lingua franca communication contexts. • Reflect on, describe and clarify the configuration of cultural identities in intercultural communication, including your own. • Define intercultural competency in terms of empathy, cultural adaptability, cultural relativisation, negotiation, and mediation. • Illustrate, contrast, and explain differences in both verbal and nonverbal communication in and across different cultures, as emergent resources in intercultural communication. • Make connections between theories of intercultural communication and your own intercultural experiences.	• Have meaningful, transnational, and intercultural experiences. • Increase intercultural awareness and build 21st Century skills through VE. • Encourage and promote intercultural dialogue, employability, and citizenship, strengthening the youth dimension of the EU neighbourhood policy (https://ec.europa.eu/ neighbourhood-enlargement/ neighbourhood/overview_en). • Develop soft skills that are often not formally recognised, such as the development of intercultural awareness, digital literacies, group work, etc. • Learn through dialogue where participants will be seeking mutual understanding and co-creating knowledge, based on their own experiences.

The duration of the module is 12 weeks and the students meet every week for two hours when attending the lecture. During this face-to-face time, the students are presented with theoretical issues related to interculturality which they discuss and engage in a debate following a critical approach. The conceptual approach in the intercultural studies discipline is complemented by their ten week compulsory participation in the *Cultural Encounters* programme in order to receive academic credit for the module. This VE and face-to-face combination bridges theory and practice, by making the virtual cultural encounters a venue for dialogue and exchange.

3. Activities and tools

Before the start of the VE, the students are provided with the necessary information and instructions regarding their participation. After registration for the VE programme, they have the option to follow a preparatory and exploratory session allowing them to become familiar with the virtual interface of the platform to be used. Throughout the semester they have technical, academic and pastoral support from the E+VE programme staff and from their lecturer at UL. Students need to complete a minimum of 70% of the weekly group-based online seminars and must engage with the different elements: video lectures, responses to video lectures, video dialogue assignments, and a weekly reflective journal. The latter is recorded in a Google form provided to each student at the end of the online seminar to allow them to write reflectively about the different opinions, perspectives, intercultural (mis-)understandings or simply the content of the seminar that are part of the course provided by SPF. Equally, the lecturer and coordinator of the module can monitor the participation and engagement of the students in the E+VE as SPF provides accurate and detailed reports about the levels of student participation and engagement.

The online dialogue interactions among the students from different European and Southern Mediterranean universities take place once a week (see Figure 1). The UL students choose a suitable time for engagement and dedicate two hours per week over a period of ten weeks to carry out the VEs. The online sessions do not coincide with face-to-face class sessions, therefore rooms in the UL library (quiet and well equipped spaces) or computer labs where Wi-Fi is guaranteed, are available for the students to use. The technical requirements to carry out the VEs are limited to internet accessibility, preferably from a laptop. However, some students choose to take part in the weekly online seminars using their mobile phones. The technical assistance offered by the support team at SPF has always been acknowledged by students as being very helpful, prompt, and responsive, as well as offering excellent academic, and organisational support.

Figure 1. Two UL students participating in the E+VE offered by SPF

In relation to the language used within the online exchanges, a considerable number of UL participants are native speakers of English. This is often perceived as a positive challenge as it brings awareness of the strong link between language and culture, as one student said:

> "feeling comfortable sharing my opinion was sometimes a challenge. Also, adjusting the way I spoke and the certain way [we] say things so that I wouldn't offend and could be understood by non-native English speakers".

Erasmus students and international students felt that participation in the VE through the medium of English is a very valuable opportunity to keep practising English while discussing and reflecting on socio-political issues. However, sometimes these students could feel at a disadvantage or not linguistically competent enough to articulate complex ideas during the discussions, as another student mentioned: "it was difficult to speak about those topics that are quite technical in a language that is not my own".

4. Evaluation, assessment, and recognition

As discussed in the previous sections, the VE is completely integrated into the module 'Communication across cultures'. The evaluation of student performance is twofold: for the online exchange offered by E+VE, SPF provides different assessment mechanisms: attendance and participation in the online dialogue sessions, completion of the video lecture responses, video dialogue assignments, and a weekly reflective journal. All these assessment components amount to 60% of the final student grade. For the face-to-face component, the lecturer of the module asks the students to write a final reflective essay based on their experience of the VE. The students have already been completing entries in a weekly reflective journal, submitted to SPF through a Google Form; this is designed to allow them to think back and consider on an individual basis their weekly experiences on the programme. When writing the final reflective essay, students can include anecdotes and observations recorded in their weekly reflective journal (see Section 3 of this case study). The final reflective assignment is worth 40% of their total grade and they need to analyse critically the whole experience of participating in the VE, and include some of the theory and concepts covered during the lectures when and where relevant.

In recent iterations of the module, a high percentage of the students were taking the module as an alternative or preparation for the Erasmus physical mobility. In those cases, the students are asked to reflect on how the VE can help them develop some of the intercultural skills they would be using if they were participating in the physical mobility or how the VE is helping them prepare for their period abroad.

During the implementation of E+VE, feedback from students is collected using an anonymous survey and their final reflective essays. Overall, the participants agree that taking part in the E+VE programme helps them to think more critically, share different views about the same topic (e.g. immigration, populism, nationalism, and identity) and broaden their consideration of other perspectives. Here are some representative student views: "[VEs] taught me to think about other perspectives", "showed the importance of being informed of global news", "encouraged us to think critically", and "challenged the views of the other participants".

Participating in online intercultural exchanges to discuss topics related to Europe and society in general represents a very different pedagogy for the students to develop learning. It must be reported that initially, it appears to them as a very unfamiliar and atypical approach. As one of the students observes:

> "the VE programme brought about a very different method of learning about society and culture. It introduced an aspect of learning that the typical academic student would not normally associate with their academic progression in university".

The majority of students agree that the VE fits effectively within the aims of the module, and adds practical and experiential aspects to their learning processes. In Table 2, there are several quotations that refer to this student perception of the VE as the experiential side of their academic module. The comments also illustrate the impact that participating in *Cultural Encounters* had on some of the students: growing awareness of global issues, strong engagement and action, development of multiple perspectives, and the development of soft skills important in intercultural and cross-cultural communication (i.e. active listening).

Table 2. Examples of experiential learning and the impact that VE had on students

Selected comments of the students (our highlights in bold)
Comment 1: "Although you hear of this [traumatic news]in the newspapers or online, **it doesn't become real until you have seen and spoken to someone going through it**".
Comment 2: "Using my group as an example, we took it upon ourselves **to make a Facebook group** so that we can all stay in contact if we so wish and I believe **that the Spanish students are helping A., the Syrian student, in finding scholarships to master's degree programmes in Europe and in Canada**. All this after just ten weeks of knowing each other".

Case study 16

Comment 3: "Our facilitator M., often asked us to say our favourite words in our native languages as an ice breaker. To which R. (one of the participants in the group the student was part of) once responded with the word حب /haʊbʌn/, meaning love in Arabic. **I began to develop an interest in the Arabic language and began learning the language on my own.** R. was amused by my desire to learn her mother tongue, then **she offered to help me**".
Comment 4: "This was what I liked the most about the VE programme: I realised that **my point of view was not the only one**, and that what I saw as normal was not like that for others. **For example**, people from Gaza only had three hours of electricity per day".
Comment 5: "In the first couple of weeks in my group some of us were coming close to blows just because of this thing about **listening, the process of learning how to listen** we were still getting there so at the start of the week there was a bit of tension about some certain topics that we weren't listening to properly".

Receiving a digital badge is a very welcome addition for many students, especially for those who enrol in our module as an alternative to Erasmus mobility. The badge guarantees them recognition for their multicultural experience after participating in the VE and their competencies in communicating effectively and carrying out discussions in a culturally diverse setting.

5. Lessons learnt and conclusion

Taking into consideration the pedagogical and learning outcomes, VE has offered the opportunity to our institution to develop internationalisation strategies by 'globalising the curriculum' (De Wit, 2016; Helm, 2015) and practise 'internationalisation at home'. The journey so far has been very positive and the students' feedback shows how their attitudes have shifted and their perspectives have broadened due to the blended learning model. In other words, the students' intercultural awareness and intercultural communication skills are enhanced. It should be highlighted that these gains and achievements form part of the essential learning objectives of the module and of the programme offered by SPF.

Issues related to student workload and time management have been raised from time to time to the extent that they might have a negative impact on student engagement. Consequently, some of the allocated face-to-face time has been reduced in order to offer students equitable opportunities with the credits gained.

Some technical problems were also present in the exchanges, which have always been overcome by the technical support team of the VE provider SPF. The types of students that take part in the VEs change from year to year as our module is a broadening module that is offered across the entire university. Every year some minor adjustments need to be applied when working in collaboration with SPF. Every iteration of the programme brings changes, challenges, but also opportunities to build bridges among people and cultures.

The digital era has undoubtedly brought the world closer to us, however, conversely within this global space, our mind-set and our digital practices could become very localised and limited to leisure and entertainment, potentially leading to the harmful growth of homophily and the *balkanisation* of our ideas and cultural practices (Currarini, Matheson, & Vega-Redondo, 2016; Yardi & Boyd, 2010). We are currently operating in an educational context at UL in which the vast majority of students display less and less engagement with socio-political and global issues in favour of more local and regional concerns (Murray & Giralt, 2019). VE brings the world to our classes, to our students – as mentioned by one of them: "I have not spoken much to foreign people before as I have not had the opportunity" – and affords future citizens the opportunity to open their minds, develop their intercultural skills, and become better prepared for a changing and diverse planet.

6. Acknowledgements

Special acknowledgements must go to my dear colleagues from the French Section, Florence Le-Baron and Marie-Thérèse Batardière, and Catherine

Jeanneau from the Language Learning Hub for our forever fruitful exchanges and discussions.

References

Baker, W. (2012). From cultural awareness to intercultural awareness: culture in ELT. *ELT Journal, 66*(1), 62-70. https://doi.org/10.1093/elt/ccr017

Batardière, M.-T., Giralt, M., Jeanneau, C., Le-Baron-Earle, F., & O'Regan, V. (2019). Promoting intercultural awareness among European university students via pre-mobility virtual exchanges. *Journal of Virtual Exchange, 2*, 1-6. https://doi.org/10.14705/rpnet.2019.jve.4

Bennett, M. J. (2009). Defining, measuring, and facilitating intercultural learning: a conceptual introduction to the Intercultural Education double supplement. *Intercultural Education, 20*(Sup1), S1-S13. https://doi.org/10.1080/14675980903370763

Currarini, S., Matheson, J., & Vega-Redondo, F. (2016). A simple model of homophily in social networks. *European Economic Review, 90*, 18-39. https://doi.org/10.1016/j.euroecorev.2016.03.011

De Wit, H. (2016). Internationalisation and the role of online intercultural exchange. In R. O'Dowd & T. Lewis (Eds), *Online intercultural exchange: policy, pedagogy, practice* (pp. 83-96). Routledge. https://doi.org/10.4324/9781315678931

Fantini, A. E. (2019). *Intercultural communicative competence in educational exchange: a multinational perspective*. Routledge. https://doi.org/10.4324/9781351251747-2

Giralt, M., & Jeanneau, C. (2016). Preparing higher education language students to their period abroad through telecollaboration: the I-TELL project. *AISHE-J: The All Ireland Journal of Teaching and Learning in Higher Education, 8*(2).

Helm, F. (2015). The practices and challenges of telecollaboration in higher education in Europe. *Language Learning & Technology, 19*(2), 197-217. https://doi.org/10125/44224

Kolb, D. A. (2014). *Experiential learning: experience as the source of learning and development*. Person Education.

Murray, L., & Giralt, M. (2019). Challenges of monolingual intercultural communication in the context of the languages connect strategy. *Teanga, The Journal of the Irish Association for Applied Linguistics, 26*, 26-51. https://doi.org/10.35903/teanga.v26i0.111

O'Dowd, R. (2018). From telecollaboration to virtual exchange: state-of-the-art and the role of UNICollaboration in moving forward. *Journal of Virtual Exchange, 1*, 1-23. https://doi.org/10.14705/rpnet.2018.jve.1

UL. (n.d.). *University of Limerick strategic plan.* https://www.ul.ie/UL_Strategic_Plan_2019-2024_Web.pdf

Yardi, S., & Boyd, D. (2010). Dynamic debates: an analysis of group polarization over time on Twitter. *Bulletin of Science, Technology & Society, 30*(5), 316–327. https://doi.org/10.1177/0270467610380011

17. Integrating Soliya's Connect programmes into a language course and into a liberal arts and sciences degree

Tatiana Bruni[1]

Abstract

This chapter presents how I integrated Virtual Exchange (VE) programmes delivered by Soliya in two courses at an international undergraduate liberal arts and sciences college. In both cases the VE programme was fully integrated in the courses as a graded element. The students of beginner Italian participated in the four-week long Connect Express. While liking the experience, they found that the VE was still too disconnected from their aim of learning a language. The students of Intercultural Communication (IC) participated in the eight-week long Connect Global. For them, the success of the experience was linked to the group composition and the English proficiency level of participants.

Keywords: language education, intercultural communication, teacher's role, pedagogy, dialogue, reflective work.

1. Context

University College Utrecht (UCU) provides English-language liberal arts and sciences undergraduate education in the Netherlands and it is part of Utrecht University, a large research university. UCU is a residential college located

---

1. University College Utrecht, Utrecht, Netherlands; t.bruni@uu.nl; https://orcid.org/0000-0003-1548-7862

How to cite this case study: Bruni, T. (2020). Integrating Soliya's Connect programmes into a language course and into a liberal arts and sciences degree. In F. Helm & A. Beaven (Eds), *Designing and implementing virtual exchange – a collection of case studies* (pp. 205-216). Research-publishing.net. https://doi.org/10.14705/rpnet.2020.45.1127

on a campus which is home to 750 students with 70 different nationalities, although the vast majority have the Dutch nationality or that of a European country. Students learn to think critically and to employ multiple perspectives by composing their own multidisciplinary curriculum combining courses from disciplines taught in the three departments and interdisciplinary courses. Because of this system, courses are not linked to a specific study year: course admission is regulated by a set of prerequisites. Class size is small, and classes are usually composed of students with different academic backgrounds and interests, and who are at different stages of their study programme. This mix is enriching for class discussion and peer-learning, albeit often challenging for instructors, who need to cater for very diverse needs and knowledge levels. The students who participated in the VEs presented in this chapter took either my beginner Italian course to fulfil their language and culture requirement, or my IC course as an elective.

2. Aims and description of the project

According to the educational vision of UCU (n.d.), "qualities fostered at the college not only enable personal growth and professional advancement, but also prepare our students to fulfil their role as citizens, enabling them to serve others" (p. 2). Several UCU graduates aspire to working in an international environment where they can make a difference, as they often formulate it themselves. It is thus paramount that they learn to have a deeper understanding of the perspectives of others around the world and practise cross-cultural dialogue and collaboration within and outside their educational setting. Soliya's VE programmes, aimed at enhancing communication and improving attitudes toward difference, seemed a meaningful tool to foster the qualities we value in our graduates, providing the students with experiences in a safe environment. Soliya is an international non-profit organisation headquartered in New York. Its mission is "to prepare rising generations to approach differences constructively and lead with empathy, in order to thrive in an interconnected world"[2].

---

2. https://www.soliya.net/about/about-us

The 11 students of my beginner Italian course participated in the four-week long *Connect Express*, which entailed one synchronous session of two hours per week in groups of ten to 12 students. The focus of this programme is communication in the digital world, through the lens of identity (including contextual salience of certain aspects of identity, and issues of identity threat). In the course guide, I explained the relevance of the VE by stating that Connect Express encourages thoughtful discourse in a digital society and explores how identity constructs and assumed archetypes influence engagement across cultural and continental divides.

Further, I explained that while only few participants in the VE would come from Italy, through participating in this exchange, students would further develop awareness of, and a critical stance on their own beliefs and attitudes. These two capabilities are important learning outcomes of the course, delivering on UCU's (n.d.) educational vision:

> "[s]harply developed thinking skills go hand in hand with critical self-reflection and an eagerness to understand the positions of others. In this way each student comes to discern for him or herself which intellectual and personal aims are truly worth pursuing" (p. 1).

The 26 students of my IC course participated in the eight-week long Connect Global programme, which includes 16 hours of synchronous communication, complemented by ten hours to complete asynchronous assignments, which include two sets of readings, a group project, and a final reflective journal. This programme is designed to provide young adults with the opportunity to establish a deeper understanding of the perspectives of others around the world on important socio-political issues and develop competences such as critical thinking, cross-cultural communication, and collaborative problem-solving. The dialogues and projects of the VE would complement class activities such as student-led discussions, case presentations, and the critical analysis of (social) media. Class activities were aimed at developing students' awareness of their own values, norms, and biases, and preparing them for engaging with cultural others through the VE project.

3. Activities and tools

In both programmes, Soliya places participants from over 200 educational organisations in the Middle East, North Africa, North America, and Europe in groups of eight to 12 peers, considering the availability each student indicated and the time zone in which they live. Each week, students meet with their group members and facilitators in virtual meeting rooms on Soliya's video conferencing platform. The platform has a round-table design, break-out rooms, group and bilateral private chat, social rooms for non-facilitated dialogue, and options for asynchronous interaction.

Before the programmes start, students are asked to run a technical test. They also participate in a short online orientation and are provided with detailed information about the programme and expectations. Programme implementers (the instructors) receive implementation manuals detailing weekly topics and assignments and advice on how to integrate the programme in their course and how to spark reflection on the programme in class sessions.

Each group is supported by facilitators trained in cross-cultural dialogue, so they can guide participants' reflections on the learning process and help them navigate through interpersonal dynamics. They support the groups through a staged group process: orientation, polite moderation, learning through difference, sincere transformation, forward looking brainstorming, and activation.

The synchronous group sessions offer a combination of planned activities and discussions on topics chosen by the participants. To ensure student commitment and participation in all components of the programmes, Soliya recommends making attendance compulsory by either offering it as a graded part of an academic course or by creating a compelling incentive structure to ensure that students will fully commit to all the elements. I chose to make the VE a graded part of my courses.

Finally, implementers receive support in the form of several types of reports:

- weekly attendance reports of each participant with absences or lateness;

- weekly reports with information about the issues that were discussed the previous week, and the topics that would be discussed the week after. These reports focus on the specific areas where there was extensive debate or discussion, so that teachers can pursue these topics in offline class discussions;

- reminders of important students' deadlines for assignments; and

- individual student performance reports.

Those reports, completed by the group facilitators, are short and provide quantitative assessments of each student in their respective groups. Students are rated on level of participation in the dialogue sessions, level of engagement with their peers and in the group sessions, the ability to practise constructive cross-cultural communication, positive contribution to the discussion and the group dynamics, and finally, their language ability. This information, together with the attendance report, helped me assess my students' performances in their dialogue groups and assign a grade based on that.

For the eight-week Connect Global programme, Soliya provided students with a list of goals for each week and indicated some activities and topics that are required over the eight weeks, to create consistency from group to group. Prior to the first session, students read two articles dealing with global and social challenges and reflected on what they consider the most important social and global challenge. We discussed these articles in class as well in advance, so that I could check that all students had engaged with the resources. The same happened for the second set of readings, which dealt with IC. Early in the programme, each group did an analysis of what they saw as the most pressing global challenges and social issues in the world today. Then, over the course of the semester, they explored those key issues collaboratively. As such, every

Case study 17

group's discussion took a slightly different path, based on the areas of interest of the students in that group, and their joint diagnosis of the global and social challenges.

During the semester, students also examined the process of dialogue, to build upon their capacity to engage with differences constructively. Other topics explored were identity, culture and stereotypes, values and social norms, life experiences and world view, youth empowerment and activation, and any topic important to the participants. In the final session, the focus was on sharing participants' visions for the future and brainstorming together on how they can make a difference – individually and collectively: how to become change-makers.

Throughout the programme, each group also worked on a collective project around the global challenges they had agreed to explore. This was done by interviewing people. Each group selected specific interview questions, then students conducted the interviews with two members of their communities. The interviews were shared, then students were paired up. Paired students shared the interviews of the other with their own community members and asked for a response to those responses. The aim of this activity was to engage with different perspectives in participants' local communities and connect members of their own community to others around the world.

4. Evaluation, assessment, and recognition

4.1. Language course

Participation in the Connect Express counted for 15% of the final grade. Full participation in this VE required students to spend approximately ten hours on programme-related activities (including two hours for preparation) during the four-week period, and to submit a reflective final paper (1,500 words) to Soliya and myself. In the table below you can see my grading sheet, based on the student performance report provided by Soliya.

Table 1. Grading sheet for participation to the VE programme – beginner Italian course

Student	Level of participation in the dialogue	Student's engagement with their peers & in the group sessions.	Student's ability to practice constructive cross-cultural communication.	Student's positive contributions to the discussions & the group dynamics.	Student's language ability.	Attendance	Paper	Final course grade
	Assessed by Soliya						assessed by Tatiana	by Tatiana
1	Active	Good	Excellent	Good	Good	2	Very good	B+
2	Very Active	Excellent	Excellent	Excellent	Excellent	4	Good	A-
3	Very Active	Good	Excellent	Good	Excellent	3	Excellent	A
4	Active	Good	Good	Good	Excellent	4	Very good	A-
5	Very Active	Excellent	Excellent	Excellent	Excellent	4 (missed more than 10 minutes of 1)	Excellent	A
6	Very Active	Excellent	Excellent	Excellent	Excellent	4 (missed more than 10 minutes of 1)	Excellent	A
7	Very Active	Excellent	Excellent	Excellent	Excellent	3	Excellent	A
8	Very Active	Excellent	Excellent	Excellent	Excellent	4 (missed more than 10 minutes of 1)	Excellent	A
9	Active	Good	Good	Average	Excellent	3	Very good	B+

Initially, students in this course found it difficult to connect with strangers, sometimes unexpectedly older than them (in their late 20's or early 30's), in an environment that forced them to have conversations because participants were monitored. One student wrote in her paper the following comment: "all the conversations have to be 'meaningful' and I kind of had the feeling that everything I had to say had to come across as interesting or intelligent". Because the interactions are not anonymous, participants felt more accountable for their words. Moreover, all students reflected on their own communicative strategies on different social media and learnt to adapt those to the new environment. They praised the platform feature that allows only one person to speak at once: other participants must ask and be granted speaking time. This enhanced deep and attentive listening, and self-reflection before speaking, something which most students admitted finding difficult. One student expressed it very effectively in his paper:

> "this ... allowed for a nice opportunity to (perhaps mandatorily so) try a new way of listening to and interpreting what someone is saying and give me time to reflect on what I thought about it before responding. This also allowed me to look at my own preconceptions about what someone is saying and think about my process of interpreting other people".

After a hesitant start however, most groups developed a safe environment and felt sufficiently connected to be able to talk intimately about topics that were at times controversial. Students commented that it was a pity that the programme was so short, because those fruitful conversations started happening in Week 3 or 4. They would have preferred shorter sessions for a longer period, so as to get to know each other better.

4.2. IC course

The VE Connect Global accounted for 25% of the final grade. The workload was approximately 25 hours, and included the following elements:

- attending all eight online two-hour dialogue sessions during the programme;

- preparing two sets of required readings;

- working collaboratively with the group peers on a project; and

- submitting a reflective paper with a summary of the interviews they conducted, reflecting on the process of engaging with the different perspectives during the project work and on the VE experience in general (1,300-1,500 words).

Students could obtain the Erasmus+ VE exchange badge if they attended 75% or more of the online sessions, submitted the paper, and wrote a VE programme evaluation. For my students, the VE was a graded element of the course, so the incentive to participate was provided by the grade rather than the badge.

However, to engage them actively with the VE, besides discussing the readings in class, I made the suggested weekly journaling mandatory. Students found it challenging to write one journal entry per week, together with doing the other assignments for the course. It was also hard for me to keep up, but it was vital: I was able to see patterns across the groups in topics discussed, but even more in the development of awareness and skills of students. Moreover, I could detect positive and negative experiences and feelings and bring them up in class, as well as give individual feedback and support where needed.

The paper for Soliya (1,500 words) was later on integrated in the course term paper (3,500 words, worth 40% of the final grade): students had to reflect on three learning experiences they had during the semester: one related to the VE, one related to an intercultural encounter in their own life, and one related to the case studies we examined. Some students experienced the VE as very enriching and eye-opening: they reported having developed critical self-reflection on their bias and on their communicative strategies. Because of that, they were able to adapt those strategies and make a more valuable contribution to the group. The facilitators played a key role, and in most papers, students expressed appreciation for how facilitators managed the sessions without taking the lead.

Nevertheless, there were also students who felt that they did not get as much out of the programme as they had expected. This was the consequence of the group composition: nine out of 16 ended up being in a group with two other class peers. In their experience, the three UCU students in each group were always present and very active, while the other group peers missed sessions or did not participate actively enough. As a consequence, my students felt that they were just going over the same conversations we were already having in class about identity, stereotyping, difference, and more.

Furthermore, some students reported that other participants were difficult to understand or lacked the confidence to speak up, due to their proficiency level of English. UCU students have an oral proficiency level of C1 or higher on the Common European Framework of Reference for languages (CEFR), while in several groups the level of other participants was considerably lower. In my students' perceptions, many group peers participated in the VE primarily to practise their English and seemed thus to withdraw from actively contributing to the dialogues on sensitive topics. Alternatively, they used the written chat function to ask clarification questions or get help with formulating their responses, so my students felt as if most of the time they were helping others with the language. On the one hand I think that there might be situations where participating in a VE is one of very few options for students to practise with their English, so VE programmes might be promoted more as an opportunity to practise the language. This could create a difference in expectations among participants. On the other hand, though, we discussed in class that language barriers occur all the time, and that students should develop strategies for adapting to the proficiency level of their interlocutors. Also, being able to help others in overcoming those barriers and expressing themselves, thus being an intercultural mediator, is one of the intercultural communicative competences which students hope to develop in my courses.

Finally, students of the IC course experienced the VE as burdensome because the weekly journaling, the interviews, and the final VE paper were all due within eight weeks, while they also had other homework to do as well. Moreover, they had expected to engage in more controversial dialogues. Nonetheless, most students realised how easily they were able to empathise and bond with other humans, connecting across (virtual) borders through shared interests and visions for a better future.

Throughout both programmes, technical issues impacted the group dynamics very much. Oftentimes not only participants but also the facilitators would have to reboot and reconnect. One of my students commented that: "although the Soliya team was very efficient and helped almost everyone in a matter of seconds, the constant interruptions impeded the members from truly becoming comfortable with each other as they stopped us from concentrating solely on the conversation and constantly reminded everyone the online nature of the meetings". Usually Soliya provides a reliable custom bandwidth optimisation to facilitate access to remote places and poor connections. The technical issues experienced during this semester were mainly due to the implementation of a new platform in the autumn of 2019.

5.   Lessons learnt and conclusion

Integrating Connect Express in the language course proved valuable at an individual level, but too disconnected from the course aims and class practices. This was because it was an English-medium programme and so was not focused on practising the target language, Italian. On the other hand, the aims of Global Connect and its focus on constructive dialogue and finding paths for becoming change-makers resonate with the college's educational vision and made it very relevant for the IC course. If teachers intend to fully integrate Soliya's VE programmes in a course, the workload should not be underestimated. In the future I would consider planning fewer face-to-face classes during the period of the programme and making the journaling less frequent. I would also adapt my syllabus to avoid too many content overlaps.

Finally, I would create recurring moments for reflection about the online sessions during class time.

Reference

UCU. (n.d.). *University College Utrecht liberal arts vision statement. a holistic approach to undergraduate education.* https://www.uu.nl/sites/default/files/ucu_vision_mission_statement_april_2017.pdf

Section 3.

Youth

18. Virtual exchange strengthens international youth work

Sandra van de Kraak[1] and Jan Lai[2]

Abstract

Pathways to Youth Leadership was an Erasmus+: Youth in Action long term training involving 24 youngsters from 12 countries. Grant cuts required squeezing the residential programme, originally planned to last three weeks, into two. That is why, after taking part in the Erasmus+ Virtual Exchange (E+VE) training, we successfully added five VE sessions to the project. Youth work relies on personal interaction, experiential learning, and non-formal education. Transferring that into online interaction has been our greatest innovation and challenge. In our field, there is resistance to online activities, but the Covid-19 pandemic is changing this. We need to practise online facilitation, develop the required skills, and define the role E+VE can play in youth work.

Keywords: youth, leadership, virtual exchange, training.

1. Context

Pathways to Youth Leadership is a long term leadership training initially proposed by the youth work organisations Breakthrough (the Netherlands), Associazione Interculturale NUR (Italy), and Think Forward (UK), embraced by a 12-organisation partnership and financed by Erasmus+: Youth in Action.

---

1. Breakthrough Foundation, Tilburg, The Netherlands; haveyourbreakthrough@gmail.com

2. Associazione Interculturale NUR, Cagliari, Italy; janniccu@gmail.com; https://orcid.org/0000-0003-0018-5909

How to cite this case study: Van de Kraak, S., & Lai, J. (2020). Virtual exchange strengthens international youth work. In F. Helm & A. Beaven (Eds), *Designing and implementing virtual exchange – a collection of case studies* (pp. 219-230). Research-publishing.net. https://doi.org/10.14705/rpnet.2020.45.1128

© 2020 Sandra van de Kraak and Jan Lai (CC BY)

Case study 18

The training involved 24 young leaders from 12 different countries, including some from the EU neighbouring South East Europe (SEE) and Mediterranean And Middle East (MEDA) regions. The target group was young adults, those new to youth work, ex-beneficiaries of Erasmus+ (either youth exchanges or European Voluntary Service), and young people looking for further training. Realities differ substantially within the participating countries, and sharing and learning from each other is an essential part of the programme. The participation of MEDA and SEE neighbouring regions brings another rich learning dimension to this process and offers an authentic platform for exploring cultural differences and similarities.

The long term training aimed to offer a platform for developing and understanding the principles and practice of youth leadership, and let leadership competences become habits to empower young people close to or involved in the partnering organisations' activities. One of the key goals of the programme is to support participants through their own flexible learning path, facilitating and validating their learning by means of digital open badges.

The team of freelance trainers leading the long term residential training course were three male and one female from Italy, The Netherlands, and the UK who already knew each other and had had an opportunity to develop a close partnership and professional approach to fostering learning through innovative, creative, and flexible methods. Having collaborated both in projects on youth leadership and youth work related competences development on one side, and on innovative digital tools-based projects in the field of youth on the other, it was natural for us to embrace the possibility offered by the E+VE pilot project.

Due to grant cuts in the design phase of the programme, the team faced a challenge when forced to squeeze a three-week residential learning programme into one based on only two weeks of mobility. This made us decide to proactively use digital tools, and to test E+VE.

To better embed the E+VE component into our programme, two trainers took part in the VE training organised by UNICollaboration. As a result of the further engagement in a collaboration between our partnership and UNICollaboration, a structured programme of five VE dialogue sessions was added to the existing programme (Figure 1).

Figure 1. The third E+VE meeting of Pathways to Youth Leadership[3]

2. Aims and description of the project

The first aim of Pathways to Youth Leadership is to train young people to develop effective leadership habits (Figure 2). A habit is not achieved in one week, therefore our training course needed to be structured over a longer time period. This posed a significant challenge in planning the course: how could we keep young people on board and engaged for long enough to achieve these habits?

---

3. Published in https://www.instagram.com/p/ByiSeLso_CY/?igshid=1e04macq4dasb

Case study 18

The main goal we wanted to reach by including in our agenda five dialogue sessions was to allow for a smoother flow of the project itself given that one of the three residential training courses we had asked for had not been funded in the final grant agreement. Besides resulting in a lack of time to deliver the full content of our project, the distribution of two residential trainings in a rather long project posed some doubts on the actual chances of maintaining a high commitment to the project among youth participants.

Fearing higher than normal drop-out rates and difficulties in retaining learning from one training to another, we turned to VE as a bridging solution between them.

Also, by programming the VE sessions to happen before the first mobility, after the second and between the two, we were able to plan content of the online sessions to fulfil three specific tasks:

- group building and ice breaking, before the first mobility to lessen the element of culture shock when arriving in a strange place abroad and meeting a lot of new people at once;

- content-development and learning-reinforcement, for the sessions between mobilities to support learners to keep on working on their effective leadership habits; and

- follow-up and evaluation, for the session planned at the end of the process to help learners recognise their learning and achievements and think in a constructive and practical way about their next steps.

So, even if participants were approximately the same across the whole project and the main methods, tools, and approaches used in each of the five sessions were also very consistent across the almost 12 months of the life-span of our project, we managed to differentiate the aim of each session according to the specific phase of the project's timeline in which it was implemented.

Figure 2. Pathways to Youth Leadership building links during a residential session[4]

3. Nuts and bolts

Our youth work activities are normally based on experiential learning, and active participation, peer learning approaches often identified as non-formal education methods. Therefore, the first VE session, before the first residential mobility, was mainly planned to support young participants in connecting with each other and the delivery team, making the step to going abroad accessible for everybody, and to create a friendly and safe learning environment. Content for this first session focused on getting-to-know-each-other and on a first understanding of the way

---
4. Published in https://www.instagram.com/p/BtjuZGYFN77/?igshid=1d3fkpy44i938

we would be working with active learning methods in a non-formal education setting (also using other software than just the video conferencing platform), shared viewing and commenting of videos and documents about 'What is Erasmus+'[5] or 'What is Youthpass'[6], a 'facilitated dialogue' in small breakout rooms about the expectations for the entire learning programme, and support for more logistics-related topics such as how to travel to the first physical mobility destination in Italy.

During the first residential training, a 'buddy system' and reflection groups were started, with the aim of creating a peer-support system among participants to help them during their learning process, in particular in the time between the two mobilities. These groups were used as support groups in the next VE sessions implemented between the two residential courses, one per month, to keep a high level of engagement among our young youth leaders.

The logistics of our VE sessions followed a standardised process in order to transform them into good habits as fast as possible. Before each session, participants received an invitation to take part, as well as information on time zones and on how to enter Zoom, complete with a fully explanatory screenshot tutorial, and an overview of the topics and content for the VE meeting.

In every step we were supported by the UNICollaboration team, who provided two dialogue facilitators for each session. Each exchange started with reinforcing a feeling of being in a safe environment for everybody. As a note-taking tool during the VE sessions we used Etherpad. Participants were thus able to take notes about their discussions in their breakout groups. We gave buddy groups time to meet within the VE session and participants frequently contacted each other outside our meetings using a specific Whatsapp chat we initiated, and we noticed that they were supporting each other to a great extent. But while the personal support and engagement goals were very easy to reach, having structured learning meetings was more difficult. Probably being the very first attempt in

---

5. https://youtu.be/TvondHqhKXM

6. https://www.youthpass.eu/downloads/13-62-157/flyer_yp_for_youth_worker.pdf

transferring non-formal education dynamics into an online environment, we paid too much attention to the 'human touch' aspects of our methods, sacrificing a little more detailed planning for the delivery of the learning content.

4. Evaluation, assessment, and recognition

Throughout the entire process we had several evaluation moments within the team and by participants via observations, checking out after each VE session, and regular Google Sheets evaluation forms. A year after the last VE meeting officially linked to the project, we had a new one, and participants are still planning and implementing their own VE meetings.

Given the blended nature of the project, the evaluation system was also structured to reflect this approach. So we had a very rich system of tools to evaluate, ranging from online questionnaires (both delivered by the trainers team and by the UNICollaboration team that supported us through the whole process) to digital open badges. We had already developed specific badges for the assessment of the learning component of the main content of the training course. These proved invaluable tools to explain the concept of recognition of learning in a non-formal education context and it engaged our young youth leaders in self assessing their new competences or even in a peer assessment process where each one could validate badge requests from the other participants; but we may have over-complicated the tool by planning too many and too specific badges. As a result, participants focused only on the few that they felt were more relevant to them, not using the whole range of options. On the other hand, we were offering a flexible learning path where young people could follow their own learning at the moment which was right for them (Figure 3).

Other tools and means to assess learning through the project included specific reflection group activities during the residential parts of the course, the issuing of Youthpass certificates, a long term self-assessment of improvements in specific leadership skills and the Erasmus+ Mobility Tool+ questionnaires.

Case study 18

Figure 3. Pathways to Youth Leadership open badge system, used by participants to recognise and validate learning

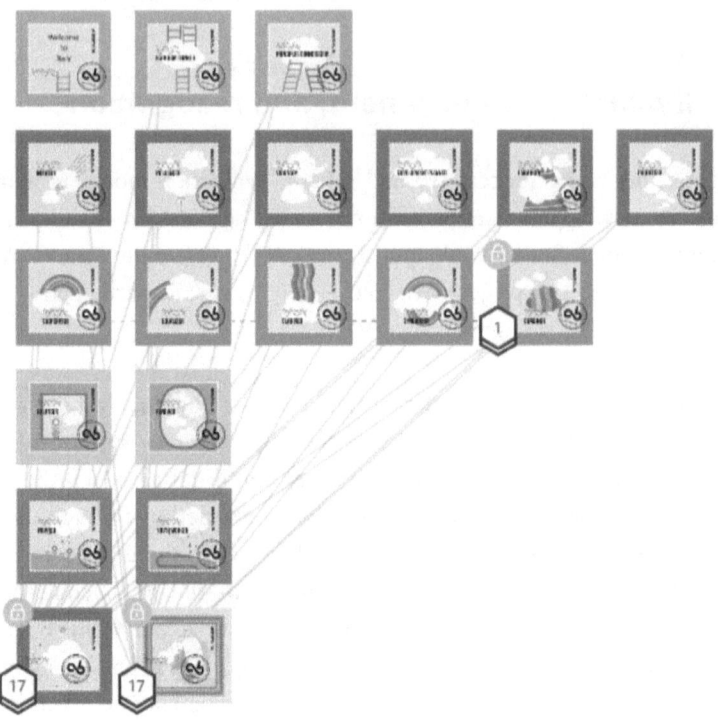

5. Lessons learnt and conclusion

As youth workers, we need to learn how to practice online facilitation in a youth world where the role of online connection is more and more relevant. We need to develop the skills needed for this and create a shared vision about what VE in youth work is and how to ensure the necessary quality. Creating a safe environment online is different from creating such a space in the physical world. Often we had too many aims for one session, and different ideas about what a VE session is (is it a practical preparation session for a training or do we want to guide our young participants in growing professionally and personally?).

How to be a good role model online and to support young people to give them the safety for a good learning path is not simply a matter of 'translating' activities that we are very much used to implementing in person into an online environment. Even finding the right icebreakers and accurately preparing a functional time scheduling was sometimes a challenge. Two members of our team followed the training course provided by UNICollaboration but even from the very early stages of such preparation it was clear to us that the strong roots in the academic world from which E+VE has sprung gave the tool and the concepts behind it a deep 'formal-education imprinting' making it less easy to implement in our field.

Also the almost total absence of previous cases from which to draw examples and guidance was an obstacle that left us almost alone (though always supported by the UNICollaboration team) in wondering and searching for the right solutions.

This was reflected in even small details such as, for instance, the choice of tools to complement the video conferencing platform of choice. Just to mention a few examples, what we could add next time is different note-taking tools, which will allow participants to also use other methods rather than just text to show their learning during VEs, for example via online post-its, posting images, etc. Through trial and error and a year-and-a-half on from our first exchange, we are in a much better position to assess our methods and tools we used during the VE sessions. Nevertheless, we still need to work on methods to support young people on how to use these tools and keep everybody on board. Tools that seem great on a computer screen also need to be usable on mobile devices in case of weak Internet connections. We often had young people who lost their connection during the VE meeting, and people dropping in and out of the virtual sessions due to technical issues. At least initially, we would recommend having three facilitators on board all with very precise tasks. One can facilitate the learning process, one can offer technical support, and one can provide individual support through the private chat function to young participants who need it. It is also crucial that the members of the facilitation team are able to trust each other's capacity in this.

Case study 18

VE meetings can be a very exciting and fun way of having learning experiences, even when they take place through a screen where you can see each other. As youth workers, we believe that people need to meet in person, but a combination of digital youth work and in person youth work is very effective. We did not always play the VE facilitator role as it had been defined in the training from UNICollaboration. The training was built on a format that for some aspects works best in the academic field and some tools typical of the youth sector needed to be kind of 'invented'. Building relationships with young people during the residentials ultimately made the VE room an easier place to navigate. However, we also saw with several young people different behaviours online and offline. In our next training, we need to better understand this and support young people in the online process to feel safe enough to be the person they want to be online and offline.

One significant lesson we learnt was linked to the fact that the working hours used for preparation, the actual VE, and the evaluation, were not financed, meaning that we delivered the whole package of five VE sessions on a totally voluntary basis. We were unaware of funding mechanisms to finance such activities. But the lesson learnt is that foreseeing a reasonable budget for recognising the facilitators' work and time can support us in devoting more time to the online activities of a project, making it easier to take into account more details that, when considered carefully, will lead to better quality in our VE delivery and outcomes.

We would also like to mention a great learning point we got from experimenting with E+VE. As mentioned, our project turned out to be one of the very first (and few) from the Erasmus+ youth funded sector and this gave us the opportunity to widely disseminate the results of the experience. We were invited to present a workshop on the project and VE innovation to the first edition of the European Academy on youth work[7] organised by seven national agencies of Erasmus+:

- Youth in Action, Agenzia Nationale Per I Giovani, Italy;
- EDUFI, Finland;
- JTBA, Lithuania;

---

7. https://www.eayw.net/

- JINT, Belgium-Flanders;
- JUGEND für Europa, Germany;
- Jugend in Aktion, Interkulturelles Zentrum, Austria;
- MOVIT, Slovenia; and
- SALTOYOUTH Resource Centres and the partnership between the European Union and the Council of Europe in the field of youth in Slovenia in May 2019.

It was a significant opportunity to share a truly innovative project in our field among colleagues, institutions, and organisations like ours. The presentation of the project aimed to introduce the tool of E+VE and in particular the current status of the E+VE pilot phase developments to colleagues and stakeholders and to find possible ways of better involving the non-formal education sector in its future steps. Participants in the workshop had the opportunity to find out how to access E+VE activities and to reflect together on how to engage in influencing their evolution, in order to better tailor the E+VE format to the needs of the youth work field. Workshop participants were youth workers, trainers, and staff of non-government organisations, national agencies, and SALTO-Youth[8] structures; nevertheless, none of them had ever heard of E+VE.

The main challenge for participants proved to be understanding the potential opportunities of the E+VE initiative. For many, if not most youth workers and trainers, it seemed difficult to imagine that a VE could be beneficial to our field of work as there is still a tendency in our non-formal education field to reject digital and virtual ways of interaction as 'not relevant', 'not useful', or simply 'not interesting'. This is quite a strange attitude if we consider the big efforts made in recent years to innovate the sector and all the progress made in the area of 'digital youth work'.

This same attitude was still quite visible, even if with a noticeably more constructive curiosity about the topic, at the end of February, 2020, when we had another chance to present the project and E+VE as a valuable support to

---

8. Support, Advanced Learning and Training Opportunities for Youth

learning even in the non-academic world. This was during the 'Exploring the digital dimension of youth workers' competences' conference, held in Vienna by the Austrian National Agency IZ – Verein zur Förderung von Vielfalt, Dialog und Bildung.

What was definitely much more effective in raising interest and attention to what we had implemented came in the first weeks of March 2020 and the progressive extension of lockdown measures across Europe due to the Covid-19 health emergency. Facing the need to forcibly find alternatives to physical mobility, our youth field has shifted towards a much more active and constructive engagement in understanding and discovering the potential of the E+VE idea and tools and this is a great opportunity for all the stakeholders of the non-formal education world as well as for E+VE alike. Creativity from the field of youth work can definitely benefit the E+VE programme in finding new and effective ways to involve and engage young people even in the virtual path to intercultural learning.

Figure 4. Exercise to support the understanding of differences in perspectives of people[9]

---

9. Published in https://www.instagram.com/p/BovxUH2nac_/?igshid=sfbhrdlv9okm

19 Intercultural competence for youth workers

Daniel Dixon[1] and Onur Tahmaz[2]

Abstract

Intercultural Competence for Youth workers (ICY)[3] was a project co-funded by the European Union Erasmus+ programme that ran for 14 months, from spring 2019 to spring 2020, and involved four organisations from Finland, Spain, Belgium, and the Netherlands. Engaging youth workers[4] and young people with fewer opportunities, the project helped youth workers improve their intercultural ability to create places – particularly in the context of sports activities – where young people feel safe, accepted, and not discriminated against. In the context of the Erasmus+ Virtual Exchange (E+VE) initiative, the partners developed a 'trial run' which included an online facilitated dialogue session to test the pedagogy and process of VE, as well as get feedback from the youth involved.

Keywords: virtual exchange, youth work, intercultural awareness, sport, social inclusion.

---

1. Asociación Cultural Social y Educativa Segundas Oportunidades, Telde, Spain; daniel.dixon@acseso.org; https://orcid.org/0000-0002-5729-3401

2. Asociación Cultural Social y Educativa Segundas Oportunidades, Telde, Spain; onur.tahmaz@acseso.org; https://orcid.org/0000-0003-4662-4604

3. https://icyerasmus.squarespace.com/

4. 'Youth worker' is used as an umbrella term and comprises the various figures – trainers, instructors, and leaders – engaged in activities with youth.

How to cite this case study: Dixon, D., & Tahmaz, O. (2020). Intercultural competence for youth workers. In F. Helm & A. Beaven (Eds), *Designing and implementing virtual exchange – a collection of case studies* (pp. 231-240). Research-publishing.net. https://doi.org/10.14705/rpnet.2020.45.1129

1. Context

The ICY project's aim was to improve social inclusion in youth groups by training youth workers and coaches in intercultural competence.

The consortium of partners was made up of:

- HNMKY, (YMCA Helsinki) Finland[5];
- Asociación Cultural Social y Educativa Segundas Oportunidades (Spain)[6];
- ChangeMakerZ, the Netherlands[7]; and
- KSC City Pirates, Belgium[8].

The professionals involved were football coaches, youth workers, trainers, facilitators, teachers, and educators. The objective was for them to share and learn from each other, exploring ways to improve intercultural competence within their organisations and beyond. The young people involved in the project were generally those with fewer opportunities, in other words from low socioeconomic and/or migrant backgrounds, unemployed, suffering from mental illness, or living in an outermost region of the EU. Most participants had found connection to their community and a safe space through sport and non-formal education, and due to the multicultural aspect of the communities involved, supporting young people and youth workers to gain effective intercultural competence skills was, and remains, a priority for the four organisations within the consortium.

In May 2018, the European Commission put forward proposals for the new EU Youth Strategy[9]. One of the main areas of further development was social inclusion. Due to the economic crisis, social exclusion among young people had

---

5. https://www.hnmky.fi/

6. https://www.acseso.org/

7. https://www.facebook.com/teamchangemakerz/

8. https://www.citypirates.be/

9. https://ec.europa.eu/youth/policy/youth-strategy_en

increased. The ICY project used sports and physical education in youth work to increase inclusion and acceptance of diversity. The core goal of the project was to increase social inclusion and solidarity in the partner organisations' youth groups by training the youth workers in inclusive methods and intercultural competence. Realising the potential of using physical education in youth work as a method of increasing social inclusion and intercultural awareness was a key goal for the partner organisations. These goals are very much in line with the objectives mentioned in the Youth Strategy proposal for the years 2019-2027. However, although sports clubs, after school programmes, and other non-formal groups, especially those using physical education in their activities, are often considered as highly effective integrators and inclusive environments for youth, they are not free from racism and discrimination (European Union Agency for Fundamental Rights, 2010). If the youth workers, instructors, trainers, and leaders are not culturally competent leaders, sports and youth clubs can be places of exclusion and racism.

The ICY project helped youth workers improve their intercultural ability to create places where young people feel safe, accepted, and not discriminated against. The objective of ICY was to share best practices to increase social inclusion in youth groups. The project partners were youth organisations that use physical activities partly or fully. Increasing social inclusion and combatting discrimination are core values of each partner organisation, but all partners also had their own strengths. The organisations were chosen from culturally distinct areas and each provided different types of activities for youth. Throughout/during the project, the partner organisations and their instructors shared their experiences, learnt methods from each other, and exchanged best practices to facilitate social inclusion. These methods supported the youth workers in their daily work by helping them deal with racism and discrimination in their groups in a constructive way. As the youth workers' intercultural competence grew, they were more equipped to promote acceptance of diversity and cultural awareness in their groups.

The partner organisations aimed to enable inclusion by giving the youth workers the tools to develop their intercultural competence. To find the best tools (i.e. methods and activities), the partners exchanged their best practices in in-person short term training events (three job shadowing rounds and one intercultural competence training). In the intercultural competence training, the instructors learnt from one another both the theoretical basis of facilitating social inclusion and practical activity ideas that can be used to promote acceptance and inclusiveness. In job shadowing events, the partners observed the methods, habits, and actions of the instructors in the host organisations. It is important to get an outside observer to point out and learn from our tacit knowledge, to verbalise it, and to transfer these learnt methods into different contexts. ICY was a fantastic opportunity to focus on finding these activities and actions that improve the intercultural competence of instructors and increase social inclusion in the youth groups as well as to collect and test them in culturally different environments. Ultimately, it is not only the instructors but the young people in their groups who benefit from these culturally sensitive instruction methods. These methods were recorded and tested in different contexts, and are now available in tool kit format[10].

During the project, the partners became aware of the E+VE initiative and with the support of UNICollaboration, developed a 'trial run' to test the pedagogy and process of VE, as well as get feedback from the youth involved. This 'project within a project' involved young people that had participated in the ICY activities.

The consortium saw the importance of keeping the momentum going between young people and youth workers that had been involved in the physical activities, and because the project was about intercultural competence, integrating E+VE seemed to meet its needs and goals. The idea was that eight young people taking part in the project would work on an asynchronous activity and also meet online for a dialogue session on the topic of intercultural competence. They would be supported in this activity by trained E+VE dialogue facilitators so they could engage on a deeper level about the topic.

---

10. https://icyerasmus.squarespace.com/mission-index-impact

2. Aims and description of the project

This was a 'trial run' for the consortium, and its main aim was to offer a way for the young people that were connected to ICY to continue learning from each other in their journey of developing intercultural competence. The work of the four organisations is mainly with physical activities, so this was also a great opportunity to test new ways of working with young people and of supporting intercultural competence development, and to see how virtual activities can complement in-person activities.

Two young people from each partner organisation (Finland, Spain, Netherlands, and Belgium), who had already met before in various transnational in-person activities, were chosen to take part. There was an asynchronous activity which involved a desk review of the ICY tool kit[11] that was designed as an output of the project, and an online facilitated dialogue session. The eight young people met online with two Erasmus+ dialogue facilitators and took part in various activities which had been planned beforehand by the facilitators at UNICollaboration and the consortium.

3. Nuts and bolts

The young people had met throughout the project in various activities and training events and took part in activities together. They then met online in a group of eight to work with the dialogue facilitators, who elicited self-group awareness and understanding by providing a safe and effective learning environment where participants could begin to engage in effective cross-cultural dialogue online. The eight participants involved were all inspired to take the skills and understanding beyond their participation in this session and continue to engage in activities, two also planning to train to become dialogue facilitators themselves.

---

11. https://issuu.com/acsesogc/docs/icy_toolkit_english__1_

Case study 19

The young people were very motivated to do this online activity and to continue with the dialogue they had started during the physical mobilities. To prepare, they met with their youth workers to reflect on what they had learnt during the project's mobilities. The consortium met with the facilitation team at UNICollaboration and explained what the project entailed, the goals and outcomes, and the UNICollaboration team then designed a session plan based on intercultural dialogue and assumptions.

The session, which took place on the Zoom video-conferencing platform, started with a warm-up and an icebreaker activity. Participants were first of all engaged in an activity where the group analysed an image of 'The Culture Iceberg' and reflected on the visible and hidden aspects of culture.

In the second main activity, they reflected on aspects of their own identity. The purpose of the activity was to explore the multiple aspects of participants' identities and how different identities are foregrounded in relation to the groups and contexts they may find themselves in.

With the support of facilitators, participants reflected on feelings related to their identities and how they may feel when their identity is threatened, or when they are identified only in relation to one aspect of their identity. According to the feedback from the young people, it was a very powerful exercise. The session finished with a time for reflection on what they had learnt.

The dialogue session was led in English and the young people with a lower proficiency level were supported by their peers; the facilitators also kept a running 'chat box' in the Zoom platform of what was being discussed. This allowed the participants to use online translation tools such as Google Translate for anything they did not fully understand, or to prepare their response to a question. This worked very well and the participants reported how they were surprised with how much they were able to achieve in a second language. The facilitators encouraged the whole group to give themselves a round of applause at the end for all working in a language other than their own.

4. Evaluation, assessment, and recognition

The group leaders met the participants in their own youth/sports centres following the session and discussed it with the participants. The feedback was overwhelmingly positive. They saw the value of connecting online and staying in contact with friends from other countries, in addition to meeting physically.

> "It was great to see the people we met in Amsterdam again, and I thought talking online would be hard but it was actually really nice" (VE participant, Spain).

> "I wasn't very nervous because I knew my friends already, but I was still a bit worried because my English is not good. It wasn't difficult though, the session was relaxed and everyone told me I was good at speaking" (VE participant, Belgium).

> "I loved this project, and the VE was a great addition to it. I have since taken part in three more [Transnational Exchange Projects (TEPs)] and begin training to become a dialogue facilitator later this year. Recently, I wondered what we would do because of the pandemic, but I am amazed with how many great opportunities I have found online" (VE participant, Spain).

5. Lessons learnt and future plans

The ICY project offered an opportunity to explore the potential of a blended model whereby following the last transnational training visit, some participants continued their engagement online. The results were extremely positive. Participants felt engaged, re-inspired, and more connected with their peers all around Europe. From the consortium's standpoint, VE was simple to arrange: people used their mobile phones or laptops, and the whole process took only a few hours while providing meaningful interaction for participants. In our project, the exchange was supported by UNICollaboration in the context of E+VE to

Case study 19

cover the topics of cultural competence and impact of cultural identity in youth work.

There is great potential in VEs both as a supportive activity (before and after transnational exchanges) and as a stand-alone learning opportunity. For some individuals, travel is not always possible due to a variety of reasons (physical, financial, family), but this should not mean that they cannot take part in multinational virtual learning events.

As organisers, we saw this project as a 'trial run'. It was added as an activity to an existing project, and only included one facilitated dialogue session, but things have certainly moved on since then.

Based on our experience from this trial exchange, and the ICY consortium's involvement in E+VE activities, we have gone on to deliver more 'robust' TEPs. These include a selection of asynchronous resources and activities (readings, short videos, forum discussions) as well as collaborative tasks in which participants from different organisations work together to produce an outcome. In addition, we have included more online facilitated dialogue sessions as these allow the participants to find their feet and delve more deeply into the topics addressed as well as to get to know one another better. With the ICY consortium, the participants were already familiar with each other, but this is not always the case. Synchronous activities should be complemented with asynchronous activities to continue with engagement of the topic outside of the dialogue sessions, bringing more value and learning opportunities.

Since this project, we have also experienced many more challenges working with young people due to the global Covid-19 pandemic. Through this 'trial run' we became much more aware of how beneficial the possibilities of delivering and supporting youth work activities online could be.

Asociación Cultural Social y Educativa Segundas Oportunidades, one of the consortium members of the ICY project, designed, planned, and implemented two large TEPs during this period.

- **Fight fakes, think critically:** a four week TEP that included 53 young people from eight organisations in Spain, Portugal, Turkey, Croatia, Latvia, Slovenia, Serbia, and Hungary. Content was provided in the form of an e-book written for this project. Asynchronous activities required participants to engage with and reflect on the content which related to elections and referendums, the climate crisis, and vaccinations. Two facilitated dialogue sessions were organised: one at the beginning of the exchange for participants to get to know one another and their different contexts, and a second one to reflect on and discuss the content of the e-book. This project is part of a larger project application that will also include a youth worker training mobility, and a youth exchange mobility.

- **CSTEP – critical thinking:** a four week cross-sectoral TEP about critical thinking which included 13 organisations, one youth theatre group, two universities, one high school, one vocational school, and eight youth organisations. These organisations were from Spain, France, Croatia, Turkey, Greece, Hungary, Italy, and Portugal, and the project involved 89 young people. Asynchronous content was delivered each week using the TED-ED platform and this content formed the basis of weekly online facilitated dialogue sessions supported by E+VE facilitators.

The participants in these TEPs received E+VE badges as recognition of their participation, which reports the acquisition of the following skills:

- digital competence;
- intercultural competence;
- openness to cultural otherness and to other beliefs, world views, and practices; and
- cooperation skills.

Although the concept of open online badges is relatively new to the participants, they are encouraged to open LinkedIn accounts and start displaying their achievements there in preparation for joining the workforce. They also use EuroPass CVs and can display their new digital badges there along with their other experiences, qualifications, and achievements.

These projects have supported youth work activities, allowing them to continue and keep young people engaged and active during trying times. They have also highlighted different models and possibilities for youth work for consortium members, and the journey continues.

We also plan to utilise VE in blended mobility programmes as soon as mobility is possible again. Facilitated dialogue and asynchronous tasks will be used as a pre-departure activity before a youth exchange mobility begins to allow the participants to engage with each other before the physical mobility. This will allow them to break the ice and start delving into the theme of the project. During the mobility, we would continue with asynchronous activities, and begin the reflection process. A final online facilitated dialogue session would be included to enable participants to continue reflecting on lessons learnt, what went well, what did not, and what they have learnt about themselves and about others. As a consortium, we see the importance of there being more than one online facilitated dialogue session, and the inclusion of asynchronous activities to complement the online facilitated dialogue sessions.

Reference

European Union Agency for Fundamental Rights (2010). *Racism, ethnic discrimination and exclusion of migrants and minorities in sport: the situation in the European Union.* Publications office of the European Union. https://fra.europa.eu/sites/default/files/fra_uploads/1207-Report-racism-sport_EN.pdf

Author index

A
Abid, Nadia vii, 5, 117
Al Karriri, Ahmed viii, 4, 167
Al Mqadma, Amani viii, 4, 167
Auffret, Katja ix, 5, 47

B
Balaman, Ufuk ix, 5, 117
Beaven, Ana vii, 1
Bruni, Tatiana ix, 4, 205

C
Cheikhrouhou, Nadia ix, 5, 6, 81
Cioltan-Drăghiciu, Andra ix, 5, 6, 37

D
Dixon, Daniel ix, 4, 231

E
Ensor, Simon x, 4, 141

F
Fernández-Raga, María x, 5, 59

G
Giralt, Marta x, 4, 5, 105, 191
Gorman, Tom x, 5, 23
Griggio, Lisa xi, 5, 127
Guth, Sarah vii, xix

H
Háhn, Judit xi, 5, 11
Helm, Francesca vii, 1
Hernández-Nanclares, Núria xi, 5, 93
Hoskins, Laüra xi, 4, 179

K
Kanninen, Mikko xii, 5, 23

Kleban, Marcin xii, 4, 141
Koris, Rita xii, 5, 69, 93

L
Lai, Jan xii, 4, 219

M
MacKinnon, Teresa xiii, 4, 141
Marchewka, Małgorzata xiii, 5, 6, 81
Mato Díaz, Francisco Javier xiii, 5, 93
Millner, Sophie C. xiii, 5, 155
Moalla, Asma xiii, 5, 117

P
Pittarello, Sara xiv, 5, 127

R
Radke, Katarzyna xiv, 5, 11
Reynolds, Alexandra xiv, 4, 179

S
Sens, Aloisia xiv, 5, 47
Stanciu, Daniela xiv, 5, 6, 37
Syrjä, Tiina xiv, 5, 23

T
Tahmaz, Onur xv, 4, 231
Trégoat, Claude xv, 4, 141

V
Van de Kraak, Sandra xv, 4, 219
Villard, Thierry xv, 5, 59
Vinagre, Margarita xv, 5, 105
Vuylsteke, Jean-François xvi, 5, 69

W
Wigham, Ciara R. xvi, 5, 105

www.ingramcontent.com/pod-product-compliance
Lightning Source LLC
Chambersburg PA
CBHW021838220426
43663CB00005B/294